THE ROMAN CAMPAGNA
IN CLASSICAL TIMES

THE ROMAN CAMPAGNA
IN CLASSICAL TIMES
By THOMAS ASHBY

New edition with introduction by
J. B. WARD-PERKINS
Director, British School at Rome

GREENWOOD PRESS, PUBLISHERS
WESTPORT, CONNECTICUT

Library of Congress Cataloging in Publication Data

Ashby, Thomas, 1874-1931.
  The Roman campagna in classical times.

  Reprint of the 1970 ed. published by E. Benn,
London, Barnes & Noble, New York.
  Includes bibliographical references and index.
  1. Campagna di Roma--Antiquities. 2. Roads,
Roman--Italy--Campagna di Roma. 3. Italy--
Antiquities. I. Title.
[DG55.C28A83 1979]   937'.6   78-12509

ISBN 0-313-21115-9

First published in 1927
First edition in this form published 1970
by Ernest Benn Limited

Reprinted with the permission of Ernest Benn Ltd.

Reprinted in 1979 by Greenwood Press, Inc.,
51 Riverside Avenue, Westport, CT 06880

Printed in the United States of America

10 9 8 7 6 5 4 3 2 1

INTRODUCTION TO THE NEW EDITION

THOMAS ASHBY was born in 1874. He studied classics at Winchester and Oxford, and at the age of sixteen his family moved to Rome, where he was befriended by the great Italian archaeologist and writer Rodolfo Lanciani. In 1901 he became the first student of the newly founded British School at Rome and after a brief spell as its Assistant Director, in 1906 he was appointed Director, a post which he held until 1925. After several years of active private life in Rome he died in 1931 at the age of fifty-seven.

His was a career in which the strands of scholarship and a deep love of Italy and its people were inextricably interwoven. Within the field of Italian historical and antiquarian studies his interests were wide, but they returned continually to the city of his adoption and to the countryside of which it is the centre, the Roman Campagna. Among the first works to be published by the British School was a series of articles in which he dealt systematically and exhaustively with the topography of the Campagna and its antiquities, articles which are still today the essential basis for any study of the areas which they covered. These were followed over the years by others dealing in no less detail with the great Roman roads of central Italy, with the topography and monuments of Rome itself, with the history of antiquarian studies in and around Rome, and with the work of the earliest Renaissance cartographers. *The Roman Campagna in Classical Times* was the mature fruit of forty years devoted study.

As generation after generation of travellers to Italy has discovered, there is nowhere else quite like the Campagna. Its appeal is insidious but not at all easy to define. The landscape is beautiful, but hardly more so than that of many other parts of Italy. Perhaps the element which distinguishes it from all others is the all-pervading sense of history. The documented story of this countryside is continuous, with hardly a break, from the moment when the first settlers from the mountains moved down into the fertile plains on either side of the river Tiber and started to clear them. Sometimes it is the living past itself that lingers on. Ever since the Bronze Age the shepherds of the Abruzzi have been driving their flocks down, as they still do today, to winter in the lowland pastures of Latium. At other times it is the ghosts of a vanished past that refuse to be laid. Many of the historic cities of Etruria and of the Latin peoples who were Rome's earliest neighbours were already dead or dying in Virgil's and Livy's day. But although the picturesque hilltop villages and townlets of Latium and southern Tuscany are almost all creations, or re-creations, of the Middle Ages, their spirit, and in many cases their actual sites, are those of a far earlier age.

Civita Castellana, for example, perched romantically on a narrow peninsula of towering cliffs above the gorges of the river Treia, was founded by early medieval refugees from the Roman city of New Falerii (*Falerii Novi*), in the open country a couple of miles to the west. The site they chose was that of Old Falerii (*Falerii Veteres*), the fortress capital of the Faliscans, whence their forefathers had been evicted by their Roman conquerors over a thousand years before. In this case nature and history conspired to reproduce not only the spirit but also much of the detail of an earlier age. At Veii, on the other hand, one may stand on the windy fields that once housed the busy streets and homes of Rome's great rival, and the lament of Propertius,

> Now within thy walls sounds the slow shepherd's horn,
> Now among thy dead they reap the cornfields
>
> (*Elegies*, IV. 10. 29-30)

has a literal truth which, to be honest, it lacked in the poet's own day, when a small Roman market town still occupied the centre of the Etruscan city. Here it was not the conqueror's sword that forcibly depopulated the ancient site; it was the security and economic prosperity of the Pax Romana that drew the inhabitants of the town out into the farms and villas of the open countryside and down to the bustle and opportunity of the great consular roads. By late antiquity the town of Veii had dwindled and died, and when in the early Middle Ages the tide of prosperity turned once more, it was on a smaller and more easily defensible promontory to the south of the ancient city that the descendants of its one-time inhabitants established the fortress settlement of *Castrum Insulae*, the modern Isola Farnese. Today, with the forces of security and economic plenty once more at work, the centres of life and activity are once again the farmsteads of the open countryside (many of them built on the sites of Roman villas) and the rapidly growing roadside town of La Storta (on the site of the Roman road station 'At the Ninth Milestone' on the Via Cassia), while medieval Isola Farnese is no more than a sleepy relic of a past age. The details of the pattern vary from place to place. But turn where one will, past and present are inextricably mingled. This is a landscape that speaks to heart and mind alike.

Ashby's qualifications for describing this countryside were unique. He loved it; he knew all the by-ways of its history; and together with his students he had walked every inch of it. His career moreover was a vital link in the chain of Italian topographical research. He was a close friend of the great medieval topographer, Giuseppe Tomassetti, whose life-long knowledge of the written documents was to crystallize in the five volumes of *La Campagna Romana*, that essential complement of Ashby's own work; and while he and Tomassetti may be said to have taken up the study of topography of Latium where Gell and Nibby had left it more than half a century before, it was he above all who shaped the tastes and talents of the young Giuseppe Lugli, the father of the very lively present-day Italian school of topographical studies. The band of those who accompanied Ashby on his explorations of the Campagna is sadly diminished; but as becomes the heroic days before the invasion of the countryside by the internal combustion engine, the tales they tell tend to have a quality slightly larger than life—of nights spent in remote country railway stations after missing the last train home; of the sinking hearts with which, at the end of a long day's tramp, they greeted the appearance on some distant horizon of some antiquity still to be explored; and dominating all the personality of Ashby himself, his flaming red beard turning grey, the obligatory half-hour nap after lunch ("Silenzio!"), and his flow of impeccably idiomatic Italian spoken in an accent which to his dying day remained obstinately British. Since his day research has added some new techniques to the equipment of the field worker—air photography, for example, or the study of the remains of domestic pottery; and the sites are far more easily accessible. But who is to say that, as things are made easier for us, we have lost something of the capacity for direct personal observation which was at the root of all that Ashby did?

He was the right man at the right place—and at the right moment. Of the Campagna that he knew so well vast tracts have vanished forever and a great deal more is vanishing daily before one's eyes. The population, which in 1921 stood at 664,000, is now over 2,500,000 and steadily rising. There are many still living who knew it when considerable stretches of market gardens and open countryside reached almost up to the Aurelianic walls. The writer of these words well remembers the late Mr. Paul Oppe describing how as a young man, walking along the Via Appia near the catacombs of San Callisto, he startled a porcupine in the undergrowth beside the road. Today the Via Appia is an enclosed park fighting for survival against the encroachment of an engulfing suburban sprawl. Where Ashby could speak of the ever-shortening interval of pasture land between the cultivation spreading outwards from Rome and that extending downwards from the Alban Hills, today it is the turn of the fields and vineyards to be squeezed out of existence by the spread of building. The coastline which he knew as "low and monotonous and very sparsely populated", is now built up almost continuously from Rome to Anzio.

Happily that is not the full story. The mile after mile of empty, rolling countryside, the romantic desolation are gone. New roads and suburbs, speculative development, the spread of light industry, the agricultural reforms of the fifties, all these have added their quota of destruction. In part compensation for this there is much fresh knowledge. The lost town of Lucus Feroniae, where later tradition held that a quarrel between Roman and Sabine merchants had once led Tullus Hostilius to declare war on his Sabine neighbours, came to light and was excavated as a direct result of the construction of the Autostrada del Sole; near Veii ploughing brought to light the church and farmbuildings of the great early medieval papal estate of Capracorum; at Palestrina it was the clearance of the havoc wrought by the Second World War that revealed in all its arrogant splendour the vast, terraced, hillside sanctuary of Fortuna Primigenia. Nor has all of this fresh knowledge been due to the pressure of events. To quote a single outstanding example, the systematic exploration and restoration of the harbour town of Ostia, probably the most important single Roman excavation of the last half-century, has not only revolutionized our understanding of the meaning of Roman architecture, but it has also brought vividly to life, for all to see, an image of the streets of Rome itself, now lost for ever beneath the buildings of later centuries.

And nothing can really destroy the setting of all this. Somehow, despite all the ravages of man's handiwork, the Alban Hills and the mountains of the Sabina still gaze across to Soracte; the clouds chase their shadows inland from the sea, towards Tivoli; and on any clear, bright winter's day when the *tramontana* is blowing, one can stand on the hills above Veii and see, spread out before one, the whole setting of Rome's earliest history. There are still many by-roads less than an hour from the centre of the city where something of the old magic still reigns. A flock of sheep grazing beside a *fontanile;* the cutting for an Etruscan road, bright with golden broom; a Roman aqueduct spanning a sheltered valley; a ruined medieval castle perched on a brown rocky cliff. All that one needs is a seeing eye, a readiness to use one's own two feet, and a feeling for the timeless presence of the past.

The Roman Campagna is not a guide book; nor is it a literary classic like George Dennis's *Cities and Cemeteries of the Etruscans*. It is the deeply felt historical interpretation of a countryside, made under conditions which are now themselves a matter of history. Other books have been, and no doubt will continue to be, written about parts of the Campagna. But nothing can replace Ashby's work. It is, and will always remain, a treasured possession of any lover of the Roman countryside.

PREFACE

H E WOULD BE INDEED UNGRATEFUL who did not mention his predecessors in this field of exploration : and it is easy to do it, for they are few in comparison with the numerous scholars who have busied themselves with the topography of Rome.

An extraordinarily fine map of the Campagna was published anonymously in 1547 by one Eufrosino della Volpaia, and was followed the next year by a book by Domenico Boccamazza, who had been the chief huntsman of Pope Leo X, describing the Campagna from the sportsman's point of view, which bears an astonishingly close relation to it. Only one copy of it was known to exist (I understand that another has recently been found at Breslau),[1] but it served as the unacknowledged model for all subsequent maps for over a century.

From that curious genius Pirro Ligorio—so much of whose good work is spoilt by his ineradicable tendency to make the truth still more picturesque by mixing it up with falsehood—a certain amount of information may be obtained : but the first investigator of the Campagna who really counts is the Danish priest Lucas Holste, the friend of Cardinal Antonio Barberini, who died in 1661 and who knew it as no one did before and as few have known it since. Unluckily neither he nor Raphael Fabretti of Urbino, the explorer of the aqueducts, was able to publish his results in full ; and while we have an annotated copy of Cluver's *Italia Antiqua* and a few maps (all now in the Barberini Library at the Vatican) from the former's hand, from the latter we have nothing but his three published works—the *De Aquaeductibus* (1680,

[1] See p. 12.

1

and the *Inscriptiones*, and a curious controversial work directed against Gronovius. In the meantime, the survey of the various farms of the Campagna, carried out by the order of Pope Alexander VII, had rendered the formation of other maps possible ; and the Jesuit Eschinardi, with the help of the surveyor Cingolani, incorporated the results in a new map, to which he wrote an important but brief text. Another explorer of whose work but little is left is the Spaniard Diego Revillas, who, like Fabretti, was much interested in the territory of Tivoli, the upper Anio valley and the aqueducts, but published nothing beyond two maps.

All these men are absolutely trustworthy—which is more than can be said for two other Jesuits, Kircher and Volpi, though in both there is wheat among the chaff. We have thus arrived at the first half of the eighteenth century : and we have to wait till the early years of the nineteenth—for the work of men like Gavin Hamilton and Thomas Jenkins was devoted only to the discovery of works of art—before, with Sir William Gell and Antonio Nibby, a new map of the Campagna was formed. The triangulation was the work of Gell, while both explored and studied the whole district—with what thoroughness is clear both from their published works and from their notebooks, which I have the good fortune to possess. At the same time the German J. H. Westphal was also making a fairly thorough exploration, but was unable to return to complete it : while Canina's various works are of a certain value but are often inaccurate in details. After them, again, there is a long interval—and indeed, until we come to the modern works of Tomassetti and Lanciani there is little of importance to record. To the latter and to my father (the best of companions while he lived) I owe my first introduction to the delights of the exploration of the Campagna; and to our mutual friends, the Misses Bulwer and the Rev. Father P. P. Mackey, O.P.—the latter an untiring investigator of its remotest corners—a number of the photographs which illustrate the present work are due. A younger pupil of Professor

2

Lanciani's, Professor Giuseppe Lugli, has done much good work on the Campagna of recent years, and is now in charge of the Italian Archaeological Survey of the district, the first portion of which, dealing with Terracina and its neighbourhood, has just appeared.

In my own descriptions and maps I have done my best to register all I could, and to them I must refer those of my readers who desire further information on points of detail.

Nor should I forget to mention the artists whose sketches and drawings may help us to realise the spirit of the Campagna. I have said that its charm defies description : but Claude, J. R. Cozens, and Turner—to name no more— may be taken as representatives of the many artists who have sought inspiration from it : and, by good fortune, attention has recently been called to their work by the publication of a well-illustrated volume dealing with each of them.

Finally, to my wife I owe much help, and to her I gratefully dedicate this book.

THOMAS ASHBY

May 1927

CONTENTS

INTRODUCTION TO THE NEW EDITION   V

PREFACE   1

LIST OF ILLUSTRATIONS   7

BIBLIOGRAPHICAL NOTE   9

SUPPLEMENTARY BIBLIOGRAPHY   11

GENERAL INTRODUCTION   15

The roads which radiate from Rome may, for our present
purpose, be divided into the following groups, beginning
on the left bank of the Tiber and working southwards
(clockwise):

I

THE ROADS LEADING TO THE SABINE COUNTRY AND THE APENNINES

     PRELIMINARY NOTE   57

I.   THE VIA SALARIA   59

II.   THE VIA NOMENTANA   82

III.   THE VIA TIBURTINA   93

II

THE ROADS LEADING TO THE ALBAN HILLS AND THE SOUTH-EAST

     PRELIMINARY NOTE   125

IV.   THE VIA PRAENESTINA   128

IVa.   THE VIA COLLATINA   143

V.   THE VIA LABICANA   146

VI.   THE VIA LATINA   153

VII.   THE VIA APPIA (WITH THE VIA ANTIATINA)   174

THE ROMAN CAMPAGNA IN CLASSICAL TIMES

III

THE ROADS LEADING TO THE SEA-COAST

	PRELIMINARY NOTE	205
VIII.	THE VIA ARDEATINA, THE ROAD TO SATRICUM, AND THE VIA LAURENTINA	207
IX.	THE VIA OSTIENSIS (WITH THE VIA CAMPANA AND THE VIA PORTUENSIS)	214

IV

THE ROADS LEADING INTO ETRURIA

	PRELIMINARY NOTE	223
X.	THE VIA AURELIA	225
XI.	THE VIA CLODIA AND THE VIA CASSIA	231

V

THE ROADS LEADING TO THE NORTH

	PRELIMINARY NOTE	245
XII.	THE VIA FLAMINIA AND THE VIA TIBERINA	247
	INDEX	255

ILLUSTRATIONS

1. FIDENAE FROM THE VILLA OF LIVIA (67)   67
2. GROTTE TORRI (79)   67
3. SULPHUR LAKE NEAR BAGNI (99)   99
4. THE LARGER BATHS, HADRIAN'S VILLA (108)   99
5. VIADUCT NEAR HADRIAN'S VILLA (111)   111
6. VILLAGE OF S. VITTORINO (111)   111
7. TEMPLES AT TIVOLI (113)   113
8. NYMPHAEUM UNDER S. ANTONIO, TIVOLI (114)   113
9. PLATFORM OF VILLA, COLLE VITRIANO (116)   116
10. TERRACE WALL OF VILLA OF BRUTUS (?) (121)   116
11. REMAINS OF VILLA OF THE GORDIANI (130)   130
12. TEMPLE AT GABII (134)   130
13. PONTE DI NONA (132)   132
14. OSA STREAM AND ALBAN HILLS (133)   132
15. VIA PRAENESTINA (136)   135
16. HUTS AT GABII (135)   135
17. CORCOLLE (137)   137
18. PASSERANO (137)   137
19. PONTE S. ANTONIO (137)   138
20. PONTE AMATO (138)   138
21. CASTEL S. PIETRO (139)   139
22. QUARRIES, CERVARA (143)   139
23. LUNGHEZZA (145)   145
24. SETTE BASSI (157)   145
25. CENTRONI (159)   159
26. VILLA OF THE QUINTILII (185)   159
27. VIA APPIA AND ALBAN HILLS (187)   187
28. CIRCUS, BOVILLAE (190)   187
29. PALAZZOLA (192)   192

30. ARICCIA (194)   192

31. EMBANKMENT OF VIA APPIA BELOW ARICCIA (196)   196

32. LAKE OF NEMI (197)   196

33. LAVINIUM (THE MODERN PRATICA) (212)   212

34. ARDEA (212)   212

35. WALLS OF ARDEA (212)   213

36. COAST AT ANZIO (213)   213

37. CASTLE, OSTIA (214)   214

38. PALAESTRA OF BATHS, OSTIA (216)   214

39. CAPITOLIUM AND DECUMANUS, OSTIA (216)   216

40. RIVER NUMICUS (217)   216

41. CASTEL FUSANO (217)   218

42. ARCO DI NOSTRA DONNA, PORTO (218)   218

43. "TEMPLE OF PORTUNUS," PORTO (218)   219

44. FLOODS NEAR PONTE GALERA (219)   219

45. TOMB ON VIA VEIENTANA (232)   232

46. GALERA, CHURCH AT (234)   232

47. PRIMA PORTA (248)   248

48. QUARRIES NEAR GROTTA OSCURA (249)   248

NOTE.—Figs. 1, 6, 13, 15, and 20 are from photographs by Mr. G. R. Swain, Photographer of the Near East Expedition of the University of Michigan; Figs. 3, 9, 11, 14, 21, 25, 29, 30, 32, 36, 37, 41, and 46 are from photographs by Miss D. E. Bulwer; Figs. 12 and 28 are from photographs by the Rev. Father P. P. Mackey, O.P.; Fig. 4 is from a photograph by Anderson, of Rome. To all of these my best thanks are due. The rest are from my own photographs. Figs. 2, 5, 8, 9, 10, and 24 have already appeared in the *Papers of the British School at Rome*, and Fig. 47 in the *Journal of Roman Studies*.

BIBLIOGRAPHICAL NOTE

(*In Chronological Order*)

Mappa della Campagna Romana del 1547 di Eufrosino della Volpaia, riprodotto dall' unico esemplare esistente nella Biblioteca Vaticana, con introduzione di Thomas Ashby (Roma, 1914).

The Breslau copy of the map of Eufrosino della Volpaia is described by Ruge in *Göttingische Nachrichten*, 1916. Beiheft, p. 82, No. 35. It is in the Stadtbibliothek (Gb. 158).

For Pirro Ligorio, see *Journal of Roman Studies*, ix. (1919) 170 *sqq.*

Holste's notes were posthumously published under the title of *Annotationes ad Cluverium* in 1666.

KIRCHER, A. *Latium* (Amsterdam, 1671).

FABRETTI, R.
De Aquis et Aquaeductibus, ed. i, Rome, 1680; ed. ii, Rome, 1788.
Ad J. Gronovium apologema. Naples, 1686.
Inscriptiones antiquae. Rome, 1699.

ESCHINARDI, F.
Espositione della Carta Cingolana dell' Agro Romano, ed. i, Rome, 1696 ; ed. ii (revised by R. Venuti), Rome, 1750.

CORRADINI and VOLPI. *Vetus Latium.* 10 vols. (Rome, 1704–45).

WESTPHAL, J. H. *Römische Kampagne* (Berlin and Stettin, 1829).

GELL, SIR W. *The Topography of Rome and its Vicinity.* Ed. i in 2 vols., London, 1834 ; ed. ii in 1 vol., London, 1846 (revised by Bunbury).

NIBBY, A. *Analisi della carta dei Dintorni di Roma*, 3 vols. (Rome, 1837 ; the 2nd edition of 1848–9 is a mere reprint.)

TOMASSETTI, G. and F. *La Campagna Romana Antica, Medioevale e moderna*, 4 vols. (Rome, 1910—in progress.)
This is a more comprehensive reissue of an earlier work (*La Campagna Romana nel Medio Evo*, published in the *Archivio della Società Romana di Storia Patria*, 1879–1907 and separately), but does not entirely supersede it.

9

LANCIANI, R. *Wanderings in the Roman Campagna* (London, 1909), and many special articles.

LUGLI, G. Various articles in the *Bullettino Comunale* from 1914 onwards on the villas of the Alban Hills (especially that of Domitian) and on the Imperial villas in the neighbourhood of Rome. The Castra Albana are dealt with in two articles in *Ausonia*, and the Via Triumphalis (on the Alban Mount) in *Memorie dell' Accademia Pontificia*, i. 1. 251 *sqq.*

My own *Classical Topography of the Roman Campagna* [1] comprises :

    I. The Viae Collatina, Praenestina, and Labicana.
       (*Papers of the British School at Rome*, i. 121 *sqq.*)

    II. The Viae Salaria, Nomentana, and Tiburtina [2] (*ib.*, iii. 1 *sqq.*).

    III. The Via Latina (*ib.*, iv. 1 *sqq.* ; v. 213 *sqq.*).
       The Via Flaminia (with Mr. R. A. L. Fell) in *Journal of Roman Studies*, xi. 125 *sqq.*, and the Via Tiberina in *Memorie dell' Accademia Pontificia*, i. 2. 129 *sqq.*, while notes on detailed points connected with the Via Clodia and the Via Salaria have appeared in *Römische Mitteilungen*, xxii. 311 *sqq.*, xxvii. 221 *sqq.*

For the aqueducts see my articles in the *Builder*, xciv. (1908, i.) and *Neue Jahrbücher*, xxiii. (1909), 246 *sqq.* ; a full list of remains, with their levels, and maps showing their exact position, will be found in Reina Corbellini and Ducci's *Livellazione degli Antichi Acquedotti Romani* (Rome, 1917).

Mr. Bradshaw's restoration of Praeneste will be found in *Papers, cit.*, ix. 233 *sqq.*

For the drawings of Claude Lorrain, see Professor A. M. Hind's volume (1925) ; for Cozens, *Drawings by John Robert Cozens* (Burlington Fine Arts Club, 1923) ; and for Turner, my own volume, *Turner's Visions of Rome* (1925).

For Hadrian's Villa see Winnefeld, H., *Die Villa des Hadrian* (Berlin, 1895).

---

[1] I am indebted to the Faculty of Archaeology, History, and Letters for permission to reproduce portions of these papers and some of the illustrations which appeared in them.

[2] A revised translation of the *Via Tiburtina* is appearing in the *Atti e Memorie della Società Tiburtina di Storia e d'Arte* (1922 *sqq.*), in the first volume of which (1921) will also be found a translation of an article on *Horace's Villa at Tivoli*, by G. H. Hallam and myself, originally published in the *Journal of Roman Studies* (iv. 121 *sqq.*).

SUPPLEMENTARY BIBLIOGRAPHY

In the forty years since this book was first published there has been a very large body of publications dealing with the individual sites and monuments of the Roman Campagna, much of it in the pages of learned journals and most of it in Italian. The following notes are intended to indicate a few only of those of a more general character, with a preference for those written in English.

TILLY, Bertha. *Vergil's Latium* (Oxford, 1947). The coastal plains and foothills to the south of the Tiber, towards Ardea, Lavinium and Laurentum, the scene of the last six books of the Aeneid.

HIGHET, G. *Poets in a Landscape* (New York and London, 1957). A sensitive and moving study of the Italy which inspired the poets of Rome's golden age, including two who, like Vergil, have intimate associations with the Campagna: Horace with Tivoli and his farm at Licenza in the Sabine Hills just behind Tivoli; and Tibullus with Pedum in what is still one of the most unspoiled corners of Latium, the foothills of the Monti Prenestini between Tivoli and Palestrina, around Gallicano.

MacKENDRICK, P. *The Mute Stones Speak* (New York and London, 1960-62). An outstanding general account of archaeological discovery in Italy, which covers many of the principal sites of the Campagna. Among these are Hadrian's Villa and Palestrina (the only recent account available in English). An excellent bibliography down to 1960.

WARD-PERKINS, J. B. 'Etruscan Towns, Roman Roads and Medieval Villages', *Geographical Journal* 128 (1962), pp. 389—405, summarizing the recent work of the British School in the South Etruscan part of the Campagna, north of Rome. For detailed accounts of this work, see the School's *Papers*, since 1955.

See also:

ASHBY, T. *The Aqueducts of Ancient Rome* (Oxford, 1935). Edited by I. A. Richmond and published posthumously.

THE ROMAN CAMPAGNA IN CLASSICAL TIMES

MORTON, H. V. *The Waters of Rome* (London, 1966).

MEIGGS, R. *Roman Ostia* (Oxford, 1960).

and, in Italian:

SILVISTRELLI, G. *Città, Castelli e Terre della Regione Romana*. 2 vols. (Rome, 1940).

ALMAGIA, R. *Le Regioni d'Italia*, vol. xi: *Lazio* (Turin, 1966).

In the absence of any commercially available published map of the classical Campagna, mention may be made of the *Carta Archeologica del Territorio di Roma* prepared by the late Giuseppe Lugli and printed for the Ufficio Speciale del Nuovo Piano Regolatore, Rome, in 1962. Copies of this can be consulted in many of the libraries of Rome. It records the lifework of the man who was Ashby's close friend and who was most directly responsible for carrying on the tradition of topographical studies which Ashby initiated.

Of the Forma Italiae, the detailed archaeological map of Italy at a scale of 1:25,000, two sheets that concern this region have been published: *Tibur* (Tivoli), vol. 1, by C. F. Giuliani (1966), and *Tellenae* (the area immediately south of Rome, between the Via Appia and the Via Ardeatina) by G. M. De Rossi (1967). Two others are in preparation and likely to appear in 1970: *Praeneste* (Palestrina) by M. P. Muzzioli, and *Gabii* (on the Via Praenestina, east of Rome) by L. Quilici.

J. B. W-P.

GENERAL
INTRODUCTION

THE ROMAN CAMPAGNA IN CLASSICAL TIMES

GENERAL INTRODUCTION [1]

THE CAMPAGNA DI ROMA is a district which certainly possesses a peculiar fascination, and creates in oneself a feeling, elusive when one attempts to define it in words, and not capable indeed—as is the case with all our higher and most intimate emotions—of being reduced to precise terms. There it is, however, none the less, and I do not wish to imagine that any of my readers have not many times felt that indefinite, yet strong desire for it which comes to one far away. " They change their skies above them, but not their hearts, that roam," says the modern poet, translating in an ideal way the well-known line of Horace.[2] He, too, has written that splendid poem of the sea and the hills—

Who hath desired the Sea ? Her excellent loneliness rather
Than forecourts of kings, and her outermost pits than the
    streets where men gather
Inland among dust under trees—inland where the slayer may
    slay him—
Inland, out of reach of her arms, and the bosom whereon
    he must lay him—
His Sea at the first that betrayed—at the last that shall never
    betray him
        His Sea that his being fulfils ?
So and no otherwise—so and no otherwise hillmen desire
    their hills.

---

[1] Portions of this introduction have appeared in the *Builder*, and others are included in the article on Latium in the 11th edition of the *Encyclopaedia Britannica* : they are reproduced here with the permission of the respective editors, which I gratefully acknowledge.

[2] Coelum non animum mutant qui trans mare currunt.

The hills and the sea have excited men's imagination from the first. And, perhaps, part of the secret is, that here we have many of the characteristics of both. The hills, when one is not actually among them, stand round and form a background to almost every view in the lower Campagna : while this, seen from the Alban or Sabine Hills, is almost indistinguishable at times from the sea by which it is bounded : in certain lights the sun will for a moment make us mistake the position of the long, low coastline, one of the most desolate in Europe.

But that which seems from above to be as flat as a sea becalmed, proves, when one descends, to be furrowed in all directions by valleys great and small, deep and shallow. The volcanic rock lends itself to erosion : so that the general level of the hill-tops is fairly uniform, or rises and falls gradually, but unless one happens to be moving along a ridge, one's course is continually up and down. And this, too, has something of the sea—of a sea once in motion, but now as it were frozen, preserving still its infinite variety ; one hill, like one wave, is never quite the same as the next. There is, too, a great impression of vastness in the landscape of the Campagna—whether we look to the low hills stretching to the sea as far as the eye can reach, or to the great mountains on the other side rising far away.

The sea itself, on the other hand, has little to do with our impressions of the Campagna : we see it in the distance from the hills, but except in the actual coast-strip we should hardly be able to guess, if we did not know, that it was, after all, so near. The coastline is low and monotonous, and very sparsely populated : and we do not see the flocks of sea-birds coming inland at the approach of stormy weather, nor hear the scream of the gulls, nor smell the salt breezes in the way that we do in the vicinity of northern seas. The sea has played, and plays still, a singularly small part in the life of Rome : it is a mere truism to say that to the average Roman, though it is far less distant, it must be far less familiar than to the average Londoner or Parisian.

But there are other elements in the charm of the Campagna—the contrast between the life of the past and the almost overwhelming solitude that reigns in the present; we think first of the little village communities that once were formidable rivals to Rome herself, which in Strabo's time even had become mere villages, the property of private individuals, so that we can hardly fix their sites —one of Sir William Gell's correspondents speaks of his search for 'the lost and mislaid cities of Latium'[1]; then we think of the free yeoman farmers who fought and died for the glory of the Republic and laid the foundations of her rapidly growing power. But when they died out the prosperity of the Campagna suffered a fatal blow: it fell into the hands of a few large proprietors and was cultivated by gangs of slaves: economically and from the point of view of public security we may compare its condition then with that of one hundred or two hundred years ago.

Country houses in the neighbourhood of Rome hardly came into vogue before the second century B.C. But the fashion spread rapidly,[2] and no doubt contributed in no small measure to the well-being of the Campagna, which was naturally benefited by the great revival of prosperity under the Empire, and especially in the times of Trajan, Hadrian, and the Antonines, when all Italy seems to have flourished as never before, until the long and gradual decadence and depopulation, which, as Professor Tomassetti has shown, reached its climax in days far nearer to our own than we are accustomed to think.

All these memories crowd in upon us, and are brought more vividly to us by the ruins that we see, picturesque in their decay, serving often as shelter to the shepherds who come from the mountains with their flocks in the winter, and whose huts and sheepskin clothes must be

---

[1] Letter of Elphinstone to Gell, Aug. 6, 1835, among some letters deposited by Mr. Craven in the Department of Greek and Roman Antiquities at the British Museum.
[2] *Builder*, LXXXVII (1905) ii. 31.

17

much the same as those of two thousand five hundred years ago.

And then the Campagna itself has so much variety, besides natural beauties of a rare order : the change of the landscape with the rising and setting of the sun, or the varying moods which it assumes with the changes of the weather—here especially rapid and difficult to forecast—add a charm to every hour.

In one's less sternly moral moments one even acquires the feeling that every fine day spent indoors, with the Campagna so close, is in a sense wasted. And has not Stevenson written a most effective apology for idlers in which he puts their case very convincingly ?

The Roman Campagna is a district in many respects unique. Most large capitals are surrounded by suburbs, residential, industrial, and so forth, which extend for several miles beyond the city proper. But Rome, for many reasons, forms an exception to the general rule. The choice of its site, commanding the only permanent crossing of the Lower Tiber, seems to have been largely dictated by commercial considerations, though in those early days a strong position was naturally selected : and this the Palatine, which was certainly the nucleus of the city, offered in a pre-eminent degree. What the ravines were like which once protected it we may see better at Veii (in the Cremera valley, for example) than in Rome itself, where there has been so much filling up and levelling down. But from early times the importance of Rome was mainly that of a ruling city and not of an emporium, though it was that incidentally, inasmuch as the accumulation of wealth led to the growth of luxury : while under the Empire the population of Rome consisted of the wealthy, of the functionaries of government, of a proletariat which toiled not but was fed by its rulers, and of numerous slaves. In those days, of course, the Campagna was covered with dwellings, but apparently rather with the country residences of the well-to-do, with the parks and gardens attached to them, than with the houses of the poor : the early villages had to a very

18

considerable extent disappeared, and except on the higher roads, where some of them lived on as post-stations, they had not been replaced by others. So that even then there were, one may say, no true suburbs.

Well before the imperial period the malaria [1] had, as we shall see, begun to make its appearance in certain districts, and after the fall of the Empire it no doubt became worse ; but it would seem that its effect in the early Middle Ages has been somewhat exaggerated, and that the period of its greatest virulence is far more recent. But other causes co-operated to reduce the number of the inhabitants of the city of Rome, so that until quite recent years the circuit of the Aurelian walls enclosed an extent of ground much larger than was required for the actual dwellings of the population, and a considerable portion of this space was occupied by gardens and culti- vated areas. When Rome became the capital of the Italian kingdom, the population soon rose from a quarter to half a million : but the financial crisis of 1890 put a stop for a time to all development, and it is only in the last few years that growth has begun once more, so much so that the population is now well over three-quarters of a million, and is still on the increase. Now, the city is spreading rapidly on every side beyond the walls : and, except for the quarter along the Via Appia and on the Aventine and Caelian, we have already lost most of the picturesqueness of the narrow lanes shut in by high walls, of the vineyards and gardens still within the city, of churches half-forgotten which seemed in their peaceful repose so far from the bustle and noise of the town. Whatever the necessities of modern life may be, and—to touch on a still more delicate point—whatever visitors or even foreign residents in Rome may have to say on the various questions of street improvements, demoli- tions, etc. (which, in one sense, are primarily the affair of the inhabitants of Rome), there is no doubt that the mediaeval feeling, which, to many lovers of Rome, was

[1] W. H. S. Jones, in *Malaria in Ancient Times*, thinks that it had not even reached Latium as early as 400 B.C.

not the least of its attractions, is disappearing fast. That this is in large measure inevitable, and that similar processes occur elsewhere, is true : but Rome occupies a unique position. It is not, and perhaps never will become, a manufacturing or commercial city, or a business centre of the first rank : it is as the seat of Government even more than as a resort of foreign residents and tourists that it has grown to its present size, and is still growing, faster perhaps than any city in the world—and yet the supply of houses is still unequal to the demand.

The Campagna Romana thus remains almost unspoilt, and there is no city which one can so quickly and easily leave behind as Rome. At an hour's distance on foot from almost any of its gates one may plunge into a solitude surprisingly profound, and forget completely that not far from a million of one's fellow-men live at so short a distance away. The greater part of the Campagna is pasture-land, and that which is under cultivation is very largely cornland, so that the population at any time of year is extremely small in proportion to the area, while in summer it is reduced to a minimum.

This state of things, which has gone on so long, will not continue very much longer, and signs of change are everywhere apparent. The law in regard to the so-called Bonifica, or improvement of the agricultural conditions of the Campagna, on which we shall touch later, and the successful war against malaria are producing considerable results. Rapid progress is already visible; new farmhouses are rising everywhere, and more land is continually coming under cultivation.

The Campagna presents considerable natural advantages ; the soil is largely volcanic and very fertile, and there is abundance of good water. Springs are plentiful, and where they fail, as in the Pomptine Marshes, artesian wells have been recently sunk with great success. Though most of it is now pasture-land and perhaps better fitted for this purpose, it seems indeed surprising that vegetables and garden produce required for the consumption of the capital are not supplied by growers in the immediate neighbourhood, but are still brought from a considerable distance : however, as usual in such cases all the world over, it is none too easy to break through the strongly established ring which has the markets of Rome in its hands.   In the meantime, the charm of the Campagna is one which it is impossible to describe : the wonderful lights that play upon its innumerable ridges and valleys, the beautiful outlines of the mountains by which it is bounded—many do not realise that from Rome one can easily see peaks in the Central Apennines which rise to over 8,000 feet above sea-level—the strange, desolate appearance of that part of it which runs towards the sea, hidden from us unless we ascend the dome of St. Peter's or the Alban or Sabine Hills, the loneliness of the flat Latin shore stretching away south-eastward towards that wonderful promontory of Monte Circeo, that dominates the whole coastline and the low-lying Pomptine Marshes, the broad, brown Tiber flowing swiftly in its winding course between high muddy banks—all these different scenes make up but a part of what few even of those who know and love it best have been able to convey to those who have but a slight acquaintance with it.

It is very doubtful, however, whether the charm of the Campagna is meant to be described in prose : one might as well expect to understand a symphony of Beethoven from a printed description, if one had never heard it and could not read the score.   It is worth recalling J. K. Jerome's remarks on the subject (*Three Men on the Bummel*, p. 118) : " Nothing is easier to write than scenery : nothing more difficult and unnecessary to read. . . .   To the average man, who has seen a dozen oil-paintings, a hundred photographs, a thousand pictures in the illustrated journals, a couple of panoramas of Niagara, the word-painting of a waterfall is tedious.

" An American friend of mine, a cultured gentleman, who loved poetry well enough for its own sake, told me that he had obtained a more correct and more satisfying idea of the Lake District from an eighteenpenny book of photographic views than from all the works of Coleridge,

Southey, and Wordsworth put together. I also remember his saying, concerning this subject of scenery in literature, that he would thank an author as much for writing an elegant description of what he had just had for dinner. But this was in reference to another argument: namely, the proper province of each art; my friend maintaining that just as canvas and colour were the wrong mediums for story-telling, so word-painting was, at its best, but a clumsy method of conveying impressions that could much better be received through the eye."

We will begin from the very beginning, with a short sketch of the geology of the Campagna. We find that Sir Archibald Geikie, in his essay on the Roman Campagna,[1] traces three distinct successive phases in the sequence of events which made the Campagna what it is : " First," he says, " came a time when the waves of the Mediterranean broke against the base of the steep front of the Apennines, and when all the low grounds around Rome, and for leagues to the north and south, lay sunk many fathoms deep. . . ." The records of this first period (marine clay, sands, and gravels) lie beneath the Seven Hills on the left bank of the Tiber, but appear in the chain of heights on the right bank that culminates in Monte Mario (455 feet above sea-level).[2] Next followed the chief period in the building up of the Campagna. A host of volcanoes rose along the sea floor on the west side of Central Italy, when ashes, dust, and stones were thrown out in such quantity and for so prolonged a time as to strew over the sea bottom a mass of material several hundred feet thick. Partly from this accumulation, and partly by an upheaval of the whole region of Italy, the sea bottom with its volcanic cones was raised up as a strip of low land bordering the high grounds of the interior, and huge volcanoes were piled up to a height of several thousand feet. On the

---

[1] *Landscape in History and other Essays* (London, 1905), p. 312.

[2] This clay has ever since Roman times supplied the material for brickmaking, and we shall see that the valleys which now separate the different summits are in large measure artificial (Lanciani, *Ruins and Excavations*, 41).

south side of the plain the group of the Alban Hills was built up by many successive eruptions. First there was a huge crater with a base about 12 miles in diameter (from Frascati to Velletri is about 10 miles). The pass of Algidus is a gap in this outer crater rim : and Rocca Priora occupies one of the highest points upon its rim, and was probably the site of an ancient town named Corbio. Within this a new and smaller one was subsequently piled up enclosing a well-marked crater with the Campo d'Annibale at its bottom, while Monte Cavo marks almost (*not* quite) the highest point on its rim. There are various subsidiary craters—the lakes of Albano and Nemi, the Valle d'Ariccia, the Lago di Turno, Lake Regillus, Prata Porci, the lake of Gabii, etc.

On the north side is an independent series of volcanoes— the lake of Bracciano, the Lago di Vico, the lake of Bolsena, etc. This volcanic activity must have greatly modified the topographical features—thus the lower part of the course of the Tiber, which originally flowed south-westward between Bolsena and Viterbo, was buried, and it had to find a new way of escape. The tufa of the Roman Campagna is not, however, according to Sir Archibald, derived from the eruptions of these two great volcanic groups, but is rather due " to local eruptions from many and generally small submarine vents, discharging here fine, there coarse materials, at different times and independent of each other " (p. 328). These would be difficult to trace, but would, he thinks, be detected by accurate study. There is certainly abundant evidence of spent volcanic activity all over the Campagna—hot springs, exhalations of sulphuretted hydrogen—let us take as an example the Solfatara on the way to Ardea, or another at the point where the Velletri railway crosses the Via Appia Nuova ; and the travertine that we find at Bagni and elsewhere is due to the deposition of carbonate of lime in solution by hot springs, which may be regarded as an accompaniment or sequel of volcanic activity.

" Lastly," says Sir Archibald, " succeeded the epoch in which the volcanic platform, no longer increased by

C

fresh eruptions, was carved by the atmospheric agencies into the topography which it presents to-day."

The district sloping down from Velletri to the dead-level of the Pomptine Marshes has not, like the western and northern slopes of the Alban Hills, drainage towards the Tiber. The subsoil, too, is differently formed : the surface consists of very absorbent materials, then comes a stratum of less permeable tufa or peperino (sometimes clay is present), and below that again more permeable materials. In ancient and probably pre-Roman times this district was drained by an elaborate system of *cuniculi,* or small drainage tunnels, about 5 feet high and 2 feet wide, which ran, not at the bottom of the valleys, where there were sometimes streams already, and where, in any case, erosion would have broken through their roofs, but along their slopes, through the less permeable tufa, their object being to drain the hills on each side of the valleys. They had probably much to do with the relative healthiness of this district in early times. Some of them have been observed to be earlier in date than the Via Appia (312 B.C.). They were studied in detail by the late M. R. de la Blanchère. When they fell into desuetude, the malaria gained the upper hand, the lack of drainage providing breeding-places for the malarial mosquito. Remains of similar drainage channels exist in many parts of the Campagna Romana and of Southern Etruria, at points where the natural drainage was not sufficient, and especially below cultivated or inhabited hills (though it was not necessary here, as in the neighbourhood of Velletri, to create a drainage system, as streams and rivers were present already as natural collectors), and streams very frequently pass through them at the present day.

The drainage channels which were dug for the various crater lakes in the neighbourhood of Rome are also interesting in this regard. That of the Alban Lake is the most famous : but all the other crater lakes are similarly provided.

As the drainage by *cuniculi* removed the moisture in the subsoil, so the drainage of the lakes by *emissaria*—

outlet channels at a low level—prevented the permeable strata below the tufa from becoming impregnated with moisture which they would have derived from the lakes of the Alban Hills. The slopes below Velletri, on the other hand, derive much of their moisture from the space between the inner and outer ring of the Alban volcano, which it was impossible to drain : and this in turn receives much moisture from the basin of the extinct inner crater.[1]

Numerous isolated palaeolithic objects of the Mousterian type have been found in the neighbourhood of Rome, in the quaternary gravels of the Tiber and Anio : but no traces of the neolithic period have come to light, as the many flint implements found sporadically round Rome probably belong to the period which succeeded the neolithic, called by Italian archaeologists the eneolithic period, inasmuch as both stone and metal (not, however, bronze, but copper) were in use.[2]

At Sgurgola, in the valley of the Sacco, a skeleton was found in a rock-cut tomb of this period which still bears traces of painting with cinnabar. A similar rock-cut tomb was found at Mandela, in the Anio valley. Both are outside the limits of the Campagna in the narrower sense, but similar tombs were found (though less accurately observed) in travertine quarries between Rome and Tivoli. Objects of the Bronze Age, too, have only been found sporadically. The earliest cemeteries and hut foundations of the Alban Hills belong to the Iron Age, and cemeteries and objects of a similar character have been found in Rome itself and in Southern Etruria, especially the characteristic hut-urns, imitated from the oblong huts. The objects found in these cemeteries show close affinity with those found in the terremare of Emilia, these last being of earlier date, and hence Pigorini and Helbig consider that the Latini were close descendants of the inhabitants of the terremare. On the other hand, the

[1] See M. R. de la Blanchère in Daremberg and Saglio, *Dictionnaire des antiquités* s.v. *Cuniculus, Emissarium,* and the same author's *Chapître d'histoire pontine* (Paris, 1889).
[2] See G. A. Colini, in *Bullettino Paleoetnologico,* xxxi. 1 (1905).

ossuaries of the Villanova type, while they occur as far south as Veii and Caere, have *never* so far been found on the left bank of the Tiber, in Latium proper.[1]

As to the dates to which these are to be attributed, there is not as yet complete accord, e.g. some archaeologists assign to the eleventh, other to the eighth century B.C., the earliest tombs of the Alban necropolis and the coeval tombs of the necropolis recently discovered in the Forum at Rome. (See B. Modestov, *Introduction à l'histoire romaine* (Paris, 1907); Pinza, *Mon. Lincei*, XV; T. E. Peet, *The Stone and Bronze Ages in Italy* (Oxford, 1909); MacIver, *Villanovans and Early Etruscans* (Oxford, 1924), who believes that the people of the terremare are only collaterally related to the Villanovans, both being descended from the peoples of the Danube and Central Europe.)

Latium [2] in ancient geography is the name given to the portion of Central Italy which was bounded on the N.W. by Etruria, on the S.W. by the Tyrrhenian Sea, on the S.E. by Campania, on the E. by Samnium, and on the N.E. by the mountainous district inhabited by the Sabini, Aequi, and Marsi. The name was, however, applied in a very different sense at different times. Latium originally meant the land of the Latini, and in this sense, which alone is in use historically, it was a tract of limited extent; but after the overthrow of the Latin Confederacy, when the neighbouring tribes of the Rutuli, Hernici, Volsci, and Aurunci, as well as the Latini properly so called, were reduced to the condition of subjects and citizens of Rome, the name of Latium was extended to comprise them all, and include the whole country from the Tiber to the mouth of the Savo, so as just to include the Mons Massicus, though the boundary was not very precisely fixed. The change thus introduced, though already manifest in the composition of the Latin league, was not formally established till the reign of Augustus, who formed

[1] See L. Pigorini in *Rendiconti dei Lincei*, ser. v., vol. xvi. (1907) 676, and xviii. 249 (1909).

[2] *Lătium*, from the same root as *lătus*, side; *lăter*, brick; πλᾰτύς, flat; Sanskrit *prath*; not connected with *lātus*, wide.

of this larger Latium and Campania taken together the first region of Italy; but it is already recognised by Strabo, as well as by Pliny, who terms the additional territory thus incorporated Latium Adjectum, while he designates the original Latium, extending from the Tiber to Circeii, as Latium Antiquum.

In this original sense Latium consisted principally of an extensive plain, now known as the Campagna di Roma, bounded towards the interior by the Apennines, which rise very abruptly from the plains to a height of between 4,000 and 5,000 feet. Several of the Latin cities, including Tibur and Praeneste, were situated on the terrace-like underfalls of these mountains,[1] while Cora, Norba, and Setia were placed in like manner on the slopes of the Volscian mountains (Monti Lepini), a rugged and lofty limestone range, which runs parallel to the main mass of the Apennines, being separated from them, however, by the valley of the Trerus (Sacco), and forms a continuous barrier from thence to Terracina.

That Rome was once ruled by a race of Etruscan princes, the Tarquins, there is, even in the minds of the most critical of historians, practically no doubt. Under their sway or that of their like, the power of Etruria extended far to the south into Campania. Their fall meant a restriction of the growing power of Rome over her neighbours, and it was some while before the infant Republic could make up the lost ground. It was only at the beginning of the fourth century B.C., according to the traditional date, that Veii fell. The power of that city was considerable, and the great network of drainage channels to the north of it cannot have been the work of isolated landowners, but must be the result of a large and carefully planned scheme. The traces of the power of Veii lasted on in the nomenclature of Imperial times. Horace in a well-known passage talks of the right bank of the Tiber as the " Etruscan bank." [2] And, in the still

---

[1] In the time of Augustus the boundary of Latium extended as far E. as Treba (Trevi), 12 miles S.E. of Sublaqueum (Subiaco).

[2] *Vidimus flavum Tiberim retortis litore Etrusco violenter undis*, etc.

more prosaic language of the inscriptions on the boundary stones placed along the right bank of the Tiber by
Augustus,[1] we find that bank referred to as Ripa Veientana
—the Veii bank—sometimes abbreviated as R.V.

The Campagna di Roma in common parlance, and as
we shall study it, includes besides Latium a considerable
portion of Southern Etruria. Near Rome, on the right
bank of the Tiber, there was probably much forest-land,
for, while roads are plentiful, ruins are scarce.

In attempting to trace the gradual spread of the power
of Rome in Latium, we cannot place overmuch reliance
upon the traditional accounts, and to discuss, with Pais
and De Sanctis and others, the question of their credibility
would take us far too long. The list of the thirty communities belonging to the Latin League, given by Dionysius
of Halicarnassus (v. 61), is, however, of great importance.
It is considered by Th. Mommsen (*Roman History*, vol. i.
p. 448) that it dates from about the year 370 B.C., to which
period belongs the closing of the Confederacy, no fresh
communities being afterwards admitted to it, and the
consequent fixing of the boundaries of Latium. The
list is as follows : Ardeates, Aricini, Bovillani (or Bolani),
Bubentani, Cabani, Carventani, Circeiates, Coriolani,
Corbintes, Corni (probably Corani), Fortinei (?), Gabini,
Laurentini, Lavinates, Labicani, Lanuvini, Nomentani,
Norbani, Praenestini, Pedani, Querquetulani, Satricani,
Scaptini, Setini (Signini (?)), Tellenii, Tiburtini, Tolerini,
Tusculani, Veliterni.

Most of these places can be identified : but Pliny the
Elder (*N.H.* iii. 69) gives us another list,[2] including at
most eight of those found in the list of Dionysius (and

[1] *C.I.L.* vi. 31547, 31555.

[2] Albani, Aesolani (probably E. of Tibur), Accienses, Abolani,
Bubetani, Bolani, Cusuetani (Carventani ?), Coriolani, Fidenates,
Foreti (Fortinei ?), Hortenses (near Corbio), Latinienses (near Rome
itself), Longani, Manates, Macrales, Munienses (Castrimoenium ?),
Numinienses, Olliculani, Octulani, Pedani, Poletaurini, Querquetulani, Sicani, Sisolienses, Tolerienses, Tutienses (not, one would think,
connected with the small stream called Tutia at the sixth mile of
the Via Salaria—Liv. xxvi. 11), Vimitellari, Velienses, Venetulani,
Vitellenses (not far from Corbio).

those among the least known), which purports to be that of the *populi Albenses,* the earlier confederation of thirty towns or villages under the supremacy of Alba Longa. It is clear that this league did not occupy any great extent of territory, for the more powerful towns of Aricia, Lanuvium, and Tusculum were outside its sway.

We are on firmer ground in dealing with the spread of the supremacy of Rome in Latium when we take account of the foundation of new colonies and the formation of new tribes, processes which as a rule go together. The information that we have as to the districts in which the sixteen earliest clans (*tribus rusticae*) were settled shows us that, except along the Tiber, Rome's dominion extended hardly more than 5 miles beyond the city gates. Thus towards the north and east we find the towns of Antemnae, Fidenae, Caenina, and Gabii [1] : on the S.E., towards Alba, the boundary of Roman territory was at the Fossae Cluiliae, 5 miles from Rome, where Coriolanus encamped, and on the S. towards Lavinium at the sixth mile, where sacrifice to Terminus was made : the Ambarvalia too were celebrated even in Strabo's day at a place called Φῆστοι, between the fifth and sixth mile. The identification of this locality with the grove of the Arval brothers at the fifth mile of the Via Campana to the W. of Rome, and of the Ambarvalia with the festival celebrated by this brotherhood in May of each year, is now generally accepted. But Roman sway must either from the first or very soon have extended to the salt-marshes at the mouth of the Tiber.[2]

---

[1] We have various traces of the early antagonism to Gabii, e.g. the opposition between *ager Romanus* and *ager Gabinus* in the augural law.

[2] For the early extension of Roman territory towards the sea, see Festus, p. 213, Müll., s.v. Pectuscum : " That part of the city is called the breastwork of the Palatine, which Romulus placed towards the enemy on the side on which the Roman territory extended furthest towards the sea, and on which the city was approached by the most gentle slope, the Roman territory being divided from the Etruscan by the river, and the other neighbouring cities having various hills facing them."

The boundary of the *ager Romanus antiquus* towards the N.W. is similarly fixed by the festival of the Robigalia at the fifth milestone of the Via Clodia.

Within this area fall the districts inhabited by the earliest tribes, so far as these are known to us. The Romilii were settled on the right bank of the Tiber near the sanctuary of the Arvales, the *tribus Galeria* perhaps a little further W., on the lower course of the stream now known as Galera, and the Fabia perhaps on the Cremera towards Veii. We know that the pagus Lemonius was on the Via Latina, and that the Pupinian tribe dwelt between Tusculum and the city, while the Papirian possibly lived nearer Tusculum, as it was to this tribe that the Roman citizens in Tusculum belonged in later days. It is possible that the Camilian was situated in the direction of Tibur, inasmuch as this town was afterwards enrolled in this tribe. The Claudian tribe, probably the last of the sixteen older *tribus rusticae,* was, according to tradition, founded in 504 B.C. Its territory lay beyond the Anio between Fidenae and Ficulea (Liv. ii. 16 ; Dion. Hal. v. 40). The locality of the *pagi* round which the other tribes were grouped is not known to us.

With the earliest extensions of the Roman territory coincided the first beginnings of the Roman road system.

After the Latin communities on the lower Anio had fallen under the dominion of Rome, we may well believe that the first portion of the Via Salaria, leading to Antemnae, Fidenae, and Crustumerium, came into existence. The formation (according to the traditional dating in 495 or 471 B.C.) of the *tribus Clustumina* (the only one of the earlier twenty-one tribes which bears a local name) is both a consequence of an extension of territory and of the establishment of the assembly of the plebs by tribes, for which an inequality of the total number of divisions was desirable (Mommsen, *History of Rome,* i. 360). The correlative of the Via Salaria was the Via Campana, so called because it led past the grove of the Arvales, along the right bank of the Tiber to the *campus*

Salinarum Romanarum,[1] the salt-marshes, from which the Via Salaria took its name, inasmuch as it was the route by which Sabine traders came from the interior to fetch the salt. To this period would also belong the Via Ficulensis, which led to Ficulea,[2] afterwards prolonged to Nomentum, and the Via Collatina, which led to Collatia. Gabii, too, became Roman in fairly early times, though at what period is uncertain, and with its subjugation must have originated the Via Gabina,[3] afterwards prolonged to Praeneste. The Via Latina is, like the Via Appia, obviously a military highway ruled straight on the map, and therefore of artificial origin. Its establishment must be connected with the fighting with the Aequi for the pass of Algidus in the fifth and fourth centuries B.C.

The three primitive roads to the Alban Hills were probably the original road to Tusculum, which later became the first part of the Via Labicana : the Via Castrimoeniensis, which led to Castrimoenium, the modern Marino ; and a road which led to Alba Longa, probably more or less along the line of the first 12 miles of the Via Appia. The road to Satricum (Conca) is also of very ancient origin. Aerial photography may be expected to throw light upon this whole question.

Tradition places the foundation of the Latin colony at Signia as early as 495 B.C., while Norba is said to have received a colony three years later. This is in accord with the archaeological evidence, and so the magnificent walls of polygonal blocks of limestone must be taken to be of Roman date. This principle must probably be widely extended. The Via Salaria can hardly have existed as a Roman highroad before the fall of Fidenae (traditionally placed in 428 B.C.), but not long after the capture of this outpost of Veii the chief city itself fell

---

[1] The ancient name is known from an inscription discovered in 1888 (Lanciani, *Bull. Comm.* 1888, 83 ; *Ruins and Excavations*, 530) which mentions the " corpus saccariorum salariorum," who were employed there as porters.

[2] Liv. iii. 52 ; *C.I.L.* xiv. 447. See Dessau, *Inscr. Lat. Sel.* 6178.

[3] Liv. ii. 11 ; iii. 6 ; v. 49.

(396 B.C.) and a road (still traceable) was probably made thither. There was also probably a road to Caere in early times, inasmuch as we hear of the flight of the Vestals thither in 389 B.C.

The origin of the rest of the roads is no doubt to be connected with the gradual establishment of the Latin League. We find that while the later (long-distance) roads bear as a rule the name of their constructor, all the short-distance roads on the left bank of the Tiber bear the names of towns which belong to it—Nomentum, Tibur, Collatia, Praeneste, Labici, Ardea, Laurentum. The Via Pedana, leading to Pedum, is only known to us from an inscription (*Bull. Soc. Antiquaires de France*, 1905, 177) discovered in Tunisia in 1905, and may be of much later origin, and was a branch of the Via Praenestina. The road to Bovillae must have been prolonged to Aricia, Lanuvium, and Velitrae, and thence to Cora, Norba, and Setia.

We can trace the advance of the Roman supremacy with greater ease after 387 B.C., inasmuch as from this year (adopting the traditional dating for what it is worth) until 299 B.C. every accession of territory is marked by the foundation of a group of new tribes ; the limit of thirty-five in all was reached in the latter year. In 387, after the departure of the Gauls, Southern Etruria was conquered and four new tribes were formed—the Arnensis (probably derived from Aro, the modern Arrone—though the ancient name does not occur in literature—the stream which forms the outlet to the lake of Bracciano [1]), Sabatina (taking its name from this very lake), Stellatina (named from the Campus Stellatinus, near Capena : cf. Festus, p. 343, Müll.), and Tromentina (which, Festus tells us, was so called from the Campus Tromentus, the situation of which we do not know).

Four years later comes the foundation of the Latin colonies of Sutrium and Nepet. In 358 B.C. Roman preponderance in the Pomptine territory was shown by the formation of the tribus Pomptina and Publilia, while in 338 and 329 respectively Antium and Tarracina

[1] Kubitschek in Pauly-Wissowa, *Real-Encyclopädie*, ii. 1204.

became colonies of Roman citizens, the former having been founded as a Latin colony in 494 B.C.

After the dissolution of the Latin League, which followed upon the defeat of the united forces of the Samnites and of those Latin and Volscian cities which had revolted against Rome, two new tribes, Maecia and Scaptia,[1] were created in 332 B.C. in connexion with the distribution of the newly acquired lands (Mommsen, *History*, i. 462). A further advance in the same direction, ending in the capture of Privernum in 329 B.C., is marked by the establishment in 318 B.C. of the tribus Oufentina (from the river Ufens, which runs below Setia, now Sezze, and Privernum, now Piperno) and the tribus Falerna (in the *ager Falernus*), while the foundation of the colonies of Cales (334) and Fregellae (328) secured the newly won South Volscian and Campanian territories, and led no doubt to a prolongation of the Via Latina. The moment had now come for the pushing forward of the Via Appia, which had perhaps run as far as Terracina in 348 B.C., but was now prolonged into the heart of the newly conquered territory of Campania to Capua, constructed (*munita*) in 312 B.C. (Liv. ix. 29; Frontinus *de aquis*, i. 5), but apparently not paved till 292 B.C., and even then with silex only from the temple of Mars, a mile beyond the Porta Capena, to Bovillae, a footpath in *saxum quadratum* being considered sufficient from the gate to the temple (Liv. x. 23, 47) until 189 B.C. (Liv. xxxviii. 28).

In 291, after the colonisation of Horace's birthplace, Venusia, with the large number of 20,000 settlers, it was doubtless taken as far as this town, Beneventum, half-way between Capua and Venusia, serving as a fortress to guard the road, and in 264 it was prolonged to Taranto and Brindisi. Other improvements were very likely made fifteen years later (in 174 B.C.). Cf. Liv. xli. 27 : *Censores vias sternendas silice in urbe, glarea extra urbem substruendas*

---

[1] Festus tells us (p. 136, Müll.) that the Maecia derived its name *a quodam castro*. Scaptia was the only member of the Latin League that gave its name to a tribe.

marginandasque primi omnium locaverunt, pontesque multis locis faciendos.

The Via Appia was always regarded as the first and best of Roman roads—Strabo classes it with the Latina and Valeria among the chief roads of Latium, probably partly owing to the fact that these three roads served the districts most in favour as country residences in his day. Compare also the enthusiastic description of Procopius (*Bell. Goth.* i. 14). Statius (*Silvae,* ii. 2) has called it *regina viarum,* and even now the Roman peasants often speak of an ancient paved road as *via appia.*

Its construction may fairly be taken to mark the period at which the roads of which we have spoken, hitherto probably mere tracks, began to be transformed into real highways. In the same year (312) the colony of Interamna Lirenas was founded, while Luceria, Suessa, and Saticula had been established a year or two previously. Sora followed nine years later. It seems to me clear that the Via Latina must have existed before the Appia.

In 299 B.C. further successes led to the establishment of two new tribes—the Teretina in the upper valley of the Trerus (Sacco) and the Aniensis, in the upper valley of the Anio—while to about the same time we must attribute the construction of two new military roads, both secured by fortresses. The southern road, the Via Valeria, which perhaps owes its name to the censor of 305 B.C., M. Valerius Maximus (Liv. ix. 43), led to Carsioli and Alba Fucens (founded as Latin colonies respectively in 298 and 303 B.C.), whence it was extended to Corfinium before the time of Strabo (v. 3. 11) and to the Adriatic under the Emperor Claudius, and the northern (afterwards the Via Flaminia) to Narnia (founded as a Latin colony in 299 B.C.). There is little doubt that the formation of the tribus Quirina (deriving its name possibly from the town of Cures) and the tribus Velina (from the river Velinus, which forms the well-known waterfalls near Terni) is to be connected with the construction of the latter highroad, though the dates are not certainly known. But the construction of the Via Flaminia as a whole is due to C. Flaminius, the censor of 220 B.C., after the subjugation of the Boii and Insubres [1]; while of the other roads on the right bank of the Tiber, the Via Clodia, the earliest, is of unknown date ; the Via Aurelia is dated by Mommsen about 177 B.C.,[2] though there was apparently a road to Caere in 389 B.C. (and indeed there must have been a route long before, in the time of the Etruscan kings), when the Vestals fled there at the time of the Gaulish invasion : while there was a route from Rome to Vada Volaterrana and Luna in 241 B.C. The line of the Via Cassia must have been used for the purposes of the campaign of 217 B.C., especially as the road from Arretium (Arezzo) to Bononia (Bologna) was made in 189 B.C. As there is no Cassius in the list of consuls between 486 and 171 B.C., we must suppose that it already existed, and took its name from the consul of 171 B.C., who reconstructed it, losing whatever name it had previously possessed.

Having traced the development of the road system, let us now consider how it was managed during the Republican period. The roads were far too important to be given up to the management of the municipal officials of the various towns through which they passed, and were kept in the hands of the central administration. The censors naturally had the management of this department, as responsible for the letting of all contracts for public works. It was by censors that the Via Appia, the Via Flaminia, and the Via Aemilia in Etruria were constructed, and we hear, further, of occasions on which their activity was exercised more generally in making roads across the country at the public expense, or in having the existing roads paved with gravel, and providing for the construction of bridges. Even at Pisaurum (174 B.C., Liv. xli. 27) the censors (who were very active) let out a paving contract. But the tendency to delegate the extra-urban functions of the censors to higher officials representing them comes out very clearly, especially

[1] Ashby and Fell in *Journal of Roman Studies*, xi. 125.
[2] *History of Rome*, i. 486 n. Anziani in *Mélanges de l'Ecole Française*, xxxiii. (1913) 242.

when the roads to be built were at some distance from Rome. This was the case in Cisalpine Gaul, where the roads were constructed by consuls [1] often during or as the sequel to a campaign. It is from this fact that we get the names *Via Consularis* and *Via Praetoria* for the great roads, which vary, as we are told, according to whether their builder was a man of consular or of praetorian rank, though of the latter no cases are known in Italy. In a number of cases, however, where the road bears the name of a family, we do not know when or by whom, whether by a censor, a consul, or a praetor, it was constructed ; and the fact that a road bears the name of a family does not always mean that it is a road of first-class importance, though the converse—that no road of great importance bears the name of a town—is true, as we have already seen.

The censors were not even exclusively responsible for the maintenance of the roads in good order. The earliest milestone known to us—one of those of the Via Appia at Mesa (ad Medias) in the Pomptine Marshes—bears the names of two aediles, though the competence of the aediles strictly ended at the first milestone (Mommsen, *Staatsrecht*, i. p. 68) : it probably belongs to the end of the fifth century of Rome, i.e. to about 255 B.C. The eleventh milestone of the Via Ostiensis, found near Malafede and preserved in the Lateran Museum, was erected by a plebeian aedile, and so was the thirtieth milestone of the Via Tiberina from Nazzano ; while the thirteenth milestone of the Via Praenestina (*infra*, p. 136) was erected by two curule aediles.[2] The original milestones were placed by the constructor of the road.

According to Plutarch, C. Gracchus was the great organiser of the Roman road system. " His chief care," he says, " was the construction of roads, in which he paid regard both to its useful and its ornamental side. For

---

[1] Also with the Via Caecilia, a road which left the Salaria at about the thirty-fifth mile and ran across the mountains to the Adriatic, and which was not improbably constructed by C. Caecilius Metellus Diadematus (consul 117 B.C.).

[2] These are all now published in *C.I.L.* i² 2. 21, 22, 829, 833.

they were driven straight across country, regardless of obstacles, paved with smoothed stone, and strengthened with mounds of rammed earth. The hollows were filled, the torrents and ravines which cut the line of the road spanned by bridges, so that the height on each side was the same, and the whole work had a regular and elegant appearance.[1] Further, he measured the whole road by miles, and set up stone pillars to mark the distances. And he disposed other stones at a less distance from each other on each side of the road, so that it might be easier for riders to mount from them without requiring a mounting-block."

As a result perhaps of his activity we find that considerable extensions of the road system were made in Italy and in the provinces at the end of the second century B.C. And at some period in the seventh century of the city— not later than 92 B.C.—a series of *curatores viarum e lege Visellia* appear. This office was not a part of the regular succession of offices, and in fact might be held in conjunction with the tribunate, aedileship, praetorship, or consulship. The repairs to the Via Caecilia recorded in an inscription now existing in the Museo delle Terme were carried out under the supervision of a tribune as *curator viarum*. Julius Caesar was curator of the Via Appia while aedile, Minucius Thermus, Cicero's friend, of the Flaminia between the praetorship and the consulship.

The foundation of the Roman Empire marks the great change in this, as in other parts of the administration. Augustus in 27 B.C. had to take exceptional measures to get the roads into order. We are told by Dio Cassius that, finding them in bad condition, he allotted them among various senators to restore at their own expense, taking over the Via Flaminia himself—and subsequently also the other roads, as the senators did not care to spend money upon them.

[1] Compare Strabo, v. 3. 8, who speaks of the roads as made by cutting through hills and filling up valleys ; and Appian (*B.C.* i. 23), who speaks of the army of contractors and workmen who served under him.

According to Suetonius, on the other hand, the roads were allotted among those who had enjoyed the honour of a triumph, the necessary funds being drawn from the booty taken. The inscription on the arch at Rimini records that it was erected in his honour in the same year (27 B.C.) because on his initiative and at his expense the Via Flaminia and the other most frequented roads of Italy had been put into order (*munitis*). This word *munire*, which is always used, is instructive—it means literally to wall (*munia* or *moenia* is the word used for city walls) or fortify, and it gives some idea of the scale upon which they were constructed. Dionysius of Halicarnassus, the historian, and Strabo, the geographer, both of whom knew the Rome of Augustus—they came to it soon after the Battle of Actium—speak of the roads, the aqueducts, and the drains as the most splendid works of Rome in which her power was most strikingly displayed.

The only bridges not repaired upon the Via Flaminia in 27 B.C. were the Pons Mulvius (Ponte Molle) and a Pons Minucius (site unknown). The coins which record this restoration of the road depict, nevertheless, the Pons Mulvius, but this is owing to the fact that a triumphal arch was erected here as well as at Rimini.

In 20 B.C. Augustus took over the care of the roads formally, and erected the much-discussed *milliarium aureum* in the Forum. This was not the starting-point of all the roads of the Empire, in the sense that it marked, as we might say, mile 0 ; for the numbering of the miles on each of the roads began from the gate of the Servian wall from which it issued. It probably merely gave the distances along the chief roads to the most important places in the Roman Empire.

Augustus delegated his functions to others, curators chosen from among those who had held the praetorship, in the case of the more important roads,[1] while those of lesser importance were either grouped under the roads of

---

[1] There is only one known instance of the holding of the *cura* of a road (the Via Aemilia) after the consulship (*Bull. Com.* 1891, 89 ; *C.I.L.* iii. 4013) ; this was under Vespasian.

the first class with which they were connected, or put under separate curators or procurators of equestrian rank. In the case of two roads—Aemilia and Flaminia—we hear of the existence of sub-curators of equestrian rank. The *viae vicinales* remained under the control of the municipal authorities, the distinction between them and the State roads (*viae publicae*) being that the latter were under the control of *curatores*.

These curators had authority up to the walls of Rome, so that there was no longer any reason for the existence of the *duoviri*, who had charge of the roads within 1 mile of the city—though we do hear of the special appointment of commissioners for limited periods for the suburban roads. They were not apparently always careful in the performance of their duties—we hear of complaints being made against them by the Senate in the time of Tiberius (Tac. *Ann.* iii. 31), and Caligula was able to gain large sums to satisfy his extravagance by having them brought to trial for misuse of public funds (Dio. Cass. lix. 15).

From the time of Nerva we find that the *curatores* frequently (though not necessarily) had also to take charge of the alimentary institutions for which Nerva was responsible. These are so remarkable as to deserve a word. For each town which received the benefit of the endowment a sum of money was set aside and lent to landed proprietors, and the annual interest which it produced formed support of the charity, which was intended to help education of children of poor parents. The investment, resting on land, was secure, and the State undertook not to withdraw the loan.

The unity of the two officers was frequent but not necessary ; we find, e.g., *praefecti alimentorum* of Flaminia and Aemilia without care of roads so as to distribute the work. An alternative method was to appoint *subcuratores viae et alimentorum*, as was done with these two very roads, to help the *curatores*. And in districts not traversed by roads of first-class importance, separate *praefecti* for *alimenta* existed.

The duties of these officials were to see that the road

D

was kept in repair, that there was no hindering of access nor encroachment by building upon them, and that they were not damaged by drains, etc., constructed by private persons. They were also empowered to punish fraudulent extortions by Customs officials. We have many inscriptions in which the curatorship of a road is part of the regular succession of offices, finding place after the praetorship, especially of the second and third centuries : after that they disappear. *Curatores* are not heard of after A.D. 315, and the office seems to have disappeared as a consequence of the administrative changes of Diocletian and Constantine.

The *praefecti praetorio*, who had for some time controlled the postal administration,[1] now took up the general control of contractors for work on roads, and thus superseded the *curatores*.

The first use of the name of a road as that of a district is when Augustus used *Aemilia* as a name of one of the regions into which he divided Italy. But *Flaminia* came into use later from being the name of an alimentary district; thus we get a *corrector Flaminiae et Piceni* (*C.I.L.* xiv. 3594).

The milestones, however, in Imperial times all bear the Emperor's name, and not titles of any other official. Augustus, Trajan, and Maxentius are responsible for a great many : those of the earlier emperors are large, round masses of travertine ; we also get neat columns of marble, especially near Rome (e.g. the first and seventh of the Via Appia on the balustrade of the Capitol), and later still small marble columns with Maxentius' inscription rudely scrawled upon them (no other word describes the sprawling carelessness of this period). Milestones near Rome are rather scarce, except in museums : and just beyond Decimo, on the Via Laurentina, is the only place where one may still be seen *in situ*—the eleventh (of

---

[1] The postal administration—which involved providing horses and vehicles for Imperial officials on journeys—for which first communities and then, as this led to abuses and exactions, the Imperial treasury paid—was separately managed by other officials.

Tiberius), while the stone set up by Maxentius is in the courtyard of the Casale or farmhouse which perpetuates the name of the tenth mile, a little nearer Rome.

There are other instances besides this of the perpetuation of distance names—the Ponte di Nona and the Valle Vigesimo, at the ninth and twentieth mile of the Via Praenestina. The posting stations were often named by distances, if there was no town near, e.g. *ad Quintanas* on the Via Labicana, and *ad Decimum* on the Via Latina ; this latter in turn gave its name to a village, the inhabitants of which were called *Decimienses*. Such names are, both in Italy and elsewhere, used in the Itineraries, official documents giving the distances along the roads of the Roman Empire. These are, it need hardly be said, preserved to us only in copies. The most important are the *Itinerarium Antonini*—it is not certain which emperor is referred to, but probably Caracalla—which is probably an unskilful excerpt from a map[1] ; and the Tabula Peutingerana, a large map of the roads of the Empire, discovered in a convent library in 1494 by Conrad Peutinger and now in Vienna—no less than 21 feet 3 inches long and only 1 foot wide—so that there is great distortion. It was copied, no doubt, from an official document, the date of which is uncertain.

The Ravenna Itinerary is very close to it, and the following pedigree is suggested by Kubitschek [2] :—

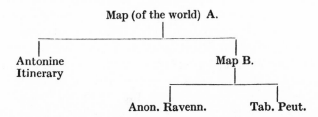

Still more valuable documents, because contemporary, are the four silver cups found at Vicarello, near the lake

---

[1] Cf. the Ravenna Itinerary, where this is expressly stated.

[2] *Oesterreiche Jahreshefte*, v. (1902) 81.

of Bracciano, which give the itinerary from Gades (Cadiz) to Rome by land, traversing Italy by the Via Flaminia. They probably belong to the time of Trajan.

The main arteries of traffic in the neighbourhood of Rome, when the system was completed, came to fall into two different classes—the short-distance roads, which were never prolonged beyond the town which they had been intended to serve, and therefore continued to bear its name ; and the long-distance roads, which had originally performed the same function, but had grown into military and commercial highways, and bore the name of the man who was responsible for their construction as such.

Besides these main thoroughfares, the Roman Campagna was well provided with branch roads, *viae vicinales* or *deverticula* or *ramuli,* called also by Livy *transversi limites* (xxii. 1. 2) or *transversi tramites* (ii. 39). The less important were under the charge of local officials, the *magistri pagorum.* These differ from the main roads in width but not in construction : they are sometimes only 8 Roman feet in width, whereas the former run from 14 to 15 feet wide in open country, going up to 18 on a steep hill, 21 on a bridge (the Ponte di Nona), or 30 (the maximum) on the great embankments of the Via Appia below Aricia and the Via Flaminia at the Muro del Peccato, and also on the bridge over the Almo on the Via Ostiensis, half-way to S. Paolo fuori le Mura.

We have a description in Vitruvius of how a road-bed should theoretically be laid, and a section corresponding to this description has been found on the Via Appia. But in the vast majority of cases in the Roman Campagna the paving-stones, massive polygonal blocks of lava (known as *selce,* and still used for paving in Rome), are laid almost direct on the volcanic soil or rock, and I have hardly ever seen what might be called the ideal or theoretical section in any Roman road. The same is the case in the calcareous mountains east of Rome, where limestone paving-blocks are often used.

In both cases, even when the surface was well levelled,

the blocks new and well laid, and the joints close, the jarring must have been considerable. This would no doubt be mitigated for travellers by having the carts slung on thongs. Examples of gravelled roads are rare, e.g. the Via Ostiensis (between the 13th and 14th kilometres).[1] There is often an edging (*crepido*), sometimes of irregular blocks of *selce*, like small paving-stones, sometimes of rectangular blocks of stone—not only on bridges but elsewhere. The best instance of parapets that I know is on the Via Flaminia, a little beyond the railway station of Civita Castellana, where the blocks measure 1 foot 8 inches thick by 2 feet 2 inches high, and there are higher blocks standing vertically at intervals of 25 metres, each 3 feet high and 2 wide.

Of bridges there are many examples, great and small. Cuttings through the hills are very frequent, and often provide, in the absence of excavation, the only evidence by which the course of a road can be traced. They are, more often than not, avoided by the mediaeval road, which the modern line generally follows. I suppose that, on the principle of *corruptio optimi pessima*, nothing would be so hard an obstacle to negotiate as a Roman road the pavement of which had been thoroughly dislocated, nor anything so difficult to repair. It was probably much easier, when it was necessary to mend the road, as, for example, on the occasion of a papal jubilee, to break the old paving-stones to pieces and make a new track close by. On these occasions tombs also fell a prey to the roadmenders. To cuttings correspond steep gradients and the observance of the direct line from point to point. But the principle of straightness was by no means uniformly observed. The Via Flaminia and the Via Labicana are two striking instances to the contrary. In portions of the course of the former the only thing to do was to keep to the watershed between two deep ravines; while the constructors of the latter seem to have taken things as they found them and to have troubled little about engineering works.

[1] *Not. Scavi.* 1913, 9.

A difficulty that confronts us at once is in regard to dating. It was a comfortable doctrine that all buildings in *opus quadratum*, or masonry of hewn stones, belonged to the Republican period ; but it will not hold water. On the other hand, we do know that neither it nor *opus reticulatum* can be placed as late as the time of Septimius Severus : and there is now little doubt that some of the brick bridges near Rome belong to the Roman period. We have, of course, a whole series of bridges in brick-faced concrete on the Via Traiana between Benevento and Bari.

To the Republic we may assign a few buildings, mostly of a sacred character—the temple at Gabii, the great substructions and other buildings connected with the temples of Fortune at Praeneste and Hercules at Tibur, a certain number of tombs and bridges—some farmhouses or *villae rusticae*—and that is about all.

The last century of the Republic with its great increase in wealth and luxury must have seen the erection of many of the great villas in the territory of Tusculum and Tibur. But it was under Augustus that the first great increase in prosperity came. He regulated the course of the Tiber both above and below Rome—it has been ascertained that the authority of the *curatores* of Tiberius extended as far as Ostia—and restored the aqueducts which supplied the city. As to the highroads, he caused them to be repaired by others, but took on the care of the Via Flaminia himself.

With him began an era of Imperial benefactions to the towns of Italy—Otricoli is a striking example of a small country town in which the greater part of the public buildings belong to his reign—and temples of Rome and Augustus were dedicated as near as Terracina.

These country towns were governed by two judicial magistrates and two officials in charge of public works (*duumviri iure dicundo* and *duumviri aediles*), who had special functions, like those of the Roman censors, every fifth year (*quinquennales*), and by a town council (*decuriones* or *curiales*). The Augustales were a body devoted to the worship of the Emperor—usually a committee of six. The trade guilds (*collegia*) also owe their rise in importance to this period. Many of the holders of these offices were people in a humble condition of life—often freedmen— and there was no doubt a good deal of vanity and naïve pomposity, such as Horace records in the case of the official at Fundi on his famous journey to Brundusium.

After the troublous years which followed the death of Nero, Vespasian's firm hand restored peace to Italy : and many of the milestones were erected by him.

Even more was done by Trajan : and that there was a general increase in prosperity in the early second century A.D., which continued until the troublous times which followed the fall of the Severi, is obvious from inscriptions and other records, which show that the revival was general all through Italy. That the district round Rome was favourably affected seems clear from the fact that a very large proportion of the remains of villas in the Campagna can be assigned to that period by the consular dates on the stamped bricks which are found in them.

There must, however, have been few parts of it which were not occupied by the country residences of wealthy Romans, by the parks and gardens connected with them, or by cultivation. Of villages we find comparatively very few, even in those times of well-being, except in the sur- rounding hills : and even in the classical period we hear that many of the old and famous cities of Latium had fallen into decay, though in a good many cases there is some poetical exaggeration in the contrast between their former greatness and their comparative unimportance in the writer's own day.

In A.D. 292, when the land tax was introduced into Italy, the first region of Augustus obtained the name of *provincia Campania*. Later on the name Latium entirely disappeared, and the name Campania extended as far as Veii and the Via Aurelia, whence the mediaeval and modern name Campagna di Roma.

It was only in the fourth and fifth centuries that here, as elsewhere, the little positions of dignity which had given pleasure to those who held them, such as the election to a seat in the municipal *curia* and the membership of or the holding of some honour in a trade guild, began, under the oppressive legislation of the Empire of that period, to be an intolerable charge. The *curiales* began to be heavily taxed, and the members of guilds and the cultivators found life so burdensome that they sought in any way they could to escape—but the clutches of the State were too strong for them.

The donation made by Constantine to various churches of Rome of numerous estates belonging to the *patrimonium Caesaris* in the neighbourhood of Rome was of great historical importance, as being the origin of the territorial dominion of the Papacy. His example was followed by others, so that the Church property in the Campagna soon became considerable ; and from the seventh century onwards, owing to the immunities and privileges which the Church enjoyed, especially its freedom from the taxes which weighed the Empire down, a certain revival of prosperity occurred. The invasions of the barbarian hordes, of course, produced a good deal of damage : but the formation of centres (*domuscultae*) in the eighth and ninth centuries was a fact of great importance—the inhabitants, indeed, formed the mediaeval militia of the Papacy. Smaller centres (the *colonia*—often formed in the remains of an ancient villa—the *curtis* or *curia*, the *castrum*,[1] the *casale*) grew up later. We may note that, owing to the growth of the Temporal Power, there was never a *dux Romae* dependent on the Exarchate of Ravenna, similar to those established by Narses in the other districts of Italy.

The papal influence was also retained by means of the suburban bishoprics, which took their rise as early as the fourth and fifth centuries A.D.

The rise of the democratic Commune of Rome [2] about

---

[1] Pratica is described in 1385 as *castrum olim, nunc reducti ad casale quod vocatur Patrica* (Lanciani in *Mon. Lincei*, xiii. (1913) 173).

[2] The Commune of Rome as such seems to have been in existence in 999 at least.

1143, and of the various trade corporations which we already find in the early eleventh century, led to struggles with the Papacy ; the Commune of Rome made various attempts to exercise supremacy in the Campagna, and levied various taxes from the twelfth century until the fifteenth. The Commune also tried to restrict the power of the barons, who, in the thirteenth century especially, though we find them feudatories of the Holy See from the tenth century onwards, threatened to become masters of the whole territory, which is still dotted over with their castles and towers. Their dominions can be traced as following strategic lines, along the ancient roads, to castles far outside the city, with intermediate fortified posts.

A little later we find treaties between the barons and the villages for the protection of the latter, which thus became dependent on the various great families, which did not begin to acquire generic titles (duke, prince, count) until the fourteenth century.

The feudal system in the Campagna did considerable damage from the economic point of view, and the wars and depredations of the barons were in large measure the cause of its depopulation : but this in mediaeval times was less serious than in comparatively recent days. This is indicated by a list of the villages of the Campagna dating from the fourteenth century, and giving the amount of salt to be purchased by each village from the Commune of Rome, which had a monopoly of the supply of salt from the marshes of Ostia. The population can be inferred from this, and is found to be about equal to that of recent times, but was differently distributed, some of the smaller centres having disappeared at the expense of the town. In the interval some of the smaller centres have perished, while the towns have grown at their expense. We find Pope Sixtus IV, in a bull of 1476, lamenting the preponderance of pasturage and attempting to revive agriculture.

It is interesting to note that the depopulation of certain parts of the Campagna caused by the prevalence of malaria was probably at its worst in the seventeenth and eighteenth centuries. We have, it is true, notices of malaria in the Middle Ages : and certainly from the accounts of the hunting expeditions of the fifteenth and sixteenth centuries we know that there was more woodland, especially on the right bank of the Tiber, than at the present day.

The actual remains of mediaeval buildings in the Campagna are numerous and important. It contains a large number of castles and towers.

The oldest castle is that of Grotta Marozza, on the prolongation of the Via Nomentana, which belongs to the eleventh century : but the majority were erected in the thirteenth. Most of them have square towers, and the round tower did not come into vogue until the fifteenth century. The name Castelli Romani, applied to the villages of the Alban Hills, comes from the emigration in the fourteenth century from Rome to these villages, those inhabiting quarters of Rome belonging to the barons emigrating to the villages which were respectively under their protection.

The isolated towers, which are especially common, form indeed quite a feature of the landscape—a series of them follows the sea-coast (most of these were constructed or renewed in the time of Pius IV and Pius V). Others, inland, of earlier date (thirteenth and fourteenth centuries) were used as watch-towers and for signalling, as outposts to the various castles : while others, often situated on the highroads, marked the limits of the various jurisdictions— of bishops, convents and abbeys, of the Pope and the Commune, and of the barons : and others again guarded the valleys, preventing the passage along them. Many, too, are the country churches, the earliest of which date in origin from the third century, frequently bearing the name of the religious body in Rome to which they belonged, and the localities called after saints—S. Silvester being a name especially frequent in wooded hill-tops, and San Cesareo occurring in places where a villa or a cult of the Caesars had existed—so that the saints come to take the place of the pagan deities. We often find the most

48

curious perversions of names little understood, which thus became corrupted in common use. Some of the country inns still mark the site of the Roman post-stations on the highroads.

In the Middle Ages it was principally Ostia that was ransacked for building material : though everywhere a good deal of damage must have been done to the buildings of the Campagna by the search for marble, both for burning into lime and for use elsewhere. Excavation for works of art only began in the Renaissance—though that did not mean that the damage ceased, but rather the contrary.

In the Renaissance, it is true, falls the erection of many fine villas in the neighbourhood of Rome—not only in the hills round the Campagna but even in certain places in the lower ground, e.g. those of Julius II at La Magliana and of Cardinal Trivulzio at Salone, and these continued to be frequented until the end of the eighteenth century, when the French Revolution dealt a fatal blow to the prosperity of the Roman nobility.

The " modern " period of the history of the Campagna Romana begins with the sixteenth century. We may note, among other points, the existence of vineyards at various places in the neighbourhood of Rome in the sixteenth century which have since entirely disappeared, and the numerous large and imposing farmhouses constructed in the Campagna at the end of the seventeenth century. It was then, as we have seen, that the worst period in its history came, and it extended over the first half at least, if not the whole, of the nineteenth century. There was a flood of literature on the subject, but, except for the draining of the Pomptine Marshes by Pius VI— and that on a partially mistaken system—little that was practical was done. But since the beginning of the present century the growth of cultivation is most remarkable, for now that the cause of malaria is known it can effectively be prevented. The discovery, made in 1900, that it is propagated by the *Anopheles claviger*, a mosquito which remains inactive by day, was epoch-making : it has rendered it possible to combat this scourge (about the cause of which the most diverse theories had previously been propounded) upon a definite plan. The marshes where it breeds were drained, or the watercourses accelerated—for the larvae cannot live in water that runs at more than a mile an hour. The houses are protected by fine mosquito-proof wire-netting, and the water supply is improved ; while quinine, the great specific both as a prophylactic and as a cure, is now sold cheaply by the State. Much remains to be done, and many of the more ignorant or careless will not adopt preventive measures : but it was proved how effective these are when rigorously applied at the British rest-camp at Taranto during the war, where malaria was practically eliminated.

A law carried in 1903 for the improvement (Bonifica) of the Agro ℩omano (the territory of the Commune of Rome beyond the immediate outskirts of the city, which, unlike that of most other cities, extends a long way out, as far as the lower limits of the territory of the various hill villages) compels the proprietors of land within a radius of some 6 miles of the city to cultivate their lands in a productive manner under penalty of expropriation : and though until recent years it was not enforced with any great stringency, it is now anything but a dead-letter, and its results are very apparent. Towards the Alban Hills especially there is now only a short interval—and in some places none at all—between the cultivation spreading outwards from Rome and that extending downwards from the hills. New farmhouses are springing up everywhere, and the aspect of the Campagna has completely changed. Whereas twenty years ago the road system resembled a starfish, the main roads being entirely unconnected, it is now more like a spider's web.

On the right bank of the Tiber is a much less fertile district, where the older marine gravels have either not been covered at all by the later volcanic deposits, or these have been removed by denudation. Probably in Roman times also population was much less dense and there were more forests. Here conditions have changed less : and there will always be districts, even in the volcanic area, where the rock comes so close to the surface that the ground is not worth cultivating, and where a universal measure of compulsion would be a mistake, and has indeed been proved to be so in more than one case—as has the institution of fixed colonies of settlers.

The permanent population of the Campagna is increasing rapidly. Under the conditions of thirty or forty years ago the greater part of it was (and much still is) under pasture, especially for sheep, which are little used for eating (except the lambs), but are kept for their wool and for their milk, out of which cheese (*pecorino*) and *ricotta* (a kind of curds) are made. They are driven down from the mountains in the autumn and back again in the summer, a custom which in some parts of Italy (e.g. in Apulia) goes back to Roman days—though probably not in the Campagna, where land was then too valuable. A large flock of sheep, with the large white dogs that guard them, is one of the most picturesque sights that can be imagined, led by the shepherds from the Abruzzi in their goatskin leggings, with all their household gods on mule-back or in carts : and not less picturesque are the thatched conical huts in which they live. Other portions, especially in or near the hills and towards the coast, are given up to woodland—small timber, used either for stakes for fencing, etc., or for charcoal-burning. Here, too, the work is done by immigrants from other parts of Italy —often from the mountains of Tuscany.

Even in 1914 more than half the territory of the Agro Romano belonged to only forty-four proprietors, many of whom worked, and still work, through *mercanti di campagna*, whose interests were purely commercial and in no sense philanthropic. But the spread of civilising agencies such as schools, the prosperity which the war brought to the agricultural classes, who were able to sell their produce at a good price, and the higher standard of living to which they have since become accustomed—it is remarkable how much more meat is eaten than before, especially by

51

those who as soldiers became used to a meat ration—have brought great changes. The spread of motor transit and of motor traction has had a very great influence, too—what were remote districts are now easily accessible, even to the poor, by means of motor-omnibuses : and motor-ploughs have done their share in bringing fresh land under cultivation and in reducing the archaeologist to despair—for they have the strength to pulverise such ancient remains as may lie in their way, so that all that is left is a sprinkling of fragments of brick and mortar on the surface of the ground.

The hill districts are very fertile—the bare limestone slopes of the Sabine mountains give way below Tivoli to gentle declivities where olive-trees centuries old flourish, and where grapes (especially the pointed pizzutelli, which are used for eating) grow well. The Alban Hills produce a great deal of wine, both red and white—very palatable, but not made carefully enough to travel nor to keep long, so that in an abundant year there is often over-production—as well as grain, vegetables, and fruit; while the upper slopes are clad with woods, which are cut every eighteen or twenty years, like those in the Campagna, but, being largely chestnut, run to a greater height than the dwarf oaks, etc., of the lower ground.

Professor Tomassetti, in his book already quoted, appeals more than once, with justice and good reason, to the proprietors and inhabitants of the Roman Campagna to show more respect for the ruins and memorials of antiquity, which are still so plentiful. He cites a case—and I could cite many more—of inexcusable and unnecessary vandalism, all the more deplorable inasmuch as every element which can help us in the reconstruction of the classical and mediaeval conditions of the Campagna is of the greatest value. That much must perish is inevitable : cultivation spreads rapidly, and discovery and destruction are almost simultaneous—I have, indeed, recorded my belief that the next fifty years may see a complete change in the economic conditions of the Campagna—but much can and should be preserved. In the meantime it is well that attention should be directed to the accurate observation of what will soon disappear; and what Professor Tomassetti has done for the Middle Ages (though his work is by no means restricted to that) others are doing for the classical period. Those who have studied the Campagna can testify to the intense pleasure and delight that it gives to wander there—and can also bear witness from their own experience that, while criticism of others may be easy, to arrive at completeness, so as to satisfy oneself that one's work is exhaustive, is quite impossible.

I

THE ROADS LEADING TO THE SABINE COUNTRY AND THE APENNINES

I. THE VIA SALARIA

II. THE VIA NOMENTANA

III. THE VIA TIBURTINA

E

I

PRELIMINARY NOTE

THE ROADS OF THE FIRST GROUP, until they reach the Apennines, lead at first through a fairly easy and undulating country—at present rather sparsely inhabited and cultivated. Both the Via Salaria and the Via Tiburtina (the latter after Tibur acquiring the name of Via Valeria) pierce the barrier of limestone mountains which lies on the east of the lower volcanic district of the Campagna, the former following a wide and not very lofty depression among the surrounding hills, which eventually takes it over to the plain of Reate, on the borders of Sabina and Umbria; while the latter, after passing Tibur, the key to the upper Anio valley, follows this for some way, and then ascends rather steeply out of it to a high-lying upland plain, and then climbs still further, crossing more than one high pass in its journey across the peninsula.

The Via Nomentana, on the other hand, never became more than a road of local importance; but the district between it and the Via Tiburtina, like the immediate environs of Tibur, was a favourite resort of the Romans; and this was especially so where it came close under the shelter of the lofty mountain barrier and into the region of the little group of conical hills known in ancient times as the Montes Corniculani. Here, in the calcareous soil, fruit-trees flourish better than the vine; and the almond and cherry blossom in the spring is a delight to behold. This district was served both by it and by a branch road of the Via Tiburtina. The district close to the Tiber, on the other hand, is of considerably less interest, and was less favoured in antiquity. The southern boundary of the district is the Anio, and the region between the two rivers is referred to as *l'Isola* (the Island) in the maps of the sixteenth century. We must, however, overstep this boundary in the last part of our survey, when we reach the neighbourhood of Tibur, in order to include not only the town itself but the villa of Hadrian in the lower country, and that line of other villas higher up on the olive-clad slopes facing towards Rome in an open situation, looking out to the sunset and the sea, with an uninterrupted view of the Campagna— the *Tibur Superbum* of which Vergil speaks.

I

THE VIA SALARIA

THE VIA SALARIA is, as we have seen, necessarily one of the oldest of Roman roads. Not only were Antemnae and Fidenae among the earliest conquests of Rome in Latium : but its name is said by our classical authorities to be derived from the fact that it was the route used by the Sabines who came to fetch salt from the marshes at the mouth of the Tiber, and we may notice that it never changed throughout history. It also followed a natural route along the river valley for a considerable way until, at the site of the ancient Eretum, it entered the hills.

The Via Salaria left Rome by the Porta Collina of the Servian wall, remains of which were found in 1872 on the site of the N.W. angle of the Finance Ministry. Immediately outside this the Via Nomentana diverged to the right, while the Via Salaria, after less than a quarter of a mile, reached its gate in the Aurelian wall, the Porta Salaria. This gate, which belonged to the time of Aurelian, had been restored by Honorius, and had two semi-circular towers. It was seriously damaged in the bombardment of September 20, 1870. Its remains were accordingly removed, and under the towers were found some interesting tombs. That on the right had concealed the monument of the boy Q. Sulpicius Maximus. The gate was then entirely reconstructed, and this purely modern building, which preserved nothing even of the ancient lines, has recently been removed. Its only title to interest was that one of its side-passages gave shelter to one of the last, if not the very last, of the public letter-writers of the modern city.

As to the initial portion of the road a difficult point is raised by the catalogues of Christian cemeteries, which take us back to the fourth century. In these we find the Via Salaria Vetus distinguished from the Via Salaria (Nova).[1] The Nova is undoubtedly the straight road from the Porta Collina to the Porta Salaria of the Aurelian wall, and so on along the line followed by the modern road; but as to the Vetus there is more question. De Rossi (*Bull. Crist.* 1894, 6 *sqq.*) makes it diverge from the Nova at the Porta Collina, identifying it with a road which passes under the Aurelian wall (which blocked its course completely) between the second and third towers to the W. of the Porta Salaria, and thence ran up to the Bivio del Leoncino, at the E. angle of the Villa Borghese. He then makes it follow the Via dei Parioli, the line of which is represented by the new Via Giovanni Paisello, sending off a branch from near the Bivio to join the Salaria Nova. Subsequent discoveries have proved him right, and the course of the road has been exactly determined.[2] The three cemeteries which the catalogues mention as existing along its course are, that of Pamphilus, that of S. Hermes, or of Basilla, and a third called "ad Septem Palumbas," "ad caput S. Iohannis," or "ad Clivum Cucumeris," the first and second of which have been discovered, the former near the point of divergence of the Via Nicola Porpora, the latter in a vineyard now belonging to the German College, rather further along, on the S.W. side of the road. The third has not yet been found, but must be upon the descent (in which traces of the ancient paving have been seen [3]) to the N.W. of the cemetery of S. Hermes.

---

[1] This addition is now generally made for convenience, though it does not occur in the catalogues.

[2] Josi in *Rivista di Archeologia Cristiana*, i. (1924) 19 *sqq.*

[3] The old Vicolo delle Tre Madonne, the Vicolo dell' Arco Oscuro (both of which diverge S.S.W. from this road), and the cross road connecting them N.E. of the Villa di Papa Giulio are all, probably, of ancient origin, as are, indeed, all the lanes in this district (*Bull. Com.* 1891, 144), which has in recent years been much altered by building operations.

If, however, we follow this descent we arrive at the foot of the Monti Parioli, not far from the Ponte Molle; and if we accept the name of Via Salaria Vetus for this road we must, if we wish to press the meaning of the name for the whole road, either suppose that it pursued a winding course (of which no traces are known) along the flat known ground to the W. and N. of Antemnae to reach the crossing of the Anio, or else abandon any attempt to connect it with the line of the road as we know it. And I think the name may be otherwise explained.

In the fourth century the closing of this road, along which a very large number of tombs existed, by the construction of the wall of Aurelian, would still be remembered; and this might have given rise to its being called *vetus* without our being obliged to suppose that it represents the original course of the road.

Immediately outside the gate, to the W. of the road, began one of the most extensive cemeteries of ancient Rome, in which thousands of tombs have been found in the last two centuries. The majority of them belong to the lower orders, and many of them are small chambers containing a number of urns for the ashes of the dead, and known as *columbaria* from the resemblance of the niches (to which the name strictly belongs, though it is in practice now used for the whole structure, which in ancient times was called *monumentum*) to those of a dovecot. This method of disposal of the remains of the dead came into vogue at the end of the Republican period, and went out of use about the beginning of the third century after Christ. Several *columbaria* belonging to the end of the Republican and the beginning of the Imperial period were found, in a very fine state of preservation, during the closing years of last century on the site of the Carmelite monastery of S. Teresa, on the Corso d' Italia. They were arranged, as if they had been the houses of the living, in four rows, separated by three narrow roads, running parallel to an ancient road which is by some identified with the Via Salaria Vetus. Subsequent building operations have shown that this huge necropolis extended as far as Via Po. It has unfortunately been impossible to preserve any of these tombs *in situ*.

Important mausolea are rare, though a striking exception is formed by the fine round mausoleum of Lucilius Paetus in the Vigna Bertone (*C.I.L.* vi. 32932). It consists of a circular base, 34 metres in diameter, of blocks of travertine, which encloses a mass of earth upon which a conical mound was probably placed. The sepulchral chamber was perhaps transformed into a Christian burying-place late in the fourth century (Marucchi, *Catacombs*, 388 *n*. 1). Here and elsewhere the tombs of the second and third centuries A.D. lie at a much higher level, and Professor Lanciani conjectures (*Pagan and Christian Rome*, 284) that the earth which Trajan excavated for the construction of his Forum was dumped here.

A cippus of the pomerium as enlarged by Claudius was found (whether *in situ* or not we do not know) in the Vigna Naro in 1738, at about 300 metres from the Porta Salaria (*C.I.L.* vi. 31537c); and a cippus of the octroi line of Marcus Aurelius was copied "in Via Salaria" by the Anonymus Einsiedlensis. If Lanciani's conjecture, that the wall of Aurelian followed the octroi line, is correct, it must originally have stood close to the gate (*Bull. Com.* 1892, 94). On the E. of the road there seem to have been hardly any tombs. A road goes off to join the Via Nomentana (the Vicolo della Fontana), forming the boundary of the Villa Albani, which very likely follows an ancient line (Lanciani, *Forma Urbis*, 3, after Bufalini). Its course is uncertain for a while; it may have fallen into the Via Nomentana at the first kilometre, but it seems more probable that it went straight on, its line being taken up again by the Vicolo degli Alberoni, in the boundary walls of which there were several paving-stones, and which seems to have followed an old line; and that it then went on through the valley and joined the cross-road known as the Vicolo di S. Agnese. Remains of Roman villas are scanty in this district, and Lanciani (*Bull. Com.* 1891, 147) cautions his readers that many of the architectural fragments to be seen in the vineyards are not of local provenance.

The cutting of the Via Po and the widening of the Via Salaria itself in connexion with the construction of a large new quarter have transformed the district almost beyond recognition : but after crossing the Viale dei Parioli, a little beyond which would fall the site of the first ancient milestone, the road preserves for about another mile the features which were characteristic of all the roads running out of Rome up till our own day. It is still a narrow cobble-paved road confined between high walls, over which are seen the trees of the villas which flank it, while gateways afford occasional glimpses of their gardens. On the left, after the Villa Grazioli, comes the Villa Savoia, the new Royal villa, the grounds of which extend as far as the confines of the fort of Antemnae. On the right was the old Villa Falconieri, part of the garden of which is still preserved.

A little further on the Vicolo di S. Agnese, a lane which almost certainly represents an ancient road, goes off at right angles in a straight line to the Via Nomentana, reaching it close to the church of S. Agnese. Just beyond it the road turns N. and begins to descend through a cutting, which has been considerably enlarged in modern times, to the valley of the Anio. On the left is the entrance to the catacombs of Priscilla. To the right is the Villa Chigi, which still preserves its fine garden.

A little further on, and still on the left of the road, is the hill, now crowned by a fort, once occupied by the primitive village of Antemnae, said to have been conquered by Romulus. The meaning of the name is explained as " ante amnem, i.e. Anienem," by Varro, *L.L.* v. 28, inasmuch as it stands at the point where the Anio falls into the Tiber, thus occupying a position of great strength. Plutarch (*Sulla*, 30) mentions it in connexion with the battle of the Porta Collina in 82 B.C. in such a manner as to indicate that it was not far from the city. Strabo mentions it, with Collatia, Fidenae, and Labici, as amongst the old fortified towns near Rome which had in his time become mere villages, some 30 stadia (4 miles) or a little more from Rome (v. 3. 2, p. 230), and Pliny (*N.H.* iii. 68) names it among the cities of Latium which had disappeared in his day. The indications given by our ancient authorities are sufficiently clear to make the identification certain, and there has never been any real doubt as to the site : while absolute certainty was brought by the excavations in connexion with the construction of the fort in 1882–86 (Lanciani, *Ruins and Excavations*, 111), when the remains of the primitive city were discovered. Some traces of walling were found both on the N. and S., at two points where the existence of gates is probable (Nibby, *Analisi*, i. 161, supposes that there were four gates in all, but Lanciani admits three only), built in somewhat irregular opus quadratum of blocks of capellaccio (an inferior variety of tufa), not very carefully squared, 0·89 m. in length on an average, and 0·59 in height (*Ruins and Excavations, cit.*). Remains of the foundations of huts were also discovered, and a good deal of local pottery, corresponding to that found in the earlier strata of the Esquiline necropolis, with a considerable admixture of Etruscan bucchero and Graeco-Chalcidian ware ; and there were (so it is said) even a few sporadic objects of the Stone Age.

The water supply of the city was well cared for : besides the springs at the foot of the hill on the N., there were several wells and a cistern within the circuit of the walls. One of the former is no less than 54 feet deep, while the cistern (*Ruins and Excavations,* Fig. 43), destroyed soon after its discovery, was of great interest.

The N. portion of the site was later on occupied by a villa at the end of the Republican or commencement of the Imperial period, considerable remains of which were found, among them a cistern divided into three chambers. Two brick stamps of the first century A.D. (*C.I.L.* xv. 670b, 864) were found loose near these ruins. On the E. side some burials under tiles were discovered, dating perhaps from the time of the abandonment of the villa : the coins found with the bodies were illegible. Two inscribed cippi were also found in use in the repairs of the villa itself.

The comparison which Professor Lanciani makes and develops between Antemnae and the early city on the Palatine is interesting and important, and it is a pity that military exigencies rendered it impossible to explore the site thoroughly, and to preserve the remains which were discovered. I do not know even where the pottery that was found is kept.

The hills on both sides of the road just above the Anio valley, the hills on the right after the crossing over the Anio, and the flat ground in the valleys both of the Anio and the Tiber, must have afforded the brick-earth which was used in the kilns of the Via Salaria. These were of considerable importance in Roman times, but have since then fallen out of use, and have no modern representatives, whereas the less important brick-fields of the Via Nomentana are still represented by a kiln near the bridge of that road over the Anio.

The Ponte Salario by which the road crosses the Anio has been thrice destroyed in comparatively recent times, and little of the ancient structure now remains except the greater portion of the small arches on each side. It was cut in 1849 for a length of 15 metres by the French in their attack on Rome (*Rapport de la Commission Mixte pour constater les dégâts, etc.* (Paris, 1850), 42). A photograph of it after it was blown up in 1867 is given in Lanciani's *Destruction of Ancient Rome*, p. 149, fig. 26. Canina (*Edifizi*, vi. tav. 178) gives views of it. It had one central arch and two smaller side-arches of tufa with voussoirs of travertine. The parapets, which were thrown into the river in 1798, bore the inscription of Narses, who restored the bridge under Justinian in A.D. 565 [1] (*C.I.L.* vi. 1199).

[1] Nibby, *op. cit.*, ii. 594, cites Procopius, *Bell. Goth.* iii. 24, *fin.*, as stating that Narses destroyed all the bridges over the Anio; but the passage runs: " Totila and the barbarians, having raised the siege, came to Tibur, after having destroyed almost all the bridges over the Tiber, so that the Romans could not easily attack them. But one bridge, which is named the Milvian, they were in no way able to destroy, because it was the nearest to the city." It

On the left of the road a little beyond the bridge is a large tomb of tufa concrete (the facing of rectangular blocks of stone has disappeared) with a chamber in the form of a Greek cross and a mediaeval tower above. The staff map marks ruins on the right also, but the loose blocks in the field at this point belong to the old bridge.

From the Ponte Salario the modern highroad follows the Tiber as far as the railway station of Passo Correse, keeping clear of the hills which flank it on the E., and hardly ever changing in level. No traces of pavement have, so far as I know, been discovered except in 1889, when a few paving-stones were found in a hole made below Villa Spada for a telegraph-pole along the railway (*Not. Scav.* 1889, 110). The ancient road, therefore, kept more under the hills than the modern, as the remains of tombs indicate, but the level was much the same. Westphal (*Römische Kampagne*, 127, 128) remarks that there are no traces of the old road along the modern one except in places, up to the sixteenth mile, large paving-stones of limestone; and remains of ancient buildings are comparatively scanty. This fact has considerably complicated the difficult problem as to the exact point at which the ancient Via Salaria left the river valley.

On the right of the road, close to the Torre Boschetto, are some remains in opus reticulatum, belonging probably to a villa. The Torre Serpentara does not seem to rest upon ancient foundations; no traces, at least, are at present to be seen, the brickwork of the lower part of the tower being mediaeval; and there are no other remains to be seen until we arrive at Fidenae.

certainly looks, however, as if Procopius had here, as in iii. 10 (where he says that Tibur lay on the Tiber about 120 stadia (15 miles)—a rough measurement—from Rome, so that Totila's occupation of it prevented the Romans from bringing provisions down by river from Tuscany !), confused the Anio with the Tiber. The Pons Milvius is, of course, the bridge by which the Via Flaminia crosses the Tiber, and there was no bridge across the Tiber above it until the Via Flaminia recrossed it near Otricoli, nor any bridge below it, except those actually within the city of Rome. Besides, it would have been the bridges over the Anio which it was important to destroy.

1. FIDENAE FROM THE VILLA OF LIVIA (p. 67).

2. GROTTE TORRI (p. 79).

To face p. 67.

Fidenae had very considerable importance in the early wars with Veii as commanding both the route up and down the Tiber valley and the bridgehead. Its site has been a good deal discussed ; but, despite what I said in the *Papers*,[1] I am now convinced that it would have been impossible to leave so strong a site as Castel Giubileo unoccupied. It commands both the crossing of the Tiber and the passage along the valley ; and the fact that the road passed between the citadel and the village—if an historic Fidenae was really so large as to extend over the hills to the E. as well—is not an insurmountable obstacle, and might indeed render it still easier to block the passage. The hill is crowned by a mediaeval farm-house which takes its name not from any papal jubilee but from the family of the Giubilei (Fig. 1).

The existence of tombs (if such they be) cut in the low tufa cliffs N. of the Villa Spada, on the hill above the E. edge of the railway, even if they are to be assigned to pre-Roman times, does not suffice to determine exactly the site of the earliest settlement. We know, on the other hand, that the Roman village of Imperial days, which grew out of the post-station, lay at the foot of the Villa Spada hill.

The accounts of its desolation are probably to some extent exaggerated : Cicero (*De Leg. Agr.* ii. 35. 96) speaks of it as almost deserted, classing it with Labici and Collatia ; Strabo mentions it with Collatia and Antemnae as an old town, the site of which had then passed into private hands ; Horace (*Epist.* i. 11. 8) and Juvenal (vi. 57, x. 100) scorn it as the type of desolation, ranking it with Gabii, which, however, enjoyed a certain amount of prosperity under the Empire (cf. *Papers*, i. 188). We hear, too, of the collapse of a temporary amphitheatre at Fidenae in A.D. 27, in which many thousand persons perished—Suetonius (*Tib.* 40) puts the number of killed at 20,000, Tacitus (*Ann.* iv. 63) the total number of casualties at 50,000. Most of the spectators must, it is true, have come from Rome : and the structure was

[1] *Op. cit.*, 17 *sqq.*

probably erected on the flat ground by the river for convenience.

We first reach the Roman post-station, which must have possessed a certain importance. Close to the road in 1889 was found the actual curia [1] of the village—a hall facing W., the back wall of which was formed by the rock itself, cut perpendicularly and cemented; while the W. wall had an arch formed by two pilasters and two columns. It was decorated with marble, and on the pavement lay a marble base, which no doubt supported a statue, with a dedication to M. Aurelius by the Senatus Fidenatium, made during the lifetime of Antoninus Pius (A.D. 140), and some fragments of other inscriptions and parts of two statues. The " Casale di Villa Spada," the farmhouse immediately to the S. of the hill, was also built upon a portion of a brick edifice of the Roman period. It has now, however, been completely destroyed.

Two other inscriptions of which we have record were probably found in the curia.

The first (*C.I.L.* xiv. 4057) is a dedication of unknown date (some time early in the second century) to the Numen Domus Augustae of a building or statue which was restored by the Senate after a fire (the place and date of its discovery are unknown); and the other (*ib.*, 4058) is a dedication to Gallienus (in which the two chief magistrates of the place still bear the title of dictator) by the Senate itself, found in 1767 " near the Villa Spada."

The village cannot have extended far to the N. of the curia, for there would have been no space for it at the foot of the hills; and, besides, about 100 yards to the N. of it (or rather more), just below the Villa Spada itself, a tomb was discovered in 1889, when the railway line was doubled, consisting of two chambers cut in the rock, the outer of which had a mosaic floor, while upon the architrave over the doorway leading to the inner chamber, which can still be seen on the edge of the line, was the inscription " *Ti(berio) Apronio Apolloni f(ilio) Fab(ia)*

---

[1] Its site is indicated on the map a little to the S.W. of the F. of Fidenae (but cf. *Ephemeris Dacoromana*, ii. 434).

Apollonio hic sepultus est." From this inscription we learn for the first time the tribe to which Fidenae belonged.

The summit of the hill has been occupied by a villa of the Imperial period, of which an open water reservoir is the most conspicuous portion remaining.

The next hill to the N. is the site selected by some authors for the city of Fidenae. Nibby (*Analisi*, ii. 61) notices the abundance of fragments of pottery (which I was unable to find), some remains in opus reticulatum near the S.W. angle of the plateau, and a subterranean passage cut in the rock (indicated also by Dennis, *Cities and Cemeteries of Etruria*, i. 48, and D on plan), which has been explored by Tomassetti (*op. cit.*, 78), who found it to lead to a reservoir with several branches and vertical shafts communicating with the upper air, of a type common in the Roman Campagna. The entrance is round-headed, about 5 feet high and a foot and a half in width, and looks like the exit of a drain.

Close by Dennis indicates a large cave (E), now closed by a gate, but which, according to him, has several ramifications (to the N.E. of which is a shaft such as Tomassetti describes, one side of which has been quarried away), and a tomb (G), and on the W. side of the hill above the railway are several more tombs.[1]

Just beyond the site of the sixth milestone a modern road goes off to a new iron bridge over the Tiber. In making the road remains of a building of the second century after Christ were discovered, including two well-preserved bathrooms heated by hypocausts.

About half a mile beyond Castel Giubileo is the Fosso della Buffalotta, and on the N. of it the Casale di Sette

[1] It may be noticed in passing that the tombs he indicates above the Casale di Villa Spada are no longer visible—perhaps owing to the fall of the rock. Some damage has very likely occurred to the tombs—though not at all recently as far as one can tell—from quarrying. Lanciani (*Storia degli Scavi*, i. 205) mentions the letting of a quarry near Castel Giubileo in 1521. But the quarries date from ancient times, and are mentioned by Vitruvius (ii. 71) and Pliny (*N.H.* xxxvi. 167) as producing soft stone. The same stone is found near Prima Porta. It is full of cinders, and is not of a very good quality (Tenney Frank, *Roman Buildings of the Republic*, 17).

F

Bagni, between which and the railway are various remains. On the E. edge of the railway, behind a signalman's house, are the concrete foundation walls (preserved to a considerable height) of a large villa, and further up remains in opus reticulatum. Further towards the E. are two water reservoirs, situated close to the *casale*. To the E. of the *casale* are large caves ; and here Dennis (*op. cit.*, 50) places the chief necropolis of Fidenae. Further to the N.E. on the top of the hill is a large reservoir, with at least three chambers, each measuring 10·9 by 2·5 metres inside, and connected by openings placed slightly on the skew to one another, so as to reduce the pressure, as in the so-called Sette Sale at Rome (really a reservoir belonging to the Golden House of Nero). The hill is bounded on the N. by the Fosso di Malpasso, which is joined by the Fosso della Buffalotta just to the E. of the road which crosses them both by the Ponte di Malpasso. The bridge consisted until 1832 of remains of three periods —opus quadratum of tufa of the original structure, a brick arch with a double ring of brickwork, the stamps in which dated from A.D. 126–129, and an arch of comparatively modern date. A view is given (Nibby, *Analisi*, i. 129) by Guattani, *Mon. Sabini*, i. tav. 2 (opp. p. 43).

The identification of the stream with the Allia (Nibby seems to refer rather to the Fosso della Buffalotta, the more important of the two) seems doubtful, inasmuch as the distance from Rome is insufficient. A mile from this point, according to Gell and Nibby, the ancient Via Salaria left the valley of the Tiber and ran towards Nomentum. The theory is, however, a very improbable one, and is conditioned by the desire to place Eretum at Grotta Marozza. The road which they indicate as the Via Salaria is in all probability a mere *deverticulum* (Hulsen and Lindner, *Alliaschlacht*, 20 *n.* 3).

We may notice that the *Tabula Peutingerana* makes a branch go to the right from Fidenae to Nomentum and join the Via Nomentana there. This may be what Nibby considers the original Via Salaria (Desjardins, *Tab. Peut.*, 176).

A mile or more further on the Casale Marcigliana rises
on a hill above the road. No traces of antiquity are
visible there at present, except for a plain marble sarcophagus in the courtyard; but Nibby (*op. cit.*, ii. 303)
saw a sepulchral cippus with the inscription *C.I.L.* xiv.
4065 (now in the Lateran), and several architectural
fragments.

Beyond Casale Marcigliana no traces of antiquity are
visible for some distance, except for a well-preserved
reservoir at the Torretta or Marcigliana Vecchia, the path
leading to which from the E.S.E. very likely follows the
line of an ancient road.

The Allia, from which the terrible defeat which the
Romans suffered at the hands of the Gauls in 390 B.C.
took its name, has been rightly identified by Hulsen and
Lindner, following Westphal (*Römische Kampagne*, 127),
Gell (*Topography of Rome and its Vicinity*, 43) and Kiepert,
with the Fosso Bettina; both Livy (v. 37) and Plutarch
(*Com.* 18) place it at about 11 miles from Rome, and
the former speaks of the stream as " Crustuminis montibus
praealto defluens alveo." But the two full accounts of
the battle which we have—that of Livy and that of
Diodorus (v. 114)—differ with regard to the site of
the battle, the former putting it on the left, the
latter on the right bank of the Tiber. The question
of the relative value of the two accounts has been much
debated. Hülsen and Lindner (*op. cit.*), after a careful
study of the ground, decided in favour of Diodorus,
as Mommsen had already done (*Hermes*, xii. 515 = *Röm.
Forsch.*, ii. 297), but their view has not been accepted
by Pais (*Storia di Roma*, i. 281, *n.* 1) nor by Richter
(*Beitrage zur röm. Topogr.* i. *Alliaschlacht und Servius-
mauer*), nor by Kromayer, the latest and the best authority
on the subject. Richter insists strongly on the fact of
the impregnability of Rome from an attack delivered by
an enemy on the right bank opposite the city, owing to
the difficulty of crossing the river. It is this fact which,
according to him, explains the importance of Fidenae
in the early wars between Rome and Veii; even admitting,

as he does, that the repeated defections and recapture of Fidenae are by no means all to be accepted as historical events, he regards it as the key to the position in all this warfare, inasmuch as it was near it that the Veientines, descending the valley of the Cremera, would naturally cross the river. He explains the flight of that portion of the Roman army which escaped to Veii (and not to Rome) by the fact that the Gauls had already cut off the passage to the city—which, even if the river did not run closer to the foot of the hills than it does now, is quite conceivable : while the absence of any effort on their part to relieve Rome may have been due to the difficulty already pointed out of crossing the river near the city and to the smallness of their numbers. Kromayer points out, too, that the ground on the left bank suits Livy's description of the battle perfectly. It is not a little curious that the Romans should have made the same mistake then as Maxentius did, centuries later, when he was defeated by Constantine, in occupying a hill with a steep descent behind them, so that when they had once given way recovery was impossible.

A little to the S. of the railway station a path ascends to Monte Rotondo, which very likely follows an ancient line. At Monte Rotondo it may have forked, one branch going to Mentana, another to join the prolongation of the Via Nomentana, though there are no certain traces of antiquity on either. The town occupies a fine position on a hill, but there is no reason for supposing that the site is that of an ancient city—Eretum certainly was not situated here, as Raphael Volaterranus (i. 54) and other authors (Cluver, *Italia antiqua*, p. 667, and, apparently, if silence gives consent, Holste) have supposed ; for, as Dessau (*C.I.L.* xiv. 439) points out, it is by no means at the right distance from Rome. Nor can Gell's identification of the site with that of Crustumerium (*op. cit.*, 190) be defended. Several sepulchral inscriptions have, not unnaturally, been collected in and near the town (*C.I.L.* xiv. 3932–3939), though only Nos. 3938–3939 seem to be still preserved, but none of them presents features of any interest and their provenance is in no case certain.

The road running due N. from Monte Rotondo probably —in fact almost certainly—follows an ancient line, though no actual traces of paving are to be seen. A large bridge with twelve arches, belonging to an aqueduct, on the W. of it, half-way to La Mola, does not seem to be ancient : there are, on the other hand, remains of a villa on the E. of it, just before it descends into the valley. At La Mola traces of antiquity are absent. It seems probable, however, that it was here that the road we have been following fell into the Via Salaria, which left the valley of the Tiber at the Osteria del Grillo, about 16 miles from the Porta Collina. The sixteenth milestone of the road was found on the river bank in 1909.

The question is intimately connected with that as to the site of Eretum, which must be sought 14 miles from Fidenae (*Tab. Peut.*), i.e. 19 miles from Rome, or 18 miles from Rome (*Itin. Ant.*).

Strabo (v. 3. i. p. 228) indicates it as a Sabine village situated above the Tiber at the point where the Via Nomentana joins the Via Salaria, and not far from the Aquae Labanae (cf. *ib.*, ii. p. 238). Vergil speaks of it in the *Aeneid* (vii. 711) with " olive-bearing Mutuesca," and Servius (*ad loc.*) tells us that its name comes " ἀπὸ τῆς Ἥρας," " id est, a Junone, quae illic colitur " (cf. Solin, ii. 10). Dionysius speaks of it in one passage (iii. 32) as lying 107 stadia (13⅜ miles) and in another (xi. 3) 140 stadia (17½ miles) from Rome, and in the latter as lying near the Tiber.

There is much difference of opinion as to its site : but it should probably be placed a little way—a mile or so— to the E. of the modern road, on the low hills above it, the exact site depending upon the view they take as to its distance from Rome. The line of the road is at present anything but clear at this point, for no traces exist on the spot. The remains, too, which are to be seen are somewhat insignificant ; nothing is preserved above-ground but mere heaps of debris. Chaupy, on the other hand, who explored the ground in 1768, gives a far more definite account, which, if it be accepted in its entirety, leaves little doubt as to the site of Eretum. He places the point where the Via Salaria leaves the valley of the Tiber at about the eighteenth ancient mile from Rome (corresponding more or less with the seventeenth modern mile), just after the Ponte di Casa Cotta, where, he says, he saw traces of pavement, some of the stones being *in situ*, while others had been removed. From this point the ancient road diverged from the modern towards the right. A little further on (p. 91) he tells us that the name of the place was Rimane.

The nature of the old ruins within the enceinte would be doubtful, as he does not further describe them, did not Gell (*op. cit.*, 204) speak of them as being of opus reticulatum, of which I cannot say that I saw any traces. But that we have here the site of Eretum (occupied apparently by a mediaeval castle, which is shown in a plan of the road preserved in the State Archives in Rome) seems increasingly probable from the fact that Chaupy, in going towards it from Torre Fiora, not along the road but across the fields, saw, " vis-à-vis l'Hôtellerie de Moricone," a considerable piece of ancient paving running towards the ruins he had discovered. He was, however, in some doubt (and this is particularly unfortunate) whether to attribute it to the prolongation of the Via Nomentana to Eretum or to another road.

Gell (*op. cit.*, 203) remarks that " it is exceedingly difficult to fix with precision upon the places mentioned by this writer, or to connect intelligibly his narrations." His own theory, that Eretum was at Grotta Marozza, is, as we have already said, incorrect : but his whole conception of the facts is vitiated by his supposition that the Via Salaria Vetus ran past Mentana. He is wrong, too, in supposing that the road which at " mile xxi falls into the Via Nomentana from the seventeenth mile of the lower Via Salaria " (i.e. that which runs N. of the Colle del Forno) must be that of which Chaupy speaks. I have already had occasion to make use of Chaupy's accounts

of what he saw, and they appear to me to be of considerable value. The doubt as to the existence of a road running from the prolongation of the Via Nomentana to
Rimane is particularly unfortunate, as no traces of any
such road are, as far as I know, to be found—and this
is an important point in the determination of the site of
Eretum. The discovery of pavement just N. of the
Ponte di Casa Cotta is not positive evidence, it is true,
that the Via Salaria left the river only there, for it is
probable that the road along the Tiber valley follows an
ancient line.

From it seems to have diverged a *deverticulum* about
half a mile N. of Casa Cotta, to judge by a cutting through
the hill to the W. of point 51, though the prolongation
of it is not clear either to the N. or the S., and it certainly
cannot belong to the Via Salaria itself. The latter must
have gone straight on, as indicated in the map, though
no traces of it now exist so far as I know : a little before
the twenty-second mile, according to my reckoning, it
reaches the church which Chaupy (*op. cit.*, 75) rightly
believed to be that of S. Anthimus, whose name the hill
on which it stands still bears. He saw there columns of
granite, of one of which Stevenson [1] observed a fragment, and, on the ascent immediately preceding it, traces
of the pavement of the ancient road. Stevenson (*Bull.
Crist.* 1896, 160) mentions the church, of which nothing
but the apse of mediaeval work now remains standing,
and his discovery of the cemetery in which the martyr
was buried a little way to the E. of Monte Maggiore. The
distance from Rome of the site of his tomb is variously
given as the twenty-second and the twenty-eighth mile.

Monte Maggiore itself may occupy an ancient site,
but there are no traces of antiquity. There are various
ancient fragments in the garden, including two circular
putealia with reliefs. None of these is necessarily of
local provenance, but may have been brought here from

[1] For all this district much valuable information is contained in
a volume of Stevenson's MS. notes, now in the Vatican (*Vat. Lat.*
10551, 55 *sqq.*).

Rome by Prince Sciarra, to whom the villa until recently belonged.

Just S. of Monte Maggiore runs the modern road to Monte Libretti. This appears to follow an ancient line : there is no pavement on the older track, which cuts off some of the windings of the present road, but there are one or two paving-stones *in situ* in the bank on the S. side of the cutting a little way to the W. of the Casa Falconieri, about 2 metres above the present level.

There are no traces of the Via Salaria, so far as I know, on the descent from Monte Maggiore to the Fosso di Carolano, but immediately after this is crossed its line may be clearly seen ascending 35° N. of E. through a deep cutting. On its S.E. edge are traces of buildings running parallel to it, mainly in brick ; they have only recently been laid bare by the removal of the brushwood, the ground having been newly brought under cultivation, and have been much destroyed, so that little but debris is visible above-ground. I saw a fragment of a pediment in white marble, from a tomb or small shrine, the top of a sepulchral cippus (none of the inscribed portion was preserved), a threshold block of sandstone 1·92 metre long by 0·68 wide, and a fragment of a brick pilaster covered with plaster painted red measuring 42 by 36 cm. This may serve to show that the large group of buildings must have been of some importance—possibly they are the ruins of a halting-place on the road half-way between Eretum and Vicus Novus.

A little way beyond, on the S.E. side of the line of the road, a large block of pudding-stone is embedded in the ground—it is probably part of the foundations of a tomb : and a little further on again, just before the point where the old line would fall into the modern path, several paving-stones of limestone may be seen in the field walls. Near the point where a modern path diverges N.N.E. the large blocks of limestone of the *crepido* are to be seen running 35° E. of N. Near this point Stevenson seems to have observed the remains of several buildings on each side of the road, especially of water reservoirs. The corn was already fairly high in places at the time of my visit, but I saw the platform of a villa on the N.W. of the road.

Near the conjectural site of the twenty-fifth milestone the road reaches a new house, and here in a field-wall are many more blocks from the *crepido* of the road : two seem to be *in situ* on the S.E. edge of the modern path, and give the width of the road as 4·50 metres (just over 15 feet) and its direction as 30° E. of N. Here is a large reservoir with four chambers, one of which I measured as 3·90 metres in width, and S.E. of it are remains of substruction walls. The Via Salaria soon reaches the Osteria della Creta (the house at 218 metres), just beyond which is the Fabbrica Palmieri. Here it is joined by the prolongation of the Via Nomentana, with which I shall deal when I come to speak of that road, and also by the modern road from Fara Sabina station, which probably does not follow an ancient line. We must, however, mention a few remains near to its course, and it may be well to include a few remarks on the site of Cures.

To the W. of the Osteria della Creta are the foundations of a villa, but no other ruins are visible until we reach the Grotta S. Andrea, which is the platform of a large villa with a cryptoporticus on its S. and W. sides ; the platform is built in rough opus quadratum of conglomerate and concrete.

The Grotta Volpe, some way to the S., is a water reservoir : and another reservoir will be found further W., just to the N. of the modern road, some distance to the S. of which, on the slopes above the Fosso Carolano, there is some brick debris.

Just before we reach the bridge over the Fosso Corese, a path diverges N.N.E. and then runs almost due N. This is the line given by Kiepert (*Carta dell' Italia Centrale*) as that of the road leading to Cures. The modern road to Fara Sabina on the W. bank of the Fosso Corese may also follow an ancient line.

The site of Cures and the excavations of 1874–75 are described by Lanciani in *Commentationes Philologae in honorem Th. Mommseni* (1877), 411 *sqq.* ; while their continuation in 1877 is mentioned in *Not. Scav.* 1877, 245. The site consists of a hill with two summits, round the base of which runs the Fosso Corese. Nibby's idea (*Analisi,* i. 537) that it included the whole triangle between the Fosso Corese and the Fosso Carolano, as far E. as point 181 on the map, is absurd. The W. summit was occupied by the necropolis, the E. by the citadel (here stands the church of S. Maria degli Arci), and the lower ground between the two by the city itself. Some traces of the walls of the citadel, and of the cutting which separated it from the rest of the town, were recognised ; while in the necropolis a few graves of the Imperial period, the bodies being buried under tiles, were discovered.

The excavations brought to light a part of the principal temple, the forum, and some remains of private houses.

Cures is, as is well known, connected with the earliest history of Rome, as the home of Titus Tatius, who, according to the legend, founded the Sabine settlement on the Quirinal, and of Numa. At the beginning of the Imperial period it is spoken of as an unimportant place, but the inscriptions seem to indicate that it rose to greater prosperity in the second century A.D., as did so many of the country towns of Italy.

The classical literature with regard to it is summarised by Mommsen in *C.I.L.* ix. 471, and by Hülsen in Pauly-Wissowa, *R.E.* iv. 1814, while Tomassetti (*op. cit.*, 119 *sqq.*) deals fully with the mediaeval history of the place. In the territory of Cures, near the twenty-fifth mile from Rome, was the cemetery of SS. Tiburtius, Hyacinthus, and Alexander (*Bull. Crist.* 1880, 107).

Capmartin de Chaupy, after having identified the site by means of the inscription *C.I.L.* ix. 4962, was so pleased with the discovery that he established himself in the Casino d' Arci, and proposed to collect there whatever he could find of the antiquities of the town (*op. cit.*, iii. 79).

About a mile and a half to the W. of Cures is the ruin known as the Grotte di Torri, which by some writers (e.g. Cluver, *Italia antiqua,* and Galletti, *Gabio antica citta di Sabina scoperta ove è ora Torri overo le grotte di Torri*) was supposed to be an ancient city, while others have found in it the site of a temple (Chaupy, *op. cit.*, iii. 82). The ruins consist, however, as a fact, of an enormous rectangular platform, measuring about 96 by 93 metres, having an outer wall faced with polygonal work, very neatly jointed, with the faces of the blocks smoothed. Just inside this polygonal wall a cryptoporticus, the walls of which are faced with opus incertum, can be traced on all sides except on the S.S.E.; and on the W.S.W. there are two passages, the outer 3·67 metres in width, the inner 4 metres, the first of which is lighted by slit windows 0·67 by 0·13 metre on the outside, where they pierce the polygonal wall. In the centre of the platform is a large water reservoir, above which is a courtyard 13·60 by 7·38 metres, surrounded by a gutter of slabs of travertine.

The total thickness of the outer wall, from the face of the polygonal blocks to the face of the opus incertum of the cryptoporticus, is only 1·2 metre, the polygonal wall being only a single block thick, so that by no possibility could it have stood alone to a height of 4 or 5 metres. The attempts that have been made to see in this building the ruins of a primitive city are therefore futile; it is nothing more than a very large villa of Roman date. It has recently been described in a paper by Giovenale (well illustrated with photographs) in *Dissertazioni dell' Accad. Pontif. d'Archeologia*, Series ii. vol. vii. 351 *sqq.*, Figs. 9–14.

On one of the blocks of the W.S.W. side at the W.N.W. angle are three phalli together (see Fig. 2), and on the N.N.W. side (low down) a lion. It may be worth noting that Gell (*op. cit.*, 193) has again misunderstood Chaupy, who places these perfectly correctly at Grotte di Torri, and not at S. Pietro, a church which apparently stood at or near the point (181 on the map) where the road turns off to the village of Corese.

After this digression we may now return to the Via Salaria, which we left at the Osteria della Creta. Just N. of this building, on the W. edge of the road, are the foundations of an ancient building, and on the hill a mile to the

N., to the E. of the Casa S. Croce, is the platform of a villa (Vespignani, *Ann. Inst.* 1834, 107). At the twenty-seventh (ancient) mile from Rome we reach the Ponte Mercato : the present bridge is new, but there are remains of an older one, not necessarily of Roman date, in concrete, 3·35 metres in width.

On the N. edge of the old road is a tomb—a round mass of concrete, within which is a square chamber with three rectangular niches, lined with brick and opus reticulatum. Beyond this a line of stones marks the course of the old road, which crosses the modern just before the site of the twenty-eighth milestone, and follows a valley in an N.E. direction. The older Roman road ran almost due N. from the Osteria Nerola, and now forms the boundary between the provinces of Rome and Perugia for a little way, and, further on, that between the communes of Fara Sabina and Ponticelli. Through the valley of which I have spoken the Via Salaria can be clearly traced. The roadway is about 6 metres wide, and the *crepidines* 0·60 metre each. On the S.E. side of it, on a projecting hill, is a large platform, upon which are some unfluted columns of pudding-stone 0·60 metre in diameter : the place bears the name of S. Margherita, but it is an ancient site, though a church may have been erected there in later times. Not far off is a round-headed channel cut in the rock, which may have served to supply water, as there are still springs in the neighbourhood. A little further on, below the road, are the remains of a building in brick and concrete. Three hundred yards beyond this is the so-called Ponte del Diavolo, an embankment wall in opus quadratum of local conglomerate, with the N.W. side alone free, by which the road is supported in its ascent on the S.E. slopes of the valley, which it now abandons for the time. It is about 20 metres in length, with a turn in the middle, according to the plan of Vespignani (*Ann. · Inst. cit.*, tav. C), 7·40 metres in height at the highest part and 10 metres in width.[1] There

[1] Vespignani makes it only 4 metres, but I quote my own measurement. It will be seen, too, that the measurements of his

is a parapet on the N.W. side 60 cm. in width, while that on the S.E. side, which must have served as a footpath, is no less than 2·30 metres wide. There are eight buttresses, and between the fifth and sixth from the S. end there is an aperture for drainage 1·87 metre in height, and varying in width from 1·7 metre at the top to 1·42 at the bottom, the two upper side stones converging slightly. The blocks are practically rectangular, the vertical joints not being always quite perpendicular, and are large, from 65 to 75 cm. in height. The lowest course projects slightly, and the buttresses project from 65 to 80 cm.

A mile and a half further is the Madonna della Quercia, and a short two miles on, the site of the post-station of ad Novas or Vicus Novus; and here we may fittingly abandon the study of the Via Salaria, which we have already followed for a considerable distance beyond what are, strictly speaking, the limits of the Roman Campagna.

plan do not agree with those of his elevation, the latter being, it would seem, correct. Apparently the scale of the former is about one-half too small, which would make the total length about 40 metres.

THE VIA NOMENTANA

THE ANCIENT VIA NOMENTANA diverged from the Via Salaria at the Porta Collina, and ran to the Porta Nomentana of the Aurelian wall, through the garden of the British Embassy, some 75 metres to the S.E. of the present Porta Pia. The Porta Nomentana had two semi-circular towers with square bases; the right-hand tower, now removed, stood upon the tomb of Q. Haterius: of this tomb only a few blocks remain and not a vestige of an inscription. The left-hand tower is well preserved.

About 60 metres of the pavement of the old road was found in the Villa Patrizi on the right of the road outside Porta Pia, and many other discoveries were made when the villa was pulled down and the headquarters of the railway administration constructed; but the present road, as far as the Città Giardino Aniene, now presents hardly any archaeological interest; new buildings have sprung up along it, and Rome is gradually spreading in this direction, so that all the old landmarks are vanishing fast.

The road took a curiously indirect course, winding considerably. It was flanked by many tombs, and a little to the N. of the Castra Pretoria are the Catacombs of S. Nicomedes. On a Roman road to the N. of these again were found tombs of the late Republican or early Imperial period, including a fine sepulchral relief of a husband and wife. Some remains of a Christian cemetery were also discovered; but nothing of these can be seen now, for the modern road is so much wider than the ancient that it conveys no idea of what it was like, and much of what I saw when I first described the road twenty years ago has disappeared completely.

The exact course of the road as far as S. Agnese has until lately been somewhat uncertain, though it can never have been far from the modern road ; but the pavement was discovered in 1902 at the corner of the Via Pasqualina (now Via Pola), 2 metres below the present ground-level. At S. Agnese, if not before, the ancient road must coincide with the modern.

On the W. is the round mausoleum of Constantia, daughter of Constantine, with the circus-shaped cemetery attached. The porphyry sarcophagus in it is now in the Sala della Croce Greca of the Vatican ; the one opposite it comes from Torre Pignattara.

In the garden attached to S. Agnese is the inscription, which runs : "*Celeri Neronis Augusti l. a. . . . o.*," which is thought by some to refer to Celer, one of the architects of the Golden House of Nero. The block of marble on which it was carved was converted into one of the capitals of the church of S. Agnese.

The Via Nomentana went on from S. Agnese as far as the bridge on the line taken by the modern road ; along this modern road on the right we see a tomb in the enclosure wall of the Villa Blanc, but it is a reconstruction of one found on the Via Flaminia. A little further on the left, opposite the Osteria Mangani, there were remains of a wall in opus quadratum, belonging either to a tomb or to the *crepido* of the road itself (the wall of massive blocks, that is, which served as its edging), and in the construction of the fort on the right, just above the railway, the foundations of a large tomb were destroyed, and also remains of earlier burials—fragments of bones mixed with " monochrome Italo-Greek iridescent pottery."

On the left-hand side of the road, some 200 yards away in the valley, is the tomb known as the Sedia del Diavolo, a very fine specimen of work of the second or third century A.D., consisting of two chambers one above the other, the upper one with fine ornamental brickwork.

In the quarries to the N. are the foundations of a villa, with an extensive system of reservoirs for water storage cut in the rock.

The Via Nomentana now descends sharply to the valley of the Anio, and we soon reach the Ponte Nomentano. Very little of the original bridge remains; it is generally believed, like the Ponte Salario, to have been rebuilt by Narses, but it has been considerably transformed even since his day, and now only has one arch in use; it is crowned by a picturesque mediaeval tower. In 1849 it was cut for a length of 7 metres by the French, in their advance on Rome.

Immediately after the bridge a hill rises on the right of the road, known as the Mons Sacer.

This mount was the historic scene of the retirement of the plebs in 494 B.C. It will be remembered how, in resentment at what was considered an unjust law, the army marched out of Rome and settled here, intending to found a new city; and how the famous speech by Menenius Agrippa on the belly and its members reconciled them to Rome. Nowadays it is a far from pleasing spot, owing to unprepossessing surroundings; but has a glorious view of the surrounding hills, and would have been a fine site for a town better laid out and built than the misnamed garden suburb (on the *lucus a non lucendo* principle) which now occupies it.

If, as a recent theory has it, the plebeians were the dispossessed aristocracy of the Regal period, their continual struggles with the patricians have a very natural basis. It is pointed out by Hülsen in support of his theory that the family names of all of the kings except Romulus and the Tarquins are those of plebeian *gentes*, as are the names of three of the hills of the Septimontium (the Caelius, Cispius, and Oppius).

Here a road diverges to the N. which is now known as the Via delle Vigne Nuove (Road of the New Vineyards). This, though now it shows little trace of antiquity, is certainly an ancient road—i.e. the Via Patinaria; the cutting made for it to the W. of Casale Mangani may be noticed and also its straightness of line. A road branches off from it on the left, which is also ancient, now called the Via della Buffalotta. To the E. of the Via Patinaria,

a little further on, is the Casale Chiari, which occupied the
site of a large villa, which is identified with the Villa of
Phaon to which Nero fled and where he committed suicide.
An interesting confirmation of this identification was a
discovery made in 1891 of the cinerary urn of Claudia
Egloge, probably the old nurse of Nero, who, as Suetonius
tells us, with Acte, provided for his burial. We also know
the name of the road : the *Catalogus Imperatorum* notes
" Nero occisus Patinaria via."

The large mediaeval tower (a later farmhouse has been
built against it) called Torre Redicicoli, further along this
road, occupies without doubt an ancient site ; there are
various fragments of coloured marble bricks, etc., to be
seen about. Beyond this the road cannot be traced, and
it most likely ran on N.E. to join the Via della Buffalotta,
to which we may now return. To the E. of it, at the
second kilometre, are traces of excavations, in which were
found remains of dwelling-houses, two statuettes, a lead
pipe, and some coins ; they (the excavations) were made
in 1831, and were closed as unsuccessful, after having
employed twenty men for two weeks. To the N.E. again
is the Casale della Cecchina. Just beyond there is a
cutting traversed by the modern road, which seems to be
of ancient origin : beyond this point there are no traces
of antiquity for some distance.

There are many paving-stones under the bridge which
crosses the stream (Fosso Buffalotta), and the road continues on the further side of it, still in a straight line
(due N.) until it passes on the left the Chiesuola Buffalotta
—a tomb of ornamental brickwork, the front being of
yellow bricks, the sides of red. Soon after this it appears
to divide into three branches, two of which turn N.W. to
cross the Fosso Formicola, while the third keeps straight
on. All the three must have fallen into the ancient road
from Malpasso to Mentana. The first of the branches,
which runs N.W., passes the remains of a villa on the S.
and those of another brick tomb which faces N.W. ; the
ruins to the N.W. of this are mediaeval, though they no
doubt occupy an ancient site. Brick debris is to be found

all over this plateau. There is a circular chamber cut in the rock on the edge of the stream, into which run three water channels ; the front of it has a plastered niche with traces of painting (rosettes, etc.), so that it may have been a fountain, the front of which was ornamented—a kind of nymphaeum, in fact. Close by are caves, which may be pre-Roman tombs.

Some way before the Fosso Buffalotta the Via di Tor S. Giovanni diverges to the right. This presents no definite traces of antiquity, but is very probably ancient, to judge by the existence of a few paving-stones at the fountain W.N.W. of the Casale Tor S. Giovanni, and of a cutting to the N.W., by which it would ascend to the plateau. About a kilometre N.N.W. of the casale are the remains of another villa in the banks of a stream, to which the road probably led. Whether it went further I do not know ; but it may well have joined the others of which we have just spoken, on the high ground E. of Casale Marcigliana.

In this district, we may say between Tor S. Giovanni and the Tiber, is to be sought the site of Crustumerium, though no remains of it exist. It is frequently mentioned in the early history of Rome : and according to Pliny and Livy it must have lain hereabouts : and though the place itself had entirely disappeared (the city was finally conquered in 500 B.C., the tribus Crustumina being formed probably in 471 B.C.), and Pliny—this time correctly—names it among the lost cities of Latium, the name seems to have clung to the district, the fertility of which, and especially the pears which it produced, remained famous.

It was apparently on the edge of the Sabine territory ; it is mentioned, with Caenina and Antemnae, among the Sabine cities in the story of the rape of the Sabine women, but among the Prisci Latini by Livy and Dionysius, and the latter tells us that it was an Alban colony of far greater antiquity than Rome. There are various opinions as to its site, and it is impossible in the present state of our knowledge to be more exact.

We now return to the Via Nomentana, which we left just beyond the bridge over the Anio. The cutting through the hill, by which the road descends to the stream before the fifth kilometre, is probably of ancient origin.

The road descends again through a cutting of ancient origin, which has recently been deepened (two ancient drains cut in the rock being thus exposed), to a bridge over the Fosso della Cecchina, in which there were some traces of ancient paving years ago. Beyond is the Casale dei Pazzi on the right, with a picturesque group of pines.

A little further along, on the right, is the brick tomb known as the Torraccio della Cecchina, or di Spuntapiedi : it is similar in construction to the Sedia del Diavolo, and is built of red and yellow bricks, the former in front, the latter at the sides. The lower chamber (not now accessible) had four niches, and was reached by a staircase on the outside, while the upper chamber has four niches also. Both retain traces of decoration in painted stucco. The construction of the dome is similar to that of the Sedia del Diavolo. The façade towards the road has two list windows, between which is a festoon in relief, cut in the brick.

The cutting made for the old road, or for the extraction of its materials, can be seen on the S.E. edge of the modern road.

A little further on the right are the Ruderi del Coazzo, of which everything standing is mediaeval, though the site is probably ancient. To the W. of them an ancient road diverges to the right (now known as the Strada Vecchia di Palombara or Via Palombarese, for it is still in use for the most part),[1] while another diverged S. to the Via Tiburtina, past the Casale S. Basilio.

At the point where the first road leaves the Via Nomentana the cutting made for it is clearly traceable, and several paving-stones may be seen a little further on : while, after a couple of miles, the cuttings which run just

[1] The first part of it, which is purely modern, turns off at Capobianco.

to the N. of the modern track are conspicuous, and there is pavement preserved in them.

On the right, on a hill across the stream, is the large Casale di Marco Simone, or Castel Cesi (for to that family it belonged until 1678). It occupies in all probability an ancient site : immediately to the E. of it are vaulted substructures in concrete; while at the casale itself is a sarcophagus with a group of the Three Graces in the centre of the front under a large niche, and two other figures on each side in smaller niches.

A mile to the N.E. is the Casale di Marco Simone Vecchio, where there are no traces of antiquity.

The rest of the road into Palombara has no particular archaeological interest, and Palombara itself will be dealt with later. We now return to the Via Nomentana.

Before the eighth kilometre-stone the modern road crosses over, leaving the ancient road on the left. There are various remains on the left of the road, of no great importance—of villas or tombs ; those at the point marked Ficulea on the Staff map belong to the former.

The Casale Coazzo apparently occupies an ancient site ; there is a wall indeed in the floor of the yard, and fragments of columns, etc., are to be seen—also many paving-stones, which, however, probably do not come from the Via Nomentana, the pavement of which, 4 metres wide, is intact for some distance.

To the N. again, on the further side of a deep valley, is the Casale della Cesarina.

Though the exact site of Ficulea remains somewhat uncertain (as is often the case with these ancient " cities " or villages of Latium), we know generally that it cannot have been very far from La Cesarina. It is certain that it lay on the road from Rome to Nomentum, between the two places, inasmuch as this road, according to Livy, was originally known as Via Ficulensis : and it was not far from Fidenae, for Varro speaks of " qui tum "—after the departure of the Gauls—" sub urbe populi, ut Ficuleates ac Fidenates et finitimi alii " ; and Dionysius places the territory allotted to the Claudian tribe between Fidehae and Ficulea. Nor was it far from the Monte Corniculani, for the same author classes it with the cities built by the aborigines. " Antemnae, Caenina, Ficulea which lay towards the Montes Corniculani and Tibur." Atticus, the friend and correspondent of Cicero, had an estate which lay on the boundary between the territory of Ficulea and Nomentum, so it is indifferently spoken of under either name : and Martial's estate at Nomentum must also have been near the edge of Ficulea, since in *Epig.* vi. 27 he calls his friend Nepos *bis vicinum*, because he lived near him in Rome and out of it dwelt at " Veteres Ficeliae," in the same neighbourhood as himself. The epithet *vetus*, which occurs also in Livy, may only refer to the fact that the origin of the place was lost in remote antiquity.

An examination of the district helps us little to fix the site ; there are no remains of an earlier date—the few ruins which we saw all belong to the Roman period, and sufficient evidence is entirely wanting.

Returning to the Via Nomentana, we find a well-preserved piece of the ancient paving on the left, and just after the tenth kilometre-stone reach the so-called " Scavi del Papa S. Alessandro," that is the basilica (there are in reality two) and cemetery of S. Alexander (probably *not* the Pope). It fell within the territory of Ficulea. There are a few galleries still preserved, but as a catacomb it is of little interest.

A little further on is the mediaeval Torraccio di Capobianco, into the upper part of which are built paving-stones and marble : it rests upon an ancient tomb, the chamber of which is of tufa concrete with a barrel vault, while the exterior was faced with slabs of travertine.

In excavations made in 1795 in the tenuta of Capobianco were found several inscriptions, one a dedication to Stata Mater, and amongst others an epitaph of a *scurra*, or jester; also a curious and interesting placard which was placed outside some baths : " In this property of Aurelia Faustiniana you can take a bath as if you were in the city, in the city fashion, and you will enjoy every comfort." Beside the inscription actual remains of the baths were found, with a mosaic pavement (which was afterwards removed to Paris), with a hypocaust under it, supported alternately by terra-cotta tubes and brick pillars, about 3 Roman feet apart. The pavement was of geometrical design, and mainly in black and white.

The pavement of the Via Nomentana is well preserved on both sides of the Casale di Capobianco; to the N.E. of it I measured the width of it as 14 feet. From Capobianco the road runs on almost due N. and considerable portions of the pavement are at first preserved. Further on is the prominent mediaeval watch-tower known as Torre Lupara. On the right of the road, at the fourteenth kilometre, is the Casale S. Antonio, which occupies a remarkably strong site, though what is to be seen there is purely mediaeval. The ancient road must now have run just to the right of the modern, which cuts through the foundations of some ancient buildings; and soon afterwards it turns off sharply to the N.E., making a steep ascent and descent, and rejoining the modern road, which keeps round the head of the Valle Valentino, just before the mediaeval Casale di Monte Gentile. According to an erroneous view, this was the site of Ficulea: whereas Nibby puts Caenina here. This place appears twice in the earliest history of Rome: (1) Romulus was sacrificing there (before the foundation of Rome) when Remus was captured by the shepherds of Numitor, and (2) it was from Acro, king of Caenina, that Romulus won the first *spolia opima*, in the battle following the rape of the Sabine women, when the people of Caenina were the first to attack the Romans, but were easily defeated and their city taken. It figures in Pliny's list of the lost towns of Latium : and of its site we really know nothing except that it must have been situated close to Rome, as it is mentioned in connexion with Crustumerium and Antemnae. It gave its name to a priesthood of the Roman State, which still existed in the time of the Empire.

On the right, further on, is the large tomb, crowned by a mediaeval tower, marked in the maps as Torre Mancini.

The road then descends steeply, and is protected on

the descent by massive supporting walls, which keep up the bank on either side : they are in reticulatum and brick, with apsidal niches alternating with projecting buttresses, and weepholes to allow the moisture to escape. Those on the right are the more conspicuous, but those on the left have recently been cleared.

The road descends steeply, and then reascends to Mentana, there being no traces of antiquity in the last portion. The modern village probably occupies the lower part of the site of the ancient Nomentum, which extended further to the E., the only side upon which there is space available ; on the other sides, especially on the W. and S., the position is well protected by ravines. There are, however, no remains of walls or of buildings attributable to it to be seen *in situ*. The site is really fixed by the distance of 14 miles from Rome given by the *Tabula Peutingerana*, which leaves no room for doubt. Monte d'Oro, where remains of villas and statuary (including a youthful Bacchus) have recently been found, is over a mile too near to Rome, whereas the 14 miles take us just up to the modern village ; and the name Mentana is obviously derived from Nomentum. Inscriptions have been found here too, in which its magistrates and priest-hoods are mentioned, though the exact site of their dis-covery is not known. As Dessau remarks, there was considerable doubt in the minds of the Romans them-selves whether Nomentum was to be considered to have belonged in origin to the Latin or to the Sabine race : though the former opinion rightly prevailed, we find that Vergil was sufficiently undecided to give both in two different passages !

Roads diverge from Mentana in various directions ; there is, in the first place, one running E. to join the road to Palombara. Another, of which we shall speak presently, runs due N. in continuation of the line of the Via Nomentana. A third runs W. to Monte Rotondo. A fourth is that which is supposed by some writers to be the Via Salaria, but wrongly.

The line of road which we have seen leaving Mentana

on the N. side runs very slightly E. of N. to join the Via Salaria near the Fabbrica Palmieri, between the twenty-fifth and twenty-sixth mile from Rome. Though there is no actual pavement *in situ* upon it, there is no doubt as to its antiquity. It may have served as an alternative route to the Via Salaria, as the distance by it is about the same, but it is a good deal more hilly ; and it does not seem to have been much frequented, inasmuch as it is not to be found in the *Tabula Peutingerana* or in the *Itineraries* : and there are very few remains of antiquity along its course.

In about another mile we reach the massive ruins of Grotta Marozza, which are those of a mediaeval fortress. The name (another form of Maria) is that of a member of the family of the Crescenzi, to whom it belonged.

The Aquae Labanae mentioned by Strabo may be placed in this neighbourhood : there is a sulphur spring a little way S. of the villa marked in our map E. of Grotta Marozza, and another two and a half miles further N.E.— the former is no doubt that which bears the name Bagni di Grotta Marozza.

To the N.E. of Grotta Marozza there are the remains of several other villas of no great importance.

Returning to the road, which we left near Grotta Marozza, we find that it continues to run in a straight line, and there are some limestone paving-stones loose in the path. At the bridge over the Fosso Buffala there are some blocks of squared stone in the stream bed and in the bridge itself, probably belonging to the earlier structure : and on the ascent beyond it paving-stones may be seen in the field walls. The road now descends to the valley of the Fiora, turning sharply to the left. In a straight line with its course up till now is the lofty Torre Fiora, which is entirely mediaeval. Its great height is necessitated by the fact that it stands in very low ground.

After this the road presents no features of interest until it joins the Via Salaria.

III

THE VIA TIBURTINA

T HE VIA TIBURTINA was one of the most important
roads that issued from the gates of Rome, carrying
a large amount both of local and of long-distance
traffic. The road itself is, however, until the last part
of its course, in no way remarkable either for the beauty
of the country it traverses or for the difficulties which
have had to be dealt with by its engineers. On the contrary, until the actual ascent to Tibur begins, the road
runs through a gently undulating and somewhat monotonous district, and has no obstacles to contend with
except the river Anio, which it twice crosses. The
ascent to Tibur too, though fairly steep, presents no
problems of engineering. The result is that the modern
road has followed the ancient line pretty closely, and no
deviations of importance are to be noticed until two-
thirds of the distance have been traversed, in the
neighbourhood of Bagni, where the change in the line is
probably due to the inundations of the sulphur springs,
which, until they were carried to the Anio by a canal
(constructed by the Commune of Tivoli with help from
Cardinals Ippolito d'Este and Bartolomeo della Cueva in
the sixteenth century) ran unchecked over the plain.

No milestones have been found between Rome and
Tibur—that given by many authors as the fourteenth
is a forgery. The positions of those which have been
discovered further along the road, however, make it
necessary that the distance between Rome and Tibur
should have been twenty miles, as the *Antonine Itinerary*
has it. This fact, however, involves us in considerable
difficulties, which will be dealt with below.

It is, further, by no means certain by which gate the original Via Tiburtina left the city. Hülsen prefers the theory that the road from the Porta Esquilina is the original Via Tiburtina, though the name " Tiburtina Vetus " is not vouched for by any classical authority and is only retained for convenience. This seems to be the most probable supposition, inasmuch as the arch erected by Augustus in 5 B.C. for the passage of the Aquae Marcia Tepula and Iulia, bearing an inscription recording his restoration of them (which was incorporated in the outer half of the Porta Tiburtina of the Aurelian wall) points to the importance of the road which passed under it, while we find that the straight road from the Porta Viminalis passed through the Aurelian wall by a small postern, which was closed at some unknown period. We may notice, too, that the earliest tombs which flanked the " Tiburtina Vetus " were found to date from the beginning of the Imperial period.

Along the first part of the course of the road various discoveries have been made, the most notable being that of the " Tomba della Medusa " excavated in 1839, which lay on the N. of the road. It is a square chamber in opus quadratum of travertine and contained three fine sarcophagi (from one of which it takes its name) which are now in the Lateran. Other discoveries of tombs, etc., were made in the course of the work of building the great modern hospital (the Policlinico) ; but they are mostly of minor importance.

Beyond the Policlinico the course of the road was not traceable, even before the changes caused by the growth of the city of to-day, but if prolonged it would fall into the line of the modern highroad near the point where it is joined by the so-called Via Cupa (dark lane), i.e. where it turns almost at right angles from N.N.E. to E. The fact that this change of direction brings it into the same straight line with the road from the Porta Viminalis is certainly an argument in favour of the claim of the latter to be regarded as the original Via Tiburtina. The question is, in fact, one of considerable difficulty, and with the evidence at our disposal it is difficult to arrive at a definite conclusion.

We may now return to the Porta Tiburtina, now known as the Porta San Lorenzo, and follow the line taken by the modern road.

The Porta Tiburtina was made up of two parts—the outer portion was formed by the aforementioned arch made by Augustus to carry the aqueducts, and on the outside Honorius added another arch and two towers flanking it. The inner arch was also constructed by Honorius, who restored the walls about A.D. 400, as the inscription records. The whole of the inner arch was removed by Pius IX in 1869. The tower on the right hand of the gate has in its base some travertine blocks from a tomb, one of which bears an inscription.

The construction of a new quarter has completely altered the appearance of the Via Tiburtina between the gate and San Lorenzo, and all traces of antiquity have entirely disappeared. At some point before the first milestone was reached the tomb of Pallas, the freedman and Finance Minister of Claudius, was situated.

The original basilica of San Lorenzo was erected by Constantine, but was quite small. Pelagius enlarged it, and Honorius III in 1218 built the forepart and destroyed the older apse, and also built the portico in front.

The name " Campo Verano," by which the modern cemetery is known, is of classical origin, coming perhaps from the possessors of the ground in Roman times. In one of the crypts of the extensive catacomb of S. Cyriaca S. Laurence was buried, and a site for the basilica was only obtained by cutting away the rock and thus destroying a portion of the catacomb, in order to bring the tomb of the saint into its right position in the church—that is, in the centre of it, immediately in front of the apse. Many discoveries have been, and still are, made in the cemetery from time to time.

A strong argument against the supposition of some writers that the Via Tiburtina passed through the Campo Verano is the fact that on the left of the modern high-

road lies the catacomb of S. Hippolytus, which, had it
not been divided from that of S. Cyriaca by the Via
Tiburtina, would not have had a name of its own. The
statue of the saint (now in the Lateran Museum) which
was found here is important as being a genuine pro-
duction of Christian Art of the third century after
Christ.

A little further on, the highroad crosses the railway to
Florence. The construction of the bridge led to the
discovery of a series of underground passages intended
for use as cisterns and converted into a place of burial
in the first century B.C.

The construction of the fort on the right of the road,
some 500 yards to the N.N.E., led to the discovery of
a large and splendid villa, belonging to the first century
A.D. The drainage of the villa was extremely well
arranged, all the rain-water being carefully collected and
conveyed by shafts into a network of passages cut in the
rock and lined with cement. At the bottom of one of
these shafts a statue of Apollo was found. The tract of
country bounded by the highroad on the S., the railway
on the W., and the Anio on the N. and E., forms the
Tenuta di Pietralata, and contains extensive tufa quarries,
some of which may be ancient.

There is nothing of interest until we reach the River
Anio, which the modern road crosses by a new bridge,
returning to the old line a mile further on ; while the old
Ponte Mammolo (a name which can be traced back as far
as A.D. 1030) lies to the right. It was built of blocks of tufa
and travertine, and one of its ancient arches still remains
in part, though damaged in 1849, when it was broken by
the French. Here the Emperor Henry V and Pope
Paschal II concluded their well-known agreement over
the investitures in 1111.

Just where the ancient road is joined by the present
line a branch road diverged from it to the N. Some
traces of its pavement and of a group of tombs connected
with it and of a large villa were found in excavations in
1878 and may still be seen, though a quarry railway has

done a certain amount of damage. Whether it went as far as the Via Nomentana is uncertain.

At Settecamini, the next point of interest, a road diverges to the left, and eventually reaches the village of Montecelio. Its antiquity—it cannot be recommended to the motorist, and is not even passable for carriages—is demonstrated by the cuttings made for it through the hills, and by the existence of some characteristic paving at one point. Some authors have, indeed, thought it to be the original Via Tiburtina ; and, while this is uncertain, it must be confessed that, without a greater detour than is taken by the later road (following the present highroad more or less), it is impossible to arrive at the distance of 20 miles from Rome which the *Itineraries* give. The numbering of the milestones beyond Tibur would naturally have been maintained, even if a later improvement, made we know not at what period, shortened the distance from Rome to Tibur to 18½ miles.

The country is bare and undulating, but was more thickly populated in antiquity : and one of the most interesting ruins in the Campagna is to be found close by the road half a mile N.E. of an extinct volcanic crater known as the Laghetto di Marco Simone. Here is an extremely well-preserved circular building constructed entirely below-ground, in the second century after Christ. It is so completely hidden that we only found it by noticing some bushes on an otherwise bare hill-side, which proved to be growing round the window on the S.W., by which alone it can now be entered. The roof is domed and, like the Pantheon, had a round hole in it to admit light and air : it is decorated with plain white mosaic, which is almost perfect—and is, so far as I know, the earliest dome in existence so decorated; the claim of that of the Imperial mausoleum at Spalato, which belongs to the time of Diocletian, being thus definitely set aside. The walls of the lower part are composed of very fine brickwork, and there is a brick cornice just below the dome. Where the entrance was, or what is the level of the floor, it is impossible to say, for the interior is full of debris ; nor have I ever found any record of it since I first came upon it about twenty years ago.

To the N.E. are the ruins of a small fortified village of the eighth century after Christ—a *curtis,* as it is called : the enclosure wall remains for some 100 yards on the W. ; but the church, which must have existed, has disappeared : while to the N.E. is a tomb of interesting construction. The internal chamber is in the form of a Greek cross, in which are four shafts for ventilation : on the top of it was a round drum. The whole was enclosed by a wall in which there were niches, constructed of concrete, faced, like the tomb itself, with opus reticulatum and brickwork, and probably belonging to the second century after Christ.

Beyond this point the road presents no features of interest, and we may return to Settecamini.

The name refers to the seven chimneys of the old farmhouse, with its fine sixteenth-century door : but the number seven alludes also to the seven sons of Santa Sinforosa, a martyr. The remains of the church dedicated to her were excavated in 1878, and still may be seen, built into a modern house, on the edge of the tramway, a couple of miles further along. Rather over a mile due S. across the Anio is Lunghezza on the Via Collatina, to which a modern winding road turns off a little further back.

On the left is the large mediaeval Castell' Arcione, recently restored, with well-preserved walls and towers and a lofty square central keep. The name is that of a family of considerable importance in Rome in the thirteenth century, to whom the castle belonged. A little way beyond it to the E. the pavement of the ancient road has come to light in a field, showing that it cut over the shoulder of the hill and avoided the windings of the modern road.

To the N. is the conspicuous farmhouse known as Tor di Sordi, taking its name from another Roman family of the Middle Ages.

A little further on the road emerges from the undulating pasture-land, which it has so far traversed, into a desolate

3. SULPHUR LAKE NEAR BAGNI (p. 99).

Anderson, Photo.

4. THE LARGER BATHS, HADRIAN'S VILLA (p. 108).

To face p. 99.

flat plain, covered by the incrustations deposited by the sulphur springs of the Aquae Albulae. They are so considerable that a small lake known as the Lago dei Tartari, which was in existence not many years ago, is now completely dried up and filled in : and if we follow the modern road to Montecelio, which turns off just here, and which probably presents an ancient line, up to the Lago della Regina, we shall find that it, too, is continually restricting its own area by the amount of deposit left on its banks (Fig. 3). The water is bluish, and strongly impregnated with sulphur and carbonate of lime. It was in use in Roman days, for on the W. bank of the lake are the considerable remains of a large building which was used as a thermal establishment—though its attribution to Marcus Agrippa and to Zenobia, the Queen of Palmyra, whom Aurelian brought in captivity to Rome, has nothing to recommend it.

The building was decorated with statues of Aesculapius, Hygeia, Apollo Lycius, etc., with columns of verde antico marble, and other works of art ; so that it must have been of a certain magnificence. A metrical inscription records that a man, whose name is unknown, dedicated to the nymph Albula, the tutelary deity of the springs, a bronze head of his wife, whose complexion had been restored by the use of the baths. Another dedication, with a portrait of himself, was set up by a man who had been suffering from the results of a wound by a wild boar at Rusellae in Etruria. Dedications to the Aquae Albulae and to Hercules by various people were also found, and this fact would seem to show in itself that they were available for public use. Another gave us only the name of Thespis, the founder of Greek tragedy, and was carved on a herma which once bore a head of him.

A short distance to the E. is the Casale S. Antonio, near which is some flat ground which has been known as Conche ever since 1386 : and inasmuch as we are told that Aurelian assigned to Zenobia a villa in the territory of Tibur, not far from the villa of Hadrian, nor from that place which is called Concae, the coincidence may be

99

H

sufficient to establish this site. If not, it is at least sufficiently curious : and we shall not find that many of the traditional names for the ancient villas in the territory of Tivoli (the remains of which are both numerous and considerable) are as well vouched for as this. Thus, the attempt to find here the villa of Regulus, a lawyer of Martial's time, is due to a false interpretation ; it was really 4 miles from Rome, not from Tivoli.

At the station of Bagni, on the highroad, is the modern bathing establishment, where in summer a bath in the sulphur water (the temperature being about 75° Fahr.) is not at all unpleasant, and the strong smell of sulphuretted hydrogen is not noticed after a short while.

Immediately to the E. of it the railway to Tivoli and the Adriatic crosses the road : and after it we come to a surprisingly well-preserved portion of the ancient road. The road-bed, flanked by large blocks of travertine, is fairly well preserved ; while its lava pavement has been taken up bodily and used in a modern wall : but on each side of it there are a number of sepulchral inscriptions still in position, on travertine *cippi*, which belonged to the tombs on each side of the road. They seem to belong to the end of the Republic. The road has been a good deal damaged by searchers for building material ; and Pope Leo X, in a letter of 1519 to the people of Tivoli, thanks them for the blocks of travertine which they had allowed him to take for the building of S. Peter's.

To the W. of the quarries is the group of half-ruined houses known as the Casaccia del Barco, one of which stands on a large ancient tomb—a mass of concrete, with a circular chamber in the interior, lined with blocks of travertine. The name is a corruption of Parco, and alludes to the hunting-park of Cardinal Ippolito d'Este. But long before his day other princes of the Church had amused themselves here in a similar way. A poem written in 1503 by Cardinal Adriano Castellesi describes a day's hunting near the Aquae Albulae in company with Cardinal Ascanio Sforza, in which he makes Diana participate and recline at rest with him. Leo X and, in

100

March 1532, Cardinal Ippolito dei Medici took part in similar sports.

The quarries must at that time have been completely abandoned, and their sheer walls of rock, covered by the deposit of the Aquae Albulae (which after the classical period must have run unchecked on the plain), would have served as a useful enclosure for the various animals that were kept there. The working of the quarries was, as a fact, resumed only a few years ago, after having been, as it seems, entirely given up since Roman times.

To that period, then, we must assign an aqueduct on arches which ends at the quarries, and can have no other *raison d'être*—despite the fact that its construction is so bad that it might be attributed to almost any age. The quarries were very extensive, and the large heap of refuse, close to the Anio, shows that the workings must have continued for many years. The quality of the travertine (Lapis Tiburtinus, or Tivoli stone, is its ancient name) is extremely good, and very different from that of the porous superficial deposit which is largely the product of the sulphur springs.

We soon reach the bridge over the Anio, passing close to a small chapel dedicated to S. Hermes, erected by Pope Hadrian IV (Nicholas Breakspeare) in 1155, perhaps on the spot where he celebrated Mass on S. Peter's Day, after he went to Tusculum with Frederic Barbarossa. Here the ancient road is joined by the modern, which presents no features of interest. The bridge is picturesque and very fairly well preserved, though the bed of the river, and consequently its level, has probably risen since Roman times, for little can be seen of the lower part of the bridge. It had five arches in stone, four of which can still be seen ; but it has been repaired in mediaeval times. It bears the name of Ponte Lucano, which is already found in the twelfth century, though its origin is unknown (for the supposed inscription of M. Plautius Lucanus is a forgery). It was, of course, an important strategic point in the Middle Ages. Close by its E. end stands the large circular mausoleum of the Plautii, which was surrounded, like the mausoleum of Hadrian in Rome, by a low square base, of which little is now left. It is a remarkably fine specimen of a Roman tomb, but the chamber in the interior, which is circular, with the vault supported by a round pillar in the centre, is not accessible. The arms of Paul II, who restored it in 1465, still remain. It was built by M. Plautius Silvanus, who was consul in 2 B.C., for himself and his wife ; as time passed his little son was buried there, then his son P. Plautius Pulcher and Tiberius Plautius Silvanus Aelianus, whose relationship to him is uncertain, but who is of interest as having taken part in Claudius's expedition to Britain.

At the tomb a road diverges to the right which, in ancient times as now, was an important link between the various roads radiating from Rome, serving as a means of communication between the Via Tiburtina and the Via Praenestina. It intersects the modern road to Poli at the Osteria delle Capannelle, and joins the Via Prae-nestina at S. Maria di Cavamonte.

Between Ponte Lucano and Tivoli the exact course of the ancient road is at first undeterminable, as the ground is under cultivation and no traces of it remain : but it is almost certain that it ran in a fairly straight line to join the lane which eventually ascends past the Tempio della Tosse. The modern road runs further to the S., and, 500 yards from the bridge, passes to the left of two ancient rectangular tombs, both built of large blocks of travertine, each of which serves as the foundation of a small modern house. The lower part of each tomb contained a chamber at the ground level, while the upper part was decorated with a bas-relief. One of the two, indeed, has still this decoration, a panel of Parian marble in which is repre-sented a man holding a horse by the bridle ; while the relief belonging to the other is now in the Villa Albani, and its subject is, according to Mrs. Strong, a priest or an initiate, though it has more often been considered to represent the favourite occupations of the deceased.

From an examination of the various MSS. of Pirro Ligorio we learn that these tombs formed part of a group

of four.   The remains of the other two were still visible
in his day, and indeed one of them he actually saw
destroyed for building material.   The relief of one of
them, representing a large lion, is in the Palazzo Barberini
in Rome, while that of the other was apparently not
preserved even then.

It is not unnatural that these monuments should have
been believed to be pillars which flanked the entrance to
Hadrian's Villa; and indeed they were imitated by
Asprucci in designing the entrance to the Villa Borghese
in Rome, close to the Muro Torto.   But their inequality
in size and other reasons make this idea an improbable
one—even though it is probably quite true that the main
road leading to Hadrian's Villa actually passed between
them.   We may well believe, however, that there was
another more direct road from Ponte Lucano, though the
evidence is not entirely sufficient.   A line which is certainly ancient, on the other hand, and is probably of older
origin, is that which runs in a fairly straight line from the
road from Ponte Lucano to Corcolle (itself a necessary line
of communication) in an E.N.E. direction.   It crosses the
road mentioned above at right angles (some of its pavement is still preserved), and then ascends through the
olives right up to the S. extremity of the city of Tivoli,
where a piece of its pavement was found in 1883, just
outside Porta S. Croce.   It would seem that this was the
most direct route from Rome to the important group of
villas to the S. of Tibur, of which we shall speak later.
But why did it start, not from Ponte Lucano, but nearly
a mile to the S. of it ?   There is nothing in the configura-
tion of the ground on either bank of the Anio to explain
the reason, nor was there, so far as I know, any crossing
of the river opposite to its termination; had there been,
it would have led into a quarry district, thoroughly
unsuitable for swift passenger traffic such as one would
have expected between these villas and Rome.

The villa begun by the Emperor Hadrian, according to
his biographer, on his return from his first journey to the
East in A.D. 125, is situated just below the olive-clad

slopes of Tivoli.[1] It recalls to our minds very different associations from those which the word " villa " brings up in England, and even the great villas of the Renaissance must give place to its vast extent. The tourist who once ignorantly spoke of it as Hadrian's village was not so far wrong as he seemed to be. Situated on a plateau between two valleys, both of them bounded by cliffs of volcanic rock—the characteristic red tufa of the Campagna Romana —its ruins occupy an extent of about 600 yards by 300, though its gardens no doubt extended a good deal further than the ruins. The site does not seem at first to be an attractive one, and its unhealthiness in mediaeval and modern times had made the choice of it appear even more strange. But at a greater elevation space for these immense buildings and the gardens which surrounded them would not have been available.

Very little is known of the history of the villa. Its construction began in A.D. 125 and went on during the next ten years, during most of which time Hadrian was absent from Rome. On his return in 135 he retired there and continued to enlarge the villa, decorating it with works of art, until in 138 he was seized by the illness which caused his death. This, however, occurred at Baiae, whither he had caused himself to be removed.

It is clear from the discovery of some imperial busts, the latest of which represents Elagabalus (A.D. 218–222), that the villa continued to be inhabited by Hadrian's successors until that date at least, and there are indeed traces of work done there as late as the time of Diocletian, when it was still known as the Palace of Hadrian. But after this we know nothing of its history for over a thousand years : that Totila took up his quarters there in A.D. 544 is a mere conjecture, unsupported by any evidence.

Earthquakes, no doubt, began the work of destruction, and then it shared in the general desolation of the Cam-

---

[1] A considerable portion of the text is reprinted from an article on Hadrian's Villa which I contributed to *Wonders of the Past*, with the permission of the Editor, which I gratefully acknowledge.

pagna. It is noteworthy that its works of art were not removed elsewhere in ancient times, and that its ruins were not made use of in the Middle Ages for habitation, but only as a quarry for building material. There are indubitable traces of the use of its marble decorations for burning into lime—the fate of so much of the ancient marble with which Roman buildings were decorated.

Pope Pius II visited it in 1461, and gives an account of it which shows that it was then in much the same condition as it is now : " Age has destroyed the form of everything ; ivy now clothes the walls that were covered with tapestries and cloth of gold ; thorns and brambles have grown where tribunes sat, and snakes dwell in queens' chambers ; so unstable is the nature of all things mortal."

With the Renaissance search began to be made for the rich series of art treasures which it contained. Some of the best finds were made in the first half of the eighteenth century, including the famous mosaic of the doves, and several portraits of Antinous, Hadrian's young favourite. Later on, the Scotsman, Gavin Hamilton, made Hadrian's Villa one of his chief centres of activity. The sculptures which he discovered went in part to the Vatican, but in the main to the Earl of Shelburne, and these last are still at Lansdowne House. Others were dispersed among various collections. The total number of works of art so far discovered in the villa, so far as we know, is well over 250, scattered all over the world in numerous public and private collections.

The villa, we are told, contained imitations of the famous buildings which Hadrian (who was one of the most travelled of Roman Emperors) had seen and admired all over the known world ; attempts have been made by the antiquaries to identify the ruins with the list of names given us—not always with success, or even with probability.

There is, however, a key to what seems a chaos of miscellaneous ruins jostling one another in picturesque confusion, and that is the orientation of different parts of the villa. If we follow the archaeologists who take this as their guiding principle, we shall find that the whole falls naturally (leaving aside a number of outlying detached buildings, such as the two theatres and the connecting links between the various portions) into four main divisions, each centring round a large open space or courtyard : the group of the Poikile, that of the main palace, that of Canopus, and that of the " Academy," really a smaller palace.

Taking these in order, we first come to the so-called Poikile, now approached by a beautiful avenue of cypresses, which derives its modern name from having been identified with the " Stoa Poikile " (the varicoloured portico) at Athens, so called from the paintings with which its walls were decorated. Whether the name be correct or not, we certainly have here a huge garden of the formal type once surrounded by a peristyle. Its shape is imitated from that of the stadium or hippodrome, a favourite one among Roman gardens.

The N. wall is still standing to a considerable extent, and was detached from the rest, with a space at each end through which a chariot could pass. It was so arranged that one could walk or drive on one side or other of it, in the shade or in the sun, according to the season, at any hour of the day. From an inscription we learn that it bore the name of " Porticus Triumphi " (which it took from the building of that name in Rome), and that seven times its length was just over a mile. This was the length of the Roman " constitutional," and evidently the ancients liked to know the precise amount of ground they were covering, for other inscriptions of the kind have been found both in Rome and at Pompeii.

The central space was no doubt occupied by a formal garden with box and laurel hedges cut into fantastic shapes. We know them not only from a letter of Pliny the Younger, but from the frescoes (and in less degree from the gardens themselves) at Pompeii, and from some of the few formal gardens of the Renaissance villas of Rome and its neighbourhood which have escaped the caprice of altering tastes.

In the centre of it is a large open tank of the same

shape as the garden itself. From the W. extremity a fine view of the desolate Campagna and of Rome itself—especially towards sunset—is to be had. This part of the garden is built out on an artificial terrace, and the arched substructures which support the main embanking wall were used to house the Imperial Guard or slaves. The so-called " Barracks of the Vigiles " in another part of the villa should rather be considered to have been a storehouse, not only for food-stuffs, but for furniture and other objects of occasional use.

The remainder of the group contains a very finely decorated room, which was probably used for a dining-room in summer, unfortunately much devastated by searchers after building material; it communicates with the so-called " stadium," perhaps simply another garden of that shape. Beyond it on the E. is another large court-yard with an open tank in the centre; under the colon-naded walk surrounding it is an underground passage, or cryptoporticus, to provide shelter from the rain or even from the Italian sun.

To the N.E. of the first group lies the second, the Imperial palace proper, which is grouped round four main court-yards of varying size. The first of these is known, quite wrongly, as the " Courtyard of the Libraries," because the Greek and Latin libraries have been thought to be recognisable in some lofty buildings of irregular plan and uncertain use on one side of it. On another is the so-called " Maritime Theatre," which is probably not, as is so often believed, the reproduction of an island with a temple upon it which Hadrian had seen in his travels, but simply an aviary. Its chief part corresponds with the description given by Varro, and a Renaissance recon-struction according to his description shows this clearly.[1]

Between this building and the so-called " Poikile " is the great hall, wrongly called the " Hall of the Philo-sophers," which, from its orientation, belongs in reality to the first group. Close by is a set of baths, the only

[1] The work of Pirro Ligorio—see p. 102, and cf. *Mem. Amer. Acad.* II. pl. vi. p. 12; *Journal of Roman Studies,* ix. 66.

portion of the villa which has been excavated in the last few years ; they have their arrangements for heating still remarkably well preserved.

At the opposite end of the courtyard is a building known as the " Hospitium " or guests' quarters—perhaps correctly, for here we have a number of small chambers, five on each side opening on to a central hall, each containing three niches for a bed. The mosaic pavements of the floors are remarkably well preserved. Close by is a terrace overlooking the valley on the N.E. which is generally identified with the Vale of Tempe, which is now planted with beautiful trees. Further on to the S.E. are other sections of the palace—the part known as the Piazza d' Oro is perhaps especially interesting nowadays to the student of architecture, for many problems relating to the construction of the dome find here their first solution, and we may trace here the origin of some of the most important features in the great buildings of the period of Constantine.

The ordinary visitor, if he is lucky enough to be there in the late spring, when there is no chance of frost or rain, will see some of the beautiful mosaic pavements with which the whole villa was once decorated, but he will have to trust to his imagination for the rest. For the concrete walls, faced in part with brickwork, in part with small volcanic stones, grey or brown, have lost the veneer of marble, painted plaster, or stucco with which they were once entirely covered both inside and out. The columns that supported the roof of the peristyles, or decorated the interior of once splendid halls, have gone, and their place is only in some measure supplied by the grey-green olives which grow in most of the open spaces of the villa. In the spring, too, the brilliant colours of the mosaics are almost surpassed by the wild violets and purple anemones for which Hadrian's Villa is famous.

The third group lies farther to the S., and contains two separate groups of baths—the smaller of very elaborate plan, with rooms of various shapes cleverly fitted in, paved with many-coloured marbles. The larger (Fig. 4) is
108

remarkable for having in one of its halls a beautiful piece of ceiling decoration in stucco. The main feature of the group, however, is the Canopus, which took its name from a city 15 miles from Alexandria on a canal branching off from the Nile, celebrated for a temple of Serapis. Hadrian constructed a reproduction of the canal and of the temple, excavating an artificial valley some 200 yards long, with a great niche at the end of it decorated with fountains. The works of art which adorned it were a mixture of pure Egyptian art and of imitations of the Roman period, and a considerable number of them have been found at various times. It is uncertain whether the fine statue of Antinous in Egyptian costume was found here or elsewhere in the villa.

Close by is the fourth and last group, the so-called " Academy," which is in reality simply a smaller palace arranged round a courtyard. It was decorated with splendid works, the mosaic of the doves, the two centaurs, the red marble faun—all now in the Capitoline Museum.

The Villa Bulgarini marks the S.E. point of Hadrian's Villa, and to the S. of it is the Colle S. Stefano, on which lie the remains of another large villa. They were treated as a part of Hadrian's Villa until recently; Winnefeld was the first to exclude them; and a few years later, from the discovery of the fragments of a slab with an inscription on each side of it, it became probable that they belonged first to one C. Julius Plancius Varus Cornutus, probably the adopted son of C. Julius Cornutus Tertullus, Pliny the Younger's colleague in the consulship in A.D. 100. It then belonged to Vibius Varus, who was governor of Cyprus under Hadrian, and consul in A.D. 134.[1] The brick-stamps begin with the middle of the first century after Christ and go down to A.D. 128.

The principal building is a large rectangular platform facing S.E., upon which there was a large peristyle 100 feet square, excavated at the end of the eighteenth century. It was surrounded by rooms, especially on the S., with

[1] Baddeley, *Villa of the Vibii Vari.* Gloucester, 1906.

a fountain on the W. At present, however, nothing is to be seen but a rectangular chamber, decorated with niches internally, at the S. angle above the deep ravine of the Fosso di Ponte Terra. In this chamber, it is said, was found a slab of marble bearing the inscription *Lucu(s) Sanctu(s)* : but whether it was originally set up here is rather doubtful, inasmuch as this could hardly be called a sacred grove. It is more likely that it was built into the enclosure wall of an actual sacred grove not far off.

The construction of this chamber is extremely irregular, though not dissimilar to that which is found in Hadrian's Villa itself. The platform was partly surrounded by a cryptoporticus, decorated with painted portraits of Greek poets. A century ago the names of some of them could be read, but they are now obliterated.

The N.E. side of the peristyle is continued N.E. by a substruction wall strengthened with buttresses. At the S.E. extremity of this wall is the supposed amphitheatre —really, it would seem, a water reservoir with four or five concentric walls of elliptical shape, the respective diameters being 184 feet (56 metres) and 112 feet (34·20 metres).

To the N. of this reservoir is a Christian baptistery, hexagonal in plan, preserved to a considerable height. It belonged no doubt to the church of S. Stephen, which gave its name to the hill. It is possible that Ligorio actually saw the church—a basilica with nave and two aisles—though nothing is now to be seen.

To the N.W. is a lower terrace with a large exedra, projecting northwards. The substruction walls probably extended even further, but cannot now be traced. Remains of other cisterns are to be seen, including a large trapezoidal open tank : and to the N.E. of this there is yet another platform with traces of buildings upon it.

These important buildings were approached by two roads, both descending southwards from Tivoli—one a branch of the road ascending to Porta S. Croce and the other a branch of the Strada di Carciano. They intersect on the Colle di S. Stefano, and both cross the deep Fosso di Ponte Terra which lies to the S. of it—the westernmost

5. VIADUCT NEAR HADRIAN'S VILLA (p. 111).

6. VILLAGE OF S. VITTORINO (p. 111).

To face p. 111.

by a large viaduct, a massive structure in concrete 56 feet
(17 metres) high and 14 feet (4·10 metres) wide, with two
tiers of arches, one below and four above. It lies in very
picturesque surroundings (Fig. 5). The other road—a lane
not more than 6½ feet wide—is crossed by a natural bridge
in the rock, spanning a cleft which, if not entirely artificial,
has certainly been enlarged by the hand of man. The
channel is about 200 feet in length, 30 in height, and 6 in
width, and is one of the many examples of the regulation
of streams by the Romans which a careful examination of
the Campagna will reveal.

After crossing the plateau to the S., the road may have
led on to the picturesque site of the village of S. Vittorino
(Fig. 6). It occupies a naturally strong position, but there
is no evidence to prove whether it was occupied in Roman
times or not.

Returning to the older—though perhaps not the oldest—
line of the Via Tiburtina, we find that, at or near the site
of the eighteenth milestone, an inscription recording the
repair of the steep ascent to Tibur (the Clivus Tiburtinus)
under the Emperors Constantius and Constans between
A.D. 340 and 350 was found in 1735. It has been re-
erected where it was found. A similar inscription may
refer to the repair of the Ponte dell' Acquoria, which
crosses the Anio below us to the left. The road to it
branches off at the top of the slope, just before which we
pass on the right the so-called Tempio della Tosse—a name
which might come from M. Turcius Secundus Apronianus,
who was in charge of the repairs to the road, and who
may have built it as his family mausoleum. It is a
picturesque octagonal structure with a domed roof and
a circular interior—perhaps a tomb : and it has been
drawn and studied by artists and architects of all times
and all nations, who of course have been specially busy
at Tivoli.

The same is the case with the next ancient building we
reach ; for a little higher up our road, in an arched passage,
goes under the huge substructions of the building known
till a century ago as the Villa of Maecenas. It was con-

structed on the road, as two inscriptions record, by two local officials, the *quattuorviri* L. Octavius Vitulus and C. Rustius Flavus, in accordance with a decision of the senate of the town : and was certainly, as many recently discovered inscriptions show, a building connected with the cult of Hercules and Augustus, and in fact formed part of the great temple of Hercules Victor, the protecting deity of Tibur. The arches support a square courtyard, surrounded by arcades, in the centre of which were structures perhaps belonging to a temple : but the whole interior of it is now occupied by a paper mill. The temple, like that of Fortune at Praeneste, extended from the Imperial period onwards right up the hill-side, being formed of a series of great terraces, supported by massive substructures and arcades : and the cella of the temple itself was here, too, circular, and is still to be seen behind the apse of the cathedral. Like the building we have been describing, it is also of opus incertum, and probably dates from before the Imperial period. It seems possible, inasmuch as a forum and a *vicus patricius* are referred to in the neighbourhood of the Cathedral of Tivoli in a document of A.D. 978, that, as Pacifici thinks, the original temple of Hercules was comparatively small, and situated in the forum of the late Republican period, to which he also attributes the arched substructions under the Piazza dell' Olmo and the massive stone arch with a large hall attached to it on the way up to the cathedral.

Then, in the Augustan Age, when, as it would appear from the inscriptions, Augustus and the Imperial House came to share the divine honours of Hercules—the old guild of worshippers of the one took on the worship of the other, so that the very treasury of Hercules came to be officially called the treasury of Hercules and Augustus. It was then that the temple was largely extended down the hill and the so-called Villa of Maecenas built. And it was then that one M. Varenus Diphilus, " Magister Herculaneus," built a hall close to the old temple, containing the public weights and measures of Tibur ; in which, perhaps, was the relief of Hercules Tunicatus

112

7. TEMPLES AT TIVOLI (p. 113).

8. NYMPHAEUM UNDER S. ANTONIO, TIVOLI (p. 114).

To face p. 113.

mentioned by Pliny, and near to which a little while ago was found in another chamber a statue of an emperor and a head of Nerva (which, however, does not fit on to it). An inscription shows that this little chamber was erected by the same man with a prayer for Augustus's safe return during one of his last journeys.

It is of this enlarged temple that the writers of the Imperial age speak—Juvenal, who mentions it as resembling the temple of Fortune at Praeneste, and Martial, who calls Tiber itself Herculeum. A reconstruction of it by a competent architect is much to be desired, as a parallel to Mr. Bradshaw's work at Praeneste.

In the lower part of the picturesque mediaeval town, then, we have to seek the site of this great sanctuary. But more famous still are the two small temples—one circular with Corinthian columns, the other rectangular with Ionic columns—which stand at the top of the town, on a rock above the old waterfall of the Anio. The rock would probably have been eaten away by now had not Gregory XVI had a new channel made to carry off the river further away from the town, out of danger.

The two temples are traditionally attributed to Vesta and the Sibyl of Tibur—for Varro adds Albunea, a water goddess worshipped on the banks of the Anio, to the nine Sibyls of whom the Greek writers speak (Fig. 7).

This lofty point, well defended by the Anio, must have been the citadel of the ancient city, though the line of its walls cannot be traced by any actual remains. It was founded, according to tradition, by Tiburtus, Corax, and Catillus, grandsons of Amphiarus of Argos, and the last has given his name to the Monte Catillo above the modern railway station. This hill Turner, among many others, climbed for a view of the town and the deep gorge of the river. Tivoli is on the edge of the Sabine mountains, guarding the pass to the upper valley of the Anio and the interior of the complicated mountain system which forms the backbone of the peninsula and extends uninterruptedly as far as the Adriatic. It must, in the days of its independence, have been a very powerful city, with roads leading to the outlying forts by which its sway was maintained.

It came into collision with the Romans in the fourth century B.C., and thrice the latter were able to celebrate triumphs over it ; but it did not lose its independence, more wisely becoming an ally of Rome. In the later centuries of the Republic, and under the Empire, it was a favourite summer resort, and both Augustus and Maecenas had villas here, and—though it be disputed by some—I think Horace also. It is certain that a house was shown as his during the time of Suetonius ; and there is no adequate reason for doubting the truth of the tradition. As Mr. G. H. Hallam has convincingly shown, no site suits Horace's frequent references to Tibur half so well as the villa of the Augustan period under the monastery of S. Antonio, facing the waterfall—giving, not on to the open Campagna, like the great villas to the S., but on to the wild and romantic gorge of the Anio, where there was room for but a few others. A good deal of this villa is still preserved, and notably a fine nymphaeum (Fig. 8).

A little further on and further down is a projecting spur covered with olives ; and here are the remains of an immense villa. The site has been called Quintiliolum since the tenth century, and the attribution to Quintilius Varus, the friend of Horace, is therefore to be accepted. The remains are picturesque : they consist of an upper terrace, upon which the house must have stood—in the sides of it is a cryptoporticus, an underground passage lighted only by a few windows, which was always cool and fresh in summer. On the lower terrace is a large open tank, and near this the great supporting wall of the S.W. end falls off sheer to the slopes below.

Here we have a choice of two routes, if we will explore the territory of Tibur on the N. We may follow on along the hill-side, where the modern road runs, sometimes above, sometimes below the railway : or we may descend to the Ponte dell' Acquoria, and thence traverse the vineyards at the foot of the hills. In either case we shall find a district full of remains of antiquity, and be able to realise

114

that the modern habit of *villeggiatura* has its roots deep in the customs of the Rome of the late Republic. If we take the first road we shall be following one of the roads which led from Tibur down to a detached fort on the hill known now as the Colle Turrita (from a mediaeval castle which crowns it) above Palombara–Marcellina railway station. The modern road has in part obliterated it, but remains of its supporting walls of large blocks of stone may still be seen, and there are similar remains within the castle. Originally the road went no further. But later on—we do not know when—it was prolonged past Marcellina, Palombara, and Moricone (we must give the modern names, because no ancient names are known to us) until it reached the Via Salaria at the twenty-sixth mile from Rome. It thus formed a very important intermediate line of communication for the whole of this district. The remains of villas which lie on its course, on sites sheltered from the E. and N.E. by the lofty Monte Gennaro and its spurs, are far too numerous to be mentioned individually; and I may only remark here that many of them have platforms of limestone in the so-called Cyclopean style.

Again, when we reach Palombara, we shall find terrace walls of rough construction on the mountain-side—several of them one above the other, which are either the sites of prehistoric settlements or (more probably) perhaps terraces for supporting the soil for cultivation—lynchets, as they would be called in England. Still, we cannot give a name to them—and the attempt to find sites for what have been called " the lost and mislaid cities of Latium " has been proved to be unsuccessful.

We may return, then, to the lower road northward from Tivoli, which crossed the Anio by the Ponte dell' Acquoria. This bridge must have had originally some seven arches, of which only that at the N. extremity is preserved; but the pavement may be seen to the N. of it, and the ancient road ran on in a straight line for a mile or two, passing to the left of the villa attributed to Ventidius Bassus with its three great terraces, between Colle Nocelle and the S. end of the Colle Vitriano, both of which have numerous remains of large villas well provided with water reservoirs. One of the former (Fig. 9) is interesting, having its lower platform supported by a wall over 160 feet in length of large limestone blocks with almost horizontal courses, strengthened by small buttresses. The magnificence of the house that once stood there is shown by the remains of coloured marbles which are to be found everywhere, and remains of a bath and of the furnaces by which it was heated may still be seen.

If we follow the road, we find it turning N.W. until it reaches an important ancient road junction, near the modern Casale Battista, close to the railway. Here, besides the road we have been following, we can trace four others. One was more or less identical in line with a modern road from the Via Tiburtina at Ponte Lucano, which runs up over flat and uninteresting country and goes on (probably not following an ancient line) to Marcellina. A second is a prolongation of the road which left the Via Tiburtina at Settecamini, and which thus formed the most direct route from Rome to this district. It goes on in an N.E. direction up and along a hill known as the Colle della Colonnella, and falls into the ancient road from Tivoli to the Via Salaria. That is the third branch ; and the fourth is the prolongation of the line we have been following, N.N.W. up the valley to the E. of the village of Montecelio, with a branch to Palombara. Montecelio itself, and S. Angelo to the W. of it, were approached from Rome by a branch of the Settecamini road ; while Palombara was also served by a branch from the Via Nomentana. The country has by now become a good deal more hilly, and, as far as appearances go, any one of the hill-towns might justifiably lay claim to the name Corniculum, as we can hardly fail to call the whole group the Montes Corniculani. If we have to assign the name Corniculum to any one of them, it would be to Montecelio (the modern corruption of the old name Monticelli). For here, under the mediaeval fortification walls of the castle which crowns the conical hill-top, there

9. PLATFORM OF VILLA, COLLE VITRIANO (p. 116).

10. TERRACE WALL OF VILLA OF BRUTUS (?) (p. 121).

To face p. 116.

are the remains of walls in rough stone, which seem to belong to the primitive enceinte.

Within the area of the castle there is also a small Roman temple, built of brick-faced concrete, resting on a stylobate about 5 feet high, and measuring some 26 by 14 feet; some pilasters with Corinthian capitals are still preserved. The brickwork is very good, and was probably meant to be left visible.

Both E. and W. of the village there is a very large villa platform—the former in the valley below, close to the fourth road mentioned as branching off from Casale Battista, and the latter on the slopes traversed by the road from Rome, on which indeed it lay. A large open oval reservoir lies above it, while the villa itself has two great terraces, the upper being about 100 paces square, with a large cryptoporticus inside its supporting wall, and the upper 240 paces one way and 140 the other.

The pavement of the old road can be seen descending the hill, and it then fell into the line of the road from Settecamini, partly represented by the modern road from the station of Montecelio to S. Angelo, on its steep conical hill. At this latter village, years ago, I searched in vain for some polygonal walls which were actually drawn by Gell close to the church of S. Liberata, to the S. of the village; and on a second visit I was equally unsuccessful, so that I can only conclude that they have been destroyed. But there are remains of antiquity of some interest at the foot of the hill, both N. and S. of the village. On the S., at Vallemara, there is a particularly well-preserved villa platform with a very perfect cryptoporticus and a large reservoir 100 Roman feet long above it, divided into three chambers each $11\frac{1}{2}$ feet wide; while there are on the N. three circular cavities, once quarries, one of which was lined with concrete in Roman days, and used to contain an open reservoir some 80 feet in diameter and 6 deep: and not far off are the terrace walls of a very large villa, one of them being no less than 240 feet long and 10 high. It is built of almost rectangular blocks of hewn stone, well jointed and smoothed at the edges; and inasmuch

117

as it lies in low ground and in a hopeless position for defence, it is impossible to identify it (as some, mistaking its age and its object, have attempted to do) with Ameriola, one of the lost cities of Latium once subdued by Tarquin the Elder. To the W. we soon reach the modern road to Palombara, into which come two branches from Mentana, both of them probably of Roman origin. The first has recently been made to take wheeled traffic, but the second is a bridle-path : it passes the little hamlet of Castel Chiodato, and where it falls into the modern road the latter turns E. and runs straight to Palombara, another village situated picturesquely on a hill, but containing no relics of antiquity. A mile or more before we reach it, to the right of the road in a sheltered valley lies the picturesque church of S. Giovanni in Argentella, containing some interesting mediaeval frescoes.

Palombara, too, was an important road centre in antiquity ; for here the road from Tibur to the Via Salaria was joined by the Via Nomentana and the road from Nomentum by a road from Casale Battista, and by another road coming S.E. from the twenty-first mile of the Via Salaria. It is not inappropriate to call attention to this fact, for until quite recent years, as we have already remarked, the ancient Roman road system in the Campagna, which resembled a spider's web, had lost all but its main lines, so that the modern roads radiated from Rome in the centre like the rays of a starfish, without any cross connexions.

From Palombara we may return to Tivoli, and complete our study of the territory by leaving the town on the S. and glancing for a few minutes at the group of villas which are to be found on the slopes of the Monte Ripoli and Monte Arcese, commanding a wonderful view over the Campagna and the Alban Hills, especially at sunset, when the sun sinks behind the great dome of S. Peter's. First of all, the Villa d'Este claims our attention ; for it will give us as good an idea as we shall get from any existing building of the elaborately decorated fountains which played such a part in the architecture of the gardens of

the villas of the classical period. The villa itself is un-
finished, and has lost the collection of statues which its
constructor, Cardinal Ippolito d'Este, had excavated here
and collected there until it became of considerable value
and importance. Most of it has been dispersed to the
four winds, and only a very few of the least valuable still
remain. But, even were this not so, we should never
visit Villa d'Este to see them only. Its charm is far
greater now, I am sure, when its fountains are moss-
grown and half-decayed, than when once decorated, as
engravings show, with rather blatant mosaics and late
Renaissance stone statues and architecture, plastered over
and painted in glaring colours, not in very good taste.
Its charm is added to by its great cypresses and the
wonderful views N. to the pointed Corniculan Hills, and
westward over the Campagna, with the modern highroad
like a white ribbon thrown down carelessly—for it does
not run straight by any means. Since the war the villa
has passed from the Hohenlohe family to the Italian
Government, and will at least be taken care of and
repaired when necessary and, we hope, kept up, but not
too drastically.

The road, after leaving Tivoli, very soon divides. The
Via di Carciano, as it is called, keeps up on the level above
the road to Rome ; and the same was done by the
channels of the great aqueducts which conveyed the water
of the river itself, or of copious and excellent springs
(which form the main supply of the modern city) in its
valley, from the upper Anio to Rome. Remains of these
channels may be seen along the road,[1] and in some places
all the four—the uppermost the Anio Novus, then the
Aquae Claudia, then the Marcia, and then the Anio Vetus
—may be seen together or not far away from one another.
Accurate levelling along the whole of their course was
necessary to distinguish one from the other, and this was

[1] The first piece visible was a portion of the channel of the Aqua
Marcia cut in the rock, passing behind a rock-cut tomb, just after
the modern Strada di S. Gregorio turns off to the right to the village
of that name. It has, however, quite recently been covered up
with earth.

undertaken for me in 1915 by three Italian engineers, the late Professor Reina and his assistants, Signor G. Corbellini and Signor G. Ducci. I will not speak of them in detail, as I hope shortly to publish a full description of them.

The Via di Carciano is also remarkable for the great beauty and age of the olive groves through which the road passes. Of the dozen or so ancient villas which may be found along its course and on the slopes below it we need only speak in detail of three. The first is just at the twenty-fifth kilometre of the modern highroad—in a place known as *pesoni* as early as the tenth century—and it has therefore been labelled Villa of the Pisones—though which Pisones we do not know. More important is the fact that here were seen in the fifteenth century a number of *hermae* (twelve or thirteen it would seem) of Greek philosophers and poets, all without heads, while sixteen others, with heads, were discovered in 1779, and are now in Madrid. At the latter date the famous head of Alexander now in the Louvre was discovered. A few years earlier, twenty-one similar *hermae*, some with heads, some without, were found a good deal higher up the hill, where there are two great villas, each with its terraces, just below the first part of the Strada di Carciano, which is a corruption of Cassianus, a name found as far back as the tenth century. What more natural, then, to suppose that one was the villa of Cassius and the other the villa of Brutus—especially as Cicero speaks of a villa of Brutus at Tivoli ? As far as date goes, the attribution would be quite possible, and the only difficulty is to decide which is which, in the absence of any other proof !

There has naturally been a good deal of confusion. From the sixteenth century to the last quarter of the nineteenth the northern one of the two, just below the summer residence of the Irish College in Rome (originally built by Cardinal Salerno for the Greek College, and therefore often called Villa dei Greci), bore the name of Cassius. Its terrace walls are faced with opus reticulatum, in which decorative patterns are made by the use of stones of various colours. On the upper terrace there is a nymphaeum with a large central niche, and a portico with Doric columns to the right of it ; while in the central one there is a cryptoporticus with an arched passage behind.

The southern villa, some 500 yards further on, immediately to the N. of the narrow bend of the highroad (called Regresso from the fact that the engine of the steam tramway has here to take the other end of the train), is quite different. The central terrace has a huge polygonal supporting wall 40 feet long and 20 high at the N. end, while at the S. it is supported by a wall of concrete faced with opus reticulatum, with buttresses connected by arches (Fig. 10) ; while the lower terrace is of opus incertum with buttresses and arches.

Now, all the earlier writers naturally call *this* the villa of Brutus ; and it only began to be called the villa of Cassius in the documents relating to the excavations of 1773, continued in the following years by order of Pope Pius VI. But in any case, it seems clear that the *hermae* were found in the southern villa—and with them statues of Apollo and eight of the Muses, and various other statues, most of which are in the Vatican, though a group of a faun and a nymph found its way through the hands of Thomas Jenkins into Charles Townley's collection and so into the British Museum.

The road goes on for some three miles through the olives, passing another villa where other polygonal walls attracted Dodwell's attention, until it reaches the farmhouse of Gericomio.[1] This was built in 1579 by Cardinal Prospero Santacroce as a refuge for his old age; and the quiet peace of this remote corner of the world certainly commends it as an appropriate haven of rest. There is perhaps no place like the Roman Campagna for losing sight of modern life for a while, and acquiring that mental repose which is so great a relief now that Rome, alas ! has become one of the noisiest cities of Europe.

---

[1] Gericomio is an Italianised form of Γεροκομεῖον, which appears as Γεροντοκομεῖον in the code of Justinian.

On the hill above Gericomio—the Monte S. Angelo in Arcese—is the site, in all probability, of the *Arx Aesulana,* where, Livy tells us, a garrison was placed when Hannibal threatened Rome in 210 B.C.   In this account it is coupled with the Alban Mount : and Horace mentions it and Tibur and Tusculum as prominent points in the view of the hills from Rome.   In Pliny's day it had perished without leaving a trace : but twenty-five years after his death in the eruption of A.D. 79 a contractor who had successfully bored a tunnel under the mountain for the Aqua Claudia restored the ruined temple of the Bona Dea on its summit.

A road ascending the mountain, and remains of (possibly) pre-Roman platforms and of Roman reservoirs, may be seen near the top, and while the ruins on the summit belong to a church of S. Angelo with a monastery mentioned in the first half of the ninth century, there are blocks of tufa, columns, and other fragments of marble, with brick-stamps of the time of Hadrian, which probably belong to the temple.

An extremely interesting letter of the humanist Flavio Biondo has recently come to light, describing an expedition which Pope Pius II made to the summit of the mountain in September 1461.[1]

[1] *Boll. di Tivoli,* i. (1919) 128.

II

THE ROADS LEADING TO THE ALBAN HILLS AND THE SOUTH-EAST

  IV. THE VIA PRAENESTINA

IVa. THE VIA COLLATINA

  V. THE VIA LABICANA

 VI. THE VIA LATINA

VII. THE VIA APPIA (WITH THE VIA ANTIATINA)

II

PRELIMINARY NOTE

THE ALBAN HILLS are the key to any advance from Rome into South Italy, as will be clear to anyone who sees them from the S.E. side of the city. They occupy the space between the sea and the Apennines with their outliers, all of which are of limestone, and therefore were above the level of the sea of the pre-volcanic period, which washed their lower slopes before the various phases of submarine volcanic activity ended in the elevation of the coast plain and the formation of numerous sub-aerial craters.

The original Alban volcano was some 12 miles in diameter at the base, while the crater was about half as much across; and the late Sir Archibald Geikie, in his book on *Landscape in History*, has explained how, in his view, the later cone was built up in the middle of the larger crater, itself enclosing a well-marked crater with the Campo di Annibale at the bottom. This central crater then became choked, and the volcanic forces, not yet at rest, had to find other outlets; the original crater rim, which is preserved from Tusculum to Nemi, was blown away on the W., and the craters of Albano and Nemi were the result: and still later on smaller craters were produced. Such portents as Livy records, when it rained stones in the Alban Hills, are due to these sporadic manifestations of volcanic activity: while the rain of blood, which he also records, is due to an entirely different cause—the charging of the atmosphere with red sand from the Sahara when a violent sirocco is blowing, and its precipitation by rain in the form of red mud—a phenomenon which I have myself seen.

K

So far as we know, the earliest appearance of man in the Alban Hills dates from the Iron Age, as indeed in Rome itself : and it may have been the continuance of volcanic activity which rendered them not comfortable for habitation at any earlier period. According to tradition, Alba Longa was founded some three hundred years before Rome by Ascanius or Iulus, the son of Aeneas ; but we do not find this interval between the earliest tombs of the Alban Hills and those of the recently discovered cemetery in the Forum, and it is therefore doubtful whether we can accept this tradition—any more than we can accept as historical the records of the wars between the two cities. We only know that there was a Confederacy of thirty communities, of which Alba was the head (though the list as handed down to us has some curious omissions), which met for sacrifices at the temple of Jupiter Latiaris, and that, on the fall of Alba Longa, Rome succeeded to the honorary presidency of it.

The routes by which the Alban Hills were approached from Rome in early days were probably (1) the road to Tusculum, followed for some distance by the later Via Labicana, leading to the northern slopes and the rim of the outer crater, (2) the road to Castrimoenium (Marino), leading to the central portion of the group, (3) the road to Satricum, leading to the S. slopes. Besides these, it is possible—though not certain—that there was an earlier road running more or less in the same direction as the later Via Appia, to the W. side of the Alban Lake : and this is one of the points that one might hope to test by aerial photography. For both the Via Latina and the Via Appia, which run in an absolutely straight line for miles, are not natural nor primitive roads, but artificial military highways of a comparatively late date.

The Via Latina was probably the earlier, though its date is not recorded ; for it led to the pass of Algidus, upon which determined attacks were made by the Aequi and Volsci in joint operations from 465 to 389 B.C. (to adopt the traditional dating), and was probably constructed at least thus far not very long after the latter year—while the foundation of Cales, near Capua, as a colony in 334 B.C. would tend to make us believe that the road had been pushed forward to that point at least as early as that date. The Via Appia, we know, was constructed some twenty years later, while we are without information as to the construction of the Via Labicana and the Via Praenestina, the former of which served the N. slopes of the Alban Hills, as well as the undulating country between them and the limestone mountains on a projecting spur of which Praeneste stood, guarding one of the routes to the S.E. ; for the Via Labicana, on its way to join the Via Latina, passes within a few miles of the town. The district between Praeneste and Tibur is furrowed by deep ravines ; but, the level of the hills between them being generally the same, they very often do not appear until one is close upon them. They presented great difficulties to the passage of the aqueducts by which the city of Rome was supplied, and some of the finest remains of these are to be found there.

On the N. and W. sides of the Alban Hills the country is much easier, and the undulations are comparatively gentle. The lower slopes are covered with the remains of ancient villas ; these are most plentiful in the lower part of the territory of Tusculum, and in that of Castrimoenium, in the neighbourhood of the modern Frascati, Castel Gandolfo, and Marino, and even nearer to Rome : though there are also many below Albano. As we approach the coast plain they become rarer, as we shall see in the sequel.

IV

THE VIA PRAENESTINA

THE VIA PRAENESTINA and the Via Labicana both began from the Porta Esquilina of the Servian wall, and from it the distances along them are calculated : but they did not bifurcate until about three-quarters of a mile further on, at the tomb of Eurysaces the baker, which stood in the fork. This monument belongs to the last century of the Republic : and in A.D. 52 Claudius built the splendid double arch (now called the Porta Maggiore) which carried the channels of the Aqua Claudia and the Anio Novus over the two roads just before they separated—so close to the tomb that when Honorius enlarged the Porta Praenestina (for Aurelian had incorporated the arch into the line of his walls as a city gate) he was able to use the tomb as the foundation of a tower, which was only removed in 1838.

As it was the highest point on the E. side of the city, it was selected by the engineers of the aqueducts from the upper valley of the Anio and from the Alban Hills as the point at which the channels should enter the city, so that as little pressure as possible was lost. It was thus the meeting-point of eight or nine aqueducts and as many roads, and therefore, as Lanciani has pointed out, one of the most important topographical centres of the ancient city.

But neither of the two roads with which we have to deal ever acquired first-class importance.

As its original name, Via Gabina, implies, the left-hand road, later the Via Praenestina, once only led as far as Gabii ; while the Via Labicana, I think, was the earliest route from Rome to Tusculum, and was later prolonged

128

to Labici, but never became a road of first-class importance. It may, however, have superseded the Via Latina as a route for long-distance traffic, as the distance to their junction on the further side of the Alban Hills is practically the same along either, whereas its summit level is considerably (650 feet) lower than that of the Via Latina at the pass of Algidus. As regards the Via Appia, the journey by the Via Labicana is only 6 miles longer to their point of junction just before Casilinum, on the nearer bank of the Volturnus, or 3 miles shorter, if we take a more direct route by Teanum instead of going round by Venafrum : while the troublesome journey by boat through the Pomptine Marshes, so vividly described by Horace, would have been avoided. But we are not told that the Via Labicana was much in use during the period preceding the improvements which Trajan made on the Via Appia ; and these must certainly have led to a definite preference being given to the latter.

The growth of Rome has led to the obliteration of all traces of antiquity on the first portion of both roads. Taking the Via Praenestina first, we may note the existence, about a mile from the gate on the left, of the largest tomb in the suburbs of Rome, a huge, low drum of concrete about 150 feet in diameter (not reckoning the stone facing, which has disappeared), with a surprisingly small chamber (only 14 by 16 feet) in the centre reached by a long passage from the N., on the side—that is, away from the road.

It belonged until lately to the Dominican Order ; and a Frenchman placed a tablet here in 1716 (" Bastile je m'apelle F(rèr)e Dominique Brulon | M'a posté sur ce tourion pour faire santinelle "), while in 1741 the Irish Dominicans put up another to commemorate Prince Charlie's visit on September 2nd.

A mile further on we cross a stream, and then the so-called military road, built to connect the circle of forts constructed round Rome in 1883. On the right is a well-preserved tomb in ornamental brickwork of the second century A.D., which, as Rivoira pointed out, provides us

129

with the earliest example known of small arches supported on brackets and themselves carrying a cornice. Another, close by, has a niche with an elegant scallop-shell pattern in stucco. Ascending the hill, we find extensive remains of ancient villas on both sides of the road. On the right there are scanty remains of various periods from the beginning of the Empire to the fourth century A.D., when various smaller buildings were united into one group, which was not a residence *de luxe*, but probably a farmhouse. The only ruin of any importance which is now preserved is a large reservoir in two stories, each of them containing six chambers, measuring 28 by 17 feet each; but the lower chambers were not lined with hydraulic cement, and only served to support the upper. The exterior is 71 feet square, but as it stands on uneven ground it has been heavily buttressed at the lower end.

On the left, the first remains we find belong to a villa of the Republican period, with an extensive system of passages lined with cement for drawing the surface water, but they have been much damaged by modern quarrying. We then come to a large reservoir with buttresses, of the middle of the second century: and then to the remains of a large octagonal hall, upon which in the Middle Ages a lofty tower was planted, giving it a most fantastic appearance. The octagon above the niches with which it was decorated (in one of them Pirro Ligorio saw and drew nearly four hundred years ago some decorations in stucco which are still fairly well preserved) gave place to a circular dome: and the use of empty jars in the vaulting to lighten the weight shows that we are in the middle of the third century (Fig. 11). Not far off is an apse with a semi-dome also stuccoed, with the vault in the form of a scallop-shell, which is probably a century earlier.

Piranesi, who gives plates of both these buildings in his *Antichita Romana*, believed them to be tombs: but the first is probably a nymphaeum, while the second may have formed part of a set of baths.

But the most important monument of all is that which gives its modern name to the site, the Tor de' Schiavi.

12. TEMPLE AT GABII (p. 134).

To face p. 130.

11. REMAINS OF VILLA OF THE GORDIANI (p. 130).

This dates only from 1571, when one Vincenzo Rossi dello Schiavo was proprietor of the farm, which previously to that was known as the *Monumentum*, from this ruin or from the lofty tower described above. It is a large circular temple tomb, like the Heroon of Romulus, son of Maxentius, on the Via Appia, and belongs, as the brick-stamps showed (they have unfortunately all been covered up or removed in the course of recent repairs to the structure), to the time of Diocletian. The exterior was decorated in stucco in imitation of marble blocks, as were his great baths. In front was a portico with columns, approached by a flight of steps. The lower story, which is underground, has a large pillar in the centre, which carries the circular vault. The lighting was by lunette windows in the attic just below the dome. Here all topographers have placed the villa of the Gordiani, and though their biographer only tells us that it was on this road, and that it had two hundred columns in a square peristyle, three basilicas with a hundred columns each, and most magnificent thermae, we must also place it here, for we shall find no other remains of sufficient magnificence. Also we must remember that, while they reigned in 238, they were descended from the Gracchi on the father's side, and from Trajan on the mother's, and that their ancestors had frequently held the consulship. It is therefore not surprising, as it would seem, that only the octagonal hall belongs to the actual period of their reign, and that the rest of the buildings are either earlier or later. It is unlikely that the villa originally extended across the road, for the belt of tombs on each side would have been a great inconvenience : though when under Constantine the Imperial domain included the villa known as *ad duas lauros* on the Via Labicana, it is most likely that it formed an uninterrupted belt of territory as far as Tor de' Schiavi. In any case, the latter villa must have occupied the whole hill-top as far as the next stream.

In the valley, just at the fourth kilometre, the modern Via Collatina diverges to the left. Tombs continue to be visible on each side of the Via Praenestina, which keeps on a fairly straight course, despite the undulations of the ground. After a couple of miles we reach the Torre di Tre Teste, a mediaeval tower and farmhouse on the N. edge of the road, which takes its name from a much-damaged relief from a tomb, with three heads representing those who were buried in it, which is built into the chapel.

A mile further on again, on the left, are some ruins of a villa (called Muraccio dell' Uomo Morto, from a late burial found there) and of its subterranean water cisterns : the springs which supplied it are by some identified with those of the Aqua Appia, but this is very doubtful.

A mile further on again we see the picturesque Tor Angela on the right, and near it some brick arches of the Aqua Alexandrina. This ran between the Via Prae-nestina and the Via Labicana, and an ancient road existed for its service, the pavement of which I saw twenty years ago ; but it has now been used to make up the bed of a modern farm road. Ruins of various buildings are to be seen on each side of the road, and much has been brought to light, and simultaneously destroyed, by the spread of cultivation.

Just beyond the twelfth kilometre-stone we reach the eighth milestone of Innocent XIII (1721–1724), which corresponds more or less with the ninth ancient mile : and hence it is that the fine bridge (Fig. 13) over the little stream here is called Pons de Nona—a name which can be traced as far back as A.D. 958. There was originally a small single-arched bridge incorporated in the far loftier structure which was later on substituted for it, to avoid the steep descent and ascent. Its total length is about 236 feet by 33 feet wide at the top (the paved roadway now removed measured 20 feet in width) and the greatest height 52. There are seven arches of hewn Gabine stone, but the bridge-heads are of red tufa quarried on the spot. It is by far the finest road bridge in the neighbourhood of Rome.

On the hill just beyond the bridge, ploughing brought to light some twenty-five years ago a large deposit of votive objects in terra-cotta, representing almost all parts of the
132

13. PONTE DI NONA (p. 132).

14. OSA STREAM AND ALBAN HILLS (p. 133).

To face p. 132.

human body (though not of the internal organs), mostly
life-size, with some small figures of cows and horses, which
betokened the presence of some temple. Excavations
were carried on ten years later, and brought to light a
number of Republican coins. These show that the sanctuary existed from about 300 B.C. to the birth of Christ.
Of the temple itself no remains came to light; but a
rectangular enclosure walled in hewn stone was found,
and just outside it were two cavities in the rock, full
of votive objects. On the other hand, a small bath was
found which may have served for the use of wayfarers.
How it got its water is uncertain : there is a cave with a
small magnesiac spring below, which may have served
to supply it, and may also have been the original cause of
the establishment of the sanctuary here. Beyond it is a
large group of tombs in opus quadratum, which lay on
each side of the ancient road, the course of which was
slightly to the N. of the modern, so that they are all on
the left of the latter. They extended for a couple of
miles with occasional interruptions, and behind them were
other buildings at large intervals; but the spread of
cultivation will soon leave but scanty traces of them, for
on the S., where there is more pasture-land, the remains
are scantier. A branch road ran off at about the tenth
ancient mile to the Via Collatina ; and at the eleventh
we reach the Osteria dell' Osa, an important meeting-
point of roads. The ancient Via Praenestina went on in
an easterly direction, whereas the modern road, which also
follows an ancient line, turns N.E. to Le Capannelle.
Then there are two roads from Lunghezza, one on each
bank of the Osa stream, diverging to the left, and two
roads going to the Via Labicana diverging to the right,
one leaving it a little beyond the eighth mile, and another
a little after the tenth, the latter forming part of an important cross-road from the Via Appia to the various
roads to the N.E. of it (the Via Cavona.)

The Via Praenestina crossed the Osa stream (Fig. 14)
a little to the S. of the modern bridge, and its pavement
may soon be seen in the track which keeps to the S. of

the long extinct crater, on the S. and E. edges of which
are the remains of the once famous city of Gabii. There
was a lake here in the Middle Ages, but it is mentioned
by no classical author ; and we are told that in the excavation of a new outlet channel in 1838 (by which it is still
drained) traces of the ancient one were discovered. It is
indeed improbable that it would have been allowed to
exist by the Romans, for it would easily have become
swampy. The road soon passes below the famous temple
(Fig. 12), a structure of about 200 B.C. It is constructed
of blocks 2 feet in height and thickness, but varying in
length, of the local stone (which was extensively used in
Roman times, and is now called sperone), which were
originally coated with stucco, so as to give the appearance
of white marble : but they are now of a beautiful brown
colour. The *cella* is well preserved to a height of about
28 feet above the podium ; it is 44 feet long and 28 feet
wide inside, and had six columns in front and at the sides
(reckoning the corner columns twice over), but none at
the back. It stands on the S. edge of the lake, and may
be distinguished from the Alban Hills by those who
know where to look ; though an even more prominent
object is the lofty mediaeval Torre di Castiglione on
the E. bank, which probably marks the site of the
acropolis.

To what divinity the temple was dedicated is uncertain : Vergil speaks of the *arva Gabinae Junonis*, and it
has generally been attributed to Juno, though others
prefer to call it the temple of Apollo, which, Livy tells
us, was struck by lightning in 176 B.C. Speculation on
this point has, however, only been open since the site of
Gabii was definitely settled, when excavations were made
around the temple in 1792 under the direction of Gavin
Hamilton, and it was found to have been surrounded on
three sides by Doric colonnades. The Forum was also
brought to light, but no traces of it remain visible, and
indeed it had been already filled up when Maria Graham
(better known as Lady Callcott, the authoress of *Little
Arthur's History of England*) passed that way in 1819 with

15. VIA PRAENESTINA (p. 136).

16. HUTS AT GABII (p. 135).

To face p. 135.

Charles Eastlake and his wife, on her way to spend the summer with them at Poli.

A large number of inscriptions and statues were found, and the former are of especial interest, showing definitely that this was the site of Gabii : for before this, though it was clearly enough indicated both by the itineraries and by our ancient authorities as situated about 12½ miles from Rome and 11 from Praeneste, it had been not infrequently misplaced. Flavio Biondo put it at Gallicano, and so did several sixteenth-century writers ; while others, and notably Pirro Ligorio, preferred Zagarolo. Fabretti, the explorer of the aqueducts, had, as usual, seen the truth. The town owed much of its then prosperity to Hadrian, in whose honour the Curia, or council chamber, received the name of Aelia Augusta ; though from the time of Augustus, or at any rate Tiberius, to that of Elagabalus, the inscriptions give us definite evidence that it was a municipality, and the Forum was adorned with portrait statues of numerous members of the Imperial House, and other works of art as well.

The language of the inscriptions is, of course, that of flattery : and in estimating the real importance and prosperity of this roadside village we should strike a mean between it and the equally excessive stress which Cicero and the poets lay upon its desolation—Horace speaks of a God-forsaken village as *Gabiis desertior atque Fidenis vicus* ; and Juvenal, as his manner is, finds it useful to point a moral, in two passages imitating Horace, in associating it with Fidenae, while in the third he speaks of " simple Gabii." But all this part of the site of the later town very likely did not fall within the compass of the ancient city at all. The Gabii which is so prominent in the earliest history of Rome lay on the E. bank of the lake, where the crater rim is a good deal higher, and was protected by cliffs, the defensive properties of which were increased by scarping and quarrying (Fig. 16). The huts which may be seen at the foot of them, which are inhabited by peasant labourers from the hills, may give an image of those in which the primitive population must have

135

L

dwelt. A remarkable rock-cut causeway leads right through the ancient city, of which no traces are to be seen—for the piece of wall near the tower is probably mediaeval, and other certain traces of fortification are scanty—while at the tower itself there is nothing but the tombstone of a certain Sextus Cloulius who lived here to the ripe old age of ninety-five.

We may now return to the Via Praenestina ; on the left we find the scanty remains of the church of S. Primitivus, the apse of which belonged to an earlier building, while on the right a branch road, the pavement of which can still be seen, runs off southward to the springs of the Aqua Alexandrina. Shortly after another road, also ancient, marked in the maps of the seventeenth century, runs off to Passerano. A little further on, to the right, I saw lying loose in a field a round drum of travertine, which proved to bear an inscription showing it to be the thirteenth milestone of the road : and it would seem to be mentioned as a landmark in documents of the eleventh and twelfth centuries in the archives of the church of S. Prassede, which owned considerable property hereabouts. Here we may see the scanty remains of an aqueduct—which has, however, a certain interest, as it must be the very one which, as an inscription records, Hadrian constructed for the benefit of Gabii. The pavement of the road, which is only used as a bridle-path, is in fine preservation, and its width is 13 or 14 feet. A branch road soon diverged due southward to the Via Labicana ; and after another mile we come to a fairly well-preserved ancient single-arched bridge, the so-called Ponte di Terra. The pavement continues for the next 2 or 3 miles (Fig. 15) almost as far as the point where the road comes into use once more ; and several ancient branch roads go off from it, though none of them can be followed very far.

Remains of the aqueducts now begin to come in sight to the S.—two great bridges of the Aqua Claudia and Anio Novus, so close together that they might easily be taken for one, much restored in later concrete and over-

17. CORCOLLE (p. 137).

18. PASSERANO (p. 137).

To face p 137.

grown with bushes; and a little before the eighteenth
ancient mile, at the Osteria di Cavamonte, we reach the
modern road from Tivoli by Ponte Lucano to Zagarolo
and the Via Labicana, which at the Osteria delle Capannelle,
some way to the N., is joined by the modern road to Poli.
We have now come to a district of long, narrow, flat-
topped ridges, separated by deep ravines, which—as the
level of the hill-top is more or less uniform—are hardly
suspected until one is close upon them. The picturesque
sites of Corcolle (Fig. 17) and Passerano (Fig. 18), which
lie between us and the Osteria delle Capannelle, may both
occupy those of ancient villages, and have often been
identified with Querquetula and Scaptia respectively,
though the evidence is in neither case sufficient. Passerano, at least, if not Corcolle, became the site of a Roman
villa, and both were used for mediaeval castles. As to
Pedum, which seems to have been of rather more importance—for, though it is mentioned, like the other two,
among Pliny's catalogue of the lost cities of Latium, yet
the name clung to the district; and both Caesar and
Tibullus had villas *in regione Pedana*, as we learn from
Cicero and from Horace respectively—it may have been
at Zagarolo, a couple of miles to the S., or it may have
been at Gallicano.

Our road, on the other hand, traverses a deep
cutting in the rock (the Cavamonte) through a narrow
ridge; and on each side of it we may see the inspection
shafts, now blocked up, by which it was possible to descend
to the aqueduct channels below. These emerge after
the cutting, and the bridge which carried them across
the next stream is used for the modern road, which goes
on to Gallicano and thence to Poli,[1] whereas the ancient

[1] By it we reach, as the ravines become deeper and wider, and
present even more formidable obstacles to their passage, the finest
remains of the great aqueducts; but to deal with them adequately
would require a volume. Suffice it to say that I hope shortly to
publish a comprehensive work on them, and that in the meantime
details may be found in the sources cited in the Bibliography. A
specimen view of one of the most picturesque bridges—the Ponte
S. Antonio (Fig. 19), which lies not far from Gericomio, may be
given here.

bridge of the Via Praenestina, the so-called Ponte Amato, is only used for foot traffic. It is a remarkably perfect specimen of a Roman road bridge (Fig. 20), and is built of massive blocks of volcanic stone; the roadway is 19 feet in width, the parapets on each side being 2 feet wide. The road then ascends to the summit of a long ridge, passing close under the large modern villa of S. Pastore, the summer quarters of the German College in Rome, and follows it, ascending gradually, until it fades into the low ground below Palestrina, the ancient Praeneste. It then runs absolutely straight for over 4 miles, and, being followed by the modern road, there is little of interest to record except some remains of pavement at intervals and two or three prominent tombs. The hills further away from the road on each side are now entirely covered with vineyards; but in ancient times, notwithstanding the difficulties of communication caused by the deep ravines, there was a fair sprinkling of ancient buildings—both of the villas of the wealthy and of the dwellings of the cultivators. As we approach Palestrina, we may notice several fine villas; one just before reaching the Ponte Sardone (an ancient road embankment much repaired), on the left, with a cryptoporticus, the decorations of which (paintings on a white ground, with decorative borders surrounding panels) are still well preserved; while a good deal higher up, near the church of S. Francesco, are two open reservoirs, one a very large one known as La Pescara.

To the S., at the cemetery, which lies on the top of its platform, is a very large villa, which is by many attributed to Hadrian, to whose time it belongs, and in which Gavin Hamilton found the so-called Braschi Antinous, a colossal statue representing him as Dionysus: it is now in the Rotunda of the Vatican Museum. Immediately to the E., on the Cave road, there is another, the attribution of which is uncertain. Certainly the district was in considerable favour as a summer resort: Augustus had a villa here (whether it was in it or elsewhere that Horace read Homer, we do not know), and Tiberius

19. PONTE S. ANTONIO (p. 137).

20. PONTE AMATO (p. 138).

To face p. 138.

21. CASTEL S. PIETRO (p. 139).

22. QUARRIES CERVARA (p. 143)

To face p. 139.

recovered from an illness here; the Younger Pliny had a villa here, and so had Marcus Aurelius.

But this is not the chief title of Praeneste to fame. In early times it was chiefly celebrated as a stronghold; and from its citadel, now Castel San Pietro (Fig. 21) on a limestone rock high above the modern town, defended by massive Cyclopean walls of large limestone blocks, two long walls descended and enclosed a roughly triangular space between them. The wealth of the rulers of this city is shown by the magnificence of the tombs of the seventh century B.C. which have been found in the lower ground below the town. Such tombs as the Barberini and the Bernardini, the contents of which are to be seen in the museums of the Villa di Papa Giulio and the Collegio Romano in Rome, show that these princes acquired their artistic treasures, with their strong Oriental characteristics (some are actually of Eastern origin and some of local workmanship), if not from Etruria itself, at any rate from the same sources as those which supplied the lords of Caere in Southern Etruria; while the bronze toilet chests, the so-called cistae, of the fourth and third centuries B.C., reveal an important renaissance of art in the beauty of their engravings.

Its commanding position close to the route to the S. through the valley of the Sacco gave it great importance, and it was one of the very few cities of the old Latin Confederacy which still survived in a flourishing condition until the later Republic: and it had received the full franchise in 90 B.C., when eight years later, after successfully standing a severe siege from Sulla, it surrendered when the Younger Marius was finally defeated at the Porta Collina. Then it was destroyed, and its territory confiscated and divided among the soldiers of Sulla; and the site of the old town was entirely given up to the huge terraces of the temple of Fortuna, in which she was worshipped as Primigenia, the first-born of Jupiter. Her responses to those who consulted the oracle were given by " lots " or slips of wood on which letters were carved. Sulla restored the temple with greatly increased magni-

ficence, the forum of the new colony occupying the lower
ground at the foot of the hill-side where the old necropolis
had been. Before his time there was no attempt at
symmetry in the planning of the town. He found it
enclosed by the two long walls descending from the citadel,
and by a base wall on the S., which he destroyed, super-
seding it with a terrace wall of his own ; the western part
of it is of massive blocks of squared stone (above this a
very large water-tank was added in Imperial times, to
correspond with the one already existing on the E., and
below it at the corner of the wall is another, faced with
brickwork and decorated with niches on the outside),
and the eastern part has arcades, which are now used
for stores, wheelwrights' shops, etc., and give the name
to the road (Via degli Arcioni) which runs along the foot
of the town ; while in the centre, between them, he made
a monumental entrance to the temple, which is not very
easy to discern among the later constructions by which
it has been filled up. The entrance was placed on the
axis of the cathedral, which occupies an ancient building
(perhaps the old Curia, or council chamber), upon the front
of which traces may still be seen of a sundial described
by Varro. It lay upon the W. side of the older forum of
the town, the site of which is partly occupied by the modern
Piazza Regina Margherita, the main square of the little
town : and on to it fronted the city treasury, a little
vaulted chamber belonging, as an inscription shows, to
a period before the time of Sulla. This lies directly
under a large rectangular hall with an apsidal termination, which fronted on to the forum, and is generally
regarded as the temple of Fortuna. The Corinthian
columns of its front, with their fine capitals, may be
seen in the modern houses, but the entrance seems to have
been from the side. The famous mosaic, with scenes upon
the Nile, which is now in the Palazzo Barberini (with many
other interesting objects of local antiquity), decorated
the apse ; but the interior (now dark, owing to the closing
of the windows on the S.) has some fine decoration still
preserved. To the W. is an area now open, but once
140

probably roofed over, and resembling a basilica in plan, which served as a means of communication between the temple and a cave in the rock, which was probably the grotto of the oracle. A beautiful coloured mosaic pavement has been found there and left in position ; it is not as complete as the other and represents various fish swimming in the sea. Before the time of Sulla the approaches to the temple were on the E. and W., on a level with the ancient forum and with the main portion of the temple, by one gate in each of the long walls ; while the modern Porta del Sole, at the S.E. corner of the town, which one enters from the electric railway station, was probably only a postern.

In the upper part of the town the remains consist mainly of terrace walls running right across it from E. to W. ; and they have naturally had a large part in fixing the position of the streets and houses of the picturesque mediaeval town, which makes great use of them as it climbs steeply up the hill-side. At the top there was a large open space surrounded by a colonnade, with a hemicycle, the steps of which still exist, leading up to a circular temple, the back wall of which still exists, in a corridor of the Palazzo Barberini.

The resemblance to the temple of Heracles at Tibur must have been close : but here we are a good deal higher up, and the view is finer and a good deal wilder : for beyond the vineyard-clad plain, furrowed by deep ravines, we see the E. side of the Alban Hills, and to the left the limestone Volscian mountains, with Artena and Segni lying high up, in positions of great natural strength, rendered even more formidable by massive walls. Truly it must have been an imposing sanctuary from many miles away : and those who wish to form some idea of its magnificence, and at the same time learn more of its history, should glance at Mr. Bradshaw's admirable restoration, which gives us a fine conception of the appearance of this great sanctuary extending over the whole hill-side.

From Praeneste there are two or three different roads southward, which join the Via Labicana at different points, which may be more fittingly dealt with in connexion with it ; while another must have run on eastward to a point a little S. of Genazzano, where it was intersected by a road from the upper Anio valley. This would take us into interesting and fascinating country, but too far into the mountains, away from the Roman Campagna in the narrower sense.

THE VIA COLLATINA

IN THE DAYS OF THE EMPIRE, at any rate, the Via
Collatina diverged from the Via Tiburtina to the
right just beyond the Arch of the Aqua Marcia,
which was converted into the Porta Tiburtina of the
Aurelian wall. It was a short and unimportant country
road, mainly used for the service of the aqueducts and
the quarries : but it must have been, as we have already
pointed out, one of the earliest elements in the Roman
road system ; and it was one of the primitive roads which
was never converted into a great highway.

The first part of the road was marked until a few years
ago by a lane called the Via Malabarba, a corruption of
Mola Barbara, which occurs in a document of the year
981 ; but it has now been completely obliterated by the
construction of a new goods-yard and engine-sheds ; and
the line of the old road (though some scanty traces of it
may still be seen below) only comes into use again 4 miles
out of Rome, being reached by a short branch on the left
from the Via Praenestina, a little beyond the Tor de'
Schiavi. It pursues a curiously sinuous course, continually
crossing and recrossing the Aqua Virgo, a remarkably
pure supply of water brought to Rome by Agrippa, the
channel of which is still in use and supplies the lower
part of the city of Rome with perhaps the best drinking
water in the world.

A mile or more to the N. of the road are the picturesque
quarries of Cervara (Fig. 22), most of which have not
been worked since Roman days : they are now overgrown
with bushes, and the dark red tufa shows up warm against
the green. Here, till Rome ceased to be a city small

143

enough for such things, was celebrated from 1815 to 1874 the famous artists' carnival, beloved especially by German artists : but, like the Carnival itself, it has died a natural death. To reach these quarries we may turn off at the large farmhouse of Cervelletta, clustering round a lofty mediaeval tower, near the fifth mile of the ancient road, or the seventh kilometre of the modern, or at the smaller farm of La Rustica, a mile to the E., which occupies the site of a villa. Twenty years ago a fine black-and-white mosaic pavement lay under the mud of the farmyard, but all has now disappeared, except a system of passages cut in the rock for the storage of water.

Three miles further on, in a low-lying valley, are the copious springs of the Aqua Virgo, now entirely enclosed to protect them from contamination. Frontinus, who was in charge of the water supply in the time of Trajan, and effected many much-needed improvements and reforms, tells us that the springs were situated within the property of Lucullus, so famous for his wealth and luxury in the last century of the Republic, which in the time of Trajan belonged to Ceionius Commodus, the adoptive son of Hadrian and father of Lucius Verus, the colleague of Marcus Aurelius. Through him it came to form part of the Imperial domain. Somewhere in this district, too, lay the springs of the Aqua Appia, constructed like the Via Appia by the blind censor of 312 B.C., whose name it bears, but they have never been identified.

Half a mile to the N., beyond the railway, is the casale of Salone, which now contains what little is left of the villa of Cardinal Agostino Trivulzio of Milan, who bought the site from the chapter of S. Maria Maggiore in 1525 ; but it returned to them after his death. It was decorated with fountains, stuccoes, and frescoes, some of which represented the adventures of Phaethon and were the work of Giammaria da Milano and Daniele da Volterra : but only faint traces of them now remain.

A mile further on the modern road turns sharply to the left, but the old road kept straight on and is marked by a cart-track : the cuttings made for it through the

23. LUNGHEZZA (p. 145).

24. SETTE BASSI (p. 157).

To face p. 145.

rock may still be seen, while a good deal of the pavement was found and removed in 1858 ; it was only 9 feet wide, which shows that the road was of minor importance. It passes through a cutting in a hill, between the sites of two Roman villas, and, after traversing some undulating country, reaches the S. extremity of the plateau on which the ancient Collatia once stood. Remains of buildings there are none ; but the site is an admirable one for an ancient city, being protected on all sides by valleys (that on the S.E. may be artificial), except on the N.W., where a narrow neck of rock (now traversed by the railway cutting) connects it with the rock on which the large fortified farmhouse of Lunghezza now stands (Fig. 23), which is well defended by the River Anio and was no doubt the citadel. Here, then, was the site of Collatia, where, as the legend tells us, Sextus Tarquinius found the fair Lucretia spinning, surrounded by her maidens. Cicero and Strabo tell us that in their time it had lost all importance, the latter classing it with Antemnae, Fidenae, and Labici as a place that had once been a stronghold but was now a hamlet in private ownership. No doubt the large villa which, as elsewhere, occupied the fine site of the acropolis was destroyed when the Strozzi of Florence built the large fortified farmhouse which now occupies the site.

From Lunghezza an ancient road appears to have run S. along each bank of the Osa stream ; that on the E. bank passed near the ruined castle known as Castellaccio, where some authorities place Collatia, but, I think, wrongly. No road, on the other hand, crossed the river in ancient times : but one has quite recently been made to join the Via Tiburtina.

V

THE VIA LABICANA

THE FIRST MILESTONE of the Via Labicana,[1] of which
we have already spoken, erected by Vespasian,
was found 200 yards outside Porta Maggiore in
1903. But the road presents no object of interest nowadays from the tomb of Eurysaces to Torre Pignattara.
This building, which stands close to the third mile of the
ancient road (the milestone, erected by Maxentius, was
found in 1687), acquired its name from the use of empty
earthenware jars in the vaulting in order to decrease the
weight. It was circular, with eight niches, and had a
domed roof; and it was the mausoleum of Helena, the
mother of Constantine, whose huge red porphyry sarcophagus was removed from here to the Lateran by Pope
Anastasius IV (in 1153–4), and only removed to the
Vatican by Pius VI, who placed it opposite to the sarcophagus of Constantia. Beneath the mausoleum are the
catacombs of SS. Peter and Marcellinus : while above-
ground was the cemetery of a cavalry corps which served
as the Imperial bodyguard : they were known as the
Equites Singulares. Many of them were recruited from
Germany, Pannonia, Dacia, etc., though also from other
provinces, and their barracks lay near the Lateran. The
tomb stood within an Imperial domain known as *ad
duas lauros* (no doubt from two fine bay-trees which grew
in it), and which must have extended by the time of Constantine as far as the Via Praenestina. Valentinian III
was murdered here by two of his officers in 455, and from

---

[1] Its official name to-day is Via Casilina, because the Via Latina
joined the Via Appia at Casilinum, the modern Capua, immediately
before the bridge over the Volturnus.

146

313 to 649 the Imperial villa was the site of the titular church (under the name of Sub Augusta) of the see of Labici. Some remains of the villa and the buildings connected with it were to be seen on the right of the road a little further on before the establishment of the Centocelle flying-ground here ; but now a certain amount has been destroyed, and the rest is not easily accessible. A number of statues were found here at the end of the eighteenth century, the best known of which is the Eros of Centocelle in the Vatican. The name of the locality (a hundred chambers) is doubtless a popular exaggeration which sprang up when the ruins were better preserved than they are now. Descending to the stream, we find on the right a modern *osteria*, built into a curious circular structure with domed roof and niches ; on a knoll behind it rises the lofty Torre di Centocelle, built of chips of volcanic stone and white marble, the latter testifying to the destruction of tombs (of which, indeed, numerous discoveries have been recorded), which must have been used for building material ; and on the left we see the finest stretch of the brick arches of the Aqua Alexandrina which is still in existence. Built by Alexander Severus, it made use of the same springs which Sixtus V afterwards brought to Rome by the Acqua Felice. Beyond this the spread of cultivation has led to the enclosure of much of what was previously pasture-land ; and in any case there is little to be seen until we notice, just to the S. of the modern bridge over which the electric railway passes, a small but finely preserved single-arched bridge of the ancient road which served to carry the traffic until its narrowness led to its abandonment only a few years ago. A few hundred yards further is the large farmhouse of Torre Nuova, surrounded by a prominent grove of pines, which forms an oasis in the desert. It belongs to the Borghese family : and in an ancient villa within the confines of the farm attached to it was found, in 1834, the large mosaic of gladiators fighting with wild beasts which adorns the large hall on the ground-floor of the Villa Borghese. In this district was situated the territory

147

of the Pupinian tribe, one of the sixteen country tribes ; here Hannibal encamped after leaving Gabii in his advance on Rome in 211 B.C., and here, despite the proverbial sterility of the district, Atilius Regulus and Fabius Maximus had their farms.

From this point the ancient road pursues a course entirely distinct from that of the modern, and, though they are never very far apart, and, indeed, come within 35 yards of one another at one point, they separate again, and do not rejoin until the mediaeval castle of Piombinara is reached, about 31 miles from Rome. The modern road, called the Via Casilina, which is now followed almost as far as Zagarolo railway station by the electric railway to Fiuggi (after which it follows the Palestrina road), passes through a district which has until lately been desolate and given up to pasture, though it is rapidly coming under cultivation : but it was fairly thickly populated in Roman times, and the road very likely follows an ancient line.

The ancient road, on the other hand, though remains of it are fairly abundant, requires careful tracing : and, indeed, it was not really known until Rosa rediscovered its line in 1856. It is not remarkable for its straightness : the country is not very difficult, and the builders of the road seem to have taken it as they found it, without attempting to alter its line from the natural course.

I am, indeed, inclined to suppose that it was the original route to Tusculum : for at the site of the ninth ancient milestone (about 2 miles from Torre Nuova) there is another ancient road continuing the previous line of the Via Labicana in a south-easterly direction. Beyond this it can be traced on the E. bank of the (now dried) volcanic crater lake of Pantano Secco [1]—the most probable of the seven candidates for identification with the Lake Regillus, where was fought the famous battle in which the great Twin Brethren helped the Romans on to defeat the Tarquins and their ally, the Prince of Tusculum. Thence it went on up, passing close to the Villa Borghese and the

[1] This lies just S. of *C. Marchese* on the map.

Villa Mondragone, to the amphitheatre of Tusculum. This is the natural prolongation of the line we have so far been following : and we have seen that such prolongations have already occurred in the case of other roads. On any other supposition, indeed, the sudden sharp turn which the Via Labicana makes from S.E. to E. is very hard to account for, as it might quite easily have been avoided and distance thereby saved, inasmuch as the country presents no natural difficulties.

For the next couple of miles the boundary of the territory of the Commune of Rome (the Agro Romano) coincides with the road—a significant fact. In this stretch it intersects the important cross-road from the Via Appia, the so-called Via Cavona, of which we have spoken already, and to which we shall return, and at the same time it crosses the subterranean aqueduct channel of the Anio Vetus ; the yellow or white calcareous deposit of this and of the other aqueducts shows up strongly against the dark brown volcanic soil of the district, and has made it possible for us to trace the course of the aqueducts through the whole of this region, which had not previously been possible. There are, indeed, more considerable remains than had previously been suspected, but they require a good deal of finding. Thus, on the W. side of the extinct crater of Prata Porci (which is one of the unsuccessful claimants to be identified with the Lake Regillus) the rock-cut channel of the Aqua Claudia is occupied by a stream for a short distance : while the deep, narrow ravine which traverses the middle of this crater contains the two bridges of this aqueduct and of the Anio Novus, running side by side, though, the arches having collapsed in both cases, only the bridge-heads remain, and are not at first sight easily recognisable. And if the existence of these bridges were not enough to render it impossible that it was a lake in historic times, we may note the discovery of a magnificent villa of the first half of the second century A.D., with lead pipes bearing the names of two men of consular rank.

The Via Labicana kept outside the crater to the N.,

and then ascended into ground which is now heavily cultivated and mostly as vineyards : so that remains of it, and of various ancient buildings (tombs, villas, etc.) adjacent to it, have been discovered, but soon afterwards destroyed. The road continues to ascend, and shortly after the ancient thirteenth milestone we have the same phenomenon as at the ninth, of one road going straight on in a southerly direction, while the other turns E. : and here, too, the explanation is that the straight road led to Labici, another of the lost cities of Latium, which is to be identified with the high-lying village of Monte Compatri (though what were seventy years ago believed to be parts of the walls of this ancient city have completely disappeared) ; while the highroad continued eastward, and crossed the railway just W. of the station which this village shares with Colonna. On the S. of Colonna lay the post-station of Ad Quintanas, which, small though it was, had a municipal constitution, and, as we learn from inscriptions, probably called itself the *respublica Labicanorum Quintanensium* : it was, indeed, important enough to send a bishop to the Council of A.D. 313, while from 313 to 649 the title of the see was Sub Augusta. From 649 till 1111 we hear of a bishop of Labici (the see is doubtless the same), to whom Tusculum was subject until that date. Then Tusculum was regarded as the more important until its destruction in 1172, though the residence of the bishop had been transferred to Rome when Labici and Tusculum became baronial castles. The site is marked by a very large tomb in the middle of the vineyards : and architectural remains, which may have decorated the forum of this roadside village, have come to light. The name has to do with the distance (15 miles) from Rome, like the village of the Decimienses at the tenth mile of the Via Latina, and it was fixed at the intersection of a number of branch roads, running back towards Frascati, up to Labici, and northward to join the modern road—in fact the Osteria della Colonna, which lies on the latter, to the N.E. of the village of Colonna (which does not appear in mediaeval records before 1093, and contains no traces of antiquity) appears to have been an important road centre also.

After this the main road continued on the level, more or less, for another 3 miles through a district rather less thickly inhabited in Roman times, which is now covered with vineyards.

At the eighteenth ancient mile, at S. Cesareo, the modern road comes up very close to it. The name has been taken to betoken that here—as elsewhere where it occurs in the Campagna—there was a villa of the Caesars : and as a fact we know that Julius Caesar had a villa in the territory of Labici, in which he made his will only sixteen days before his death. Further, in the low ground to the E. there are the remains of a large nymphaeum, which may belong to a late reconstruction of this villa. A number of classical works of art have been found here and hereabouts, and a few are still preserved in the Villa Rospigliosi on the hill ; while it is not impossible that two inscriptions dedicated by Romulus, son of Maxentius, to his father and mother before Maxentius became Emperor, were found here.

S. Cesareo was another important road centre, and probably coincides with the post-station of Ad Statuas— though whether it took its name from the statues that decorated the interior of the Imperial villa is uncertain— it is more likely that there was some group of statues standing in the open. Roads diverge on the right to Monte Compatri and the pass of Algidus on the Via Latina, while the modern road, which, as we have seen, probably represents an ancient line, must do so from this point onwards as far as Palestrina, the pavement being pre-served for long stretches (despite modern destruction) along the present road from Zagarolo station to the former town.

The Via Labicana now continues in a south-easterly direction, the modern road keeping parallel to it, but at a certain distance. Two ancient roads from Praeneste come down to join it, one of which went on to the pass of Algidus : and three more came from the present highroad, which now takes the north side of the narrow valley which is traversed by the modern railway, and on the edge of which the villages of Labico (an erroneous identification) and Valmontone stand. All these go on to the Via Latina; and the district, desolate and uninteresting in itself, through which two main roads pass, appears to have been surprisingly rich in means of communication, considering how comparatively sparsely populated it was in ancient times—for though traces of ancient habitation are not lacking, the country was not attractive enough for us to find many villas. The Via Labicana is clearly marked enough, and the pavement preserved for considerable stretches, but all modern authorities, except the French Abbé Capmartin de Chaupy, wrongly make it coincide with the present highroad; and it was therefore interesting to be able to follow it step by step on foot for 12 miles or so—which is the only way of studying the Campagna in detail.

The *Itineraries* tell us of two junctions of the Via Labicana with the Via Latina—one at Ad Pictas, 25 miles from Rome, and another at Ad Bivium, 30 miles from the city. The latter was close to the small catacombs of S. Ilario, which have been almost entirely rifled. Some of the inscriptions are in the large Palazzo Doria at Valmontone. They lie in the side of the low hill a mile and a half W. of the railway station of Segni, in the Sacco valley, above which stands the mediaeval castle of Piombinara, with a tower (now ruined) so lofty as to command a view over all this low country, furrowed with ravines, and to allow of signalling back to other castles in the hills and forward to other towers down the Sacco valley.

VI

THE VIA LATINA

A FTER DIVERGING HALF A MILE outside the Porta Capena, the Via Latina took another 500 yards to reach the gate called the Porta Latina, by which it left the Aurelian wall. Numerous discoveries of tombs have been made both inside and outside the gate; and they seem to have been second only to those of the Via Appia in number, if not in importance, and to have extended a considerable way outside the city. Juvenal speaks of it, with the Flaminia, as a road along which illustrious men were buried. But remains above-ground are comparatively few and need not detain us.

The Via Latina runs in an absolutely straight line for the first 11 miles out of Rome, in a south-easterly direction, with a slight turn a little after the first mile. This in itself would convey the impression that we have here to do with a military highway, like the Via Appia—and possibly one of slightly earlier origin; for the pass of Algidus through which it led was of especial importance in the wars against the Aequi in 465–389 B.C.; while, inasmuch as a Latin colony was founded at Cales in 334 B.C., we must suppose that by then a road led that far. And this road was not the Via Labicana, but the Via Latina, which in the time of Augustus, as Strabo tells us, was the principal road of the two, and was indeed grouped by him with the Appia and the Valeria as one of the three most famous of Roman roads. The administration of the two was, as we have seen, placed under one curator; and this was natural, as the two eventually became alternative routes for the first 30 miles; and the Labicana may easily have superseded the Latina at a later date.

153

The line of the road, marked until a few years ago by
a lane, is now being obliterated by modern buildings : and
we only get it again clearly after crossing the Via Appia
Nuova, which issues from the Porta S. Giovanni. At
the intersection a road to Castrimoenium diverged to the
right, the line of which is followed for some miles by the
railway to Albano, which has obliterated it almost completely. Following the Via Latina to the left, we find a
fine group of tombs, well known to visitors to Rome,
with the pavement of the road well preserved. Several
of them were lofty tombs in ornamental brickwork, in
two stories or even three, including the subterranean
chamber. The most prominent is on the right : the
upper part is entirely new, but the subterranean chamber,
with its fine decoration in white stucco on the barrel
vault, is still well preserved. It is called the tomb of the
Valerii—for no adequate reason that I can discover. It
probably belongs to the middle of the second century.
Almost opposite to it is the tomb of the Pancratii—not
the name of a family, but of the burial club which owned
the tomb : and here, too, the ceiling of the second subterranean chamber has very fine decorations in painted
stucco. There is a huge sarcophagus in the centre ;
while in the first chamber, which appears to be later in
date, six were found. The superstructure has disappeared,
and we only have the pavement of the room on the ground-
floor level, with representations of sea-monsters. To the
left of this tomb are the remains of the basilica of
S. Stephen, which had been built into a large villa, now
covered up, but which was perhaps Imperial property in
the time of Alexander Severus. The church had been
founded by Pope Leo I, as an inscription records, at the
dying wish of Demetrias, perhaps the daughter of Anicius
Olybrius, who was consul in A.D. 395. The foundations,
for there is nothing more, are those of a very large basilica ;
the confession may be seen in the centre, with the apse
and the baptistery behind, and some remains of older
walls of the villa. With the two tombs and the road it
is Government property : but just beyond we emerge

into a farm, where a modern quarry has come up almost to the line of the Via Latina. There were some more brick tombs on the left, but the first came down in the earthquake of January 1915, while another is used as a barn. Both of them formed objects of study for the architects of the Renaissance.

On the left we see the lofty ruined aqueduct of the Aqua Claudia and Anio Novus, and the lower conduit, with thick cemented piers and narrow arches, of the Acqua Felice, which has made use of, and almost entirely destroyed, the remains of the Aqua Marcia. The crossing of the former over the latter is, however, well preserved inside the Tor Fiscale, a lofty mediaeval tower. About 500 yards further on the aqueducts must have crossed again; and in the long narrow space between them the Goths formed an entrenched camp when besieging Rome in 539, which is very clearly described by Procopius.

The Via Latina itself passed to the E. of the Aqua Claudia just before the tower, and was never recrossed by it; but the Aqua Marcia crossed it thrice in the next couple of miles before leaving it on the left; while both aqueducts passed under the road in their subterranean course some 8 miles from the city. At this point there are seven tombs on the left of the road, one of them close to the new railway to Naples, which, like those mentioned above, seem to have aroused the interest of an unknown Spanish architect of about 1570, whose drawings, with many others of archaeological interest, are preserved in the Royal Library at Windsor Castle. Further E., just between the present railway and the embankment of a still older railway line (given up in 1890), are the remains of a large villa, supplied with water from the Aqua Marcia, which runs close by. The supply entered at the bottom of an extremely well-preserved pentagonal reservoir in two stories, ornamented with niches on the outside. The villa itself is not very well preserved, but belongs to the time of Hadrian, as is indicated by the very large number of brick-stamps, mostly dating from A.D. 123, which I found there. It is also interesting as providing the earliest known example of the use of empty amphorae in the vaulting in order to decrease its weight. The many fragments of fine marbles show that it was once a building of considerable magnificence : the principal buildings were grouped round a courtyard. Passing through the arches of the Acqua Felice, we return to the Via Latina, and at about the fifth ancient mile reach the picturesque farm of Roma Vecchia, in the courtyard of which are a number of interesting marble fragments of inscriptions, etc. It lies close to the long line of arches of the Aqua Claudia, which without much interruption runs from the Naples railway as far as Capannelle, where the aqueduct emerged from the ground. The rapidly flowing stream which passes by it is the so-called Marrana Mariana, by which Pope Calixtus II in 1122 brought the water of some springs just above Grottaferrata (which Agrippa had tapped for the Aqua Julia) into Rome, making use, in the upper portion of its course, of a natural stream, which runs into the Anio, then availing himself where he could (as we shall see further on) of the channels of the ancient aqueducts of the Aqua Claudia, and, where he could not, digging a new channel for the purpose.

The name of the farm of Sette Bassi comes from the ruins of an enormous villa (one of the most prominent in the lower Campagna) a little less than a mile away, which, to the imagination of the peasants, seemed large enough to be called " old Rome." But, inasmuch as the villa of the Quintilii on the Via Appia was no whit less imposing, it, too, acquired the same name ; and the two were distinguished as " Roma Vecchia di Frascati " and " Roma Vecchia di Albano," according to the destinations of the two roads on which they lie. Indeed, we sometimes find mention of a third " Roma Vecchia fuori di Porta Maggiore "—which would be the villa at Tor de' Schiavi. The point is not without importance ; for many works of ancient art in the various museums of the world have their provenance indicated simply as " Roma Vecchia," and this is generally understood to refer to the villa of the Quintilii. After careful consideration, however, I think we may conclude that the excavations of 1775 and the following years were made by Gavin Hamilton in the villa of Sette Bassi on the Via Latina, and that we must therefore attribute to it two busts, an Endymion, an Ariadne, a relief of three Bacchantes, and one or two other works, most of which are now in the British Museum. But it is very likely that by about 1780 he was at work at the villa of the Quintilii also, and it is certain that the excavations of 1789–92, which were carried on for the express benefit of the Vatican Museum, were made there. And, unless or until some other source of information turns up, there are many other works of art which cannot be assigned with certainty to either—so carelessly were such details noted in the late eighteenth century, when the recovery of works of art was the main object of excavation.

The villa on the Via Latina is known by various other names in the sixteenth century. It was thought to be that of Licinius Murena, and Hamilton quoted a common belief that it had been that of Phyllis, the nurse of Domitian, who buried his body in her country house on the Via Latina—we are told no more. Others call it the Palace of Lucretia—without any reason at all: while the name Sette Bassi appears in the form Septembassi, the first time in a document of 955, and has, of course, led to the conjecture that the villa once belonged to a Septimius Bassus, of whom no one has ever heard. There would be more point in comparing it with the name Bassi or Vassi, which appears in the neighbourhood of Tivoli (where it has led to a villa near the villa of Quintilius Varus being assigned to Ventidius Bassus).

All that we can say for certain is that, while the villa, as we know it, falls into three distinct periods, which are clearly distinguishable by differences in construction, the interval in date between them is extremely small, and all the three periods fall within the first forty years of the second century after Christ.

The earliest portion is built of concrete faced with brickwork (see the right of Fig. 24), or brickwork mixed with opus reticulatum; while in the second portion the

157

latter predominates; but in the huge constructions of the third and latest part of the villa we get bands of brick-work running like red stripes across the rest of the wall facing, which is of small rectangular blocks of dark, ash-grey peperino from the Alban Hills. To this belongs the great hall, with two tiers of three windows in its back wall, extending for the whole height of the building, with three openings divided by pillars (centre of Fig. 24), giving on to the colonnaded walk which looked on to the court-yard or garden round which the main part of the villa was grouped. Other halls are a good deal more ruined, but we can still recognise the traces of them; and behind them ran a terrace with a view towards the city on the N.W. All this side of the villa was supported by a most compli-cated system of vaulted chambers, in which we get the earliest case known to students of architecture of the intersection of ribs of tiles to form a cross vault. Rivoira, in his *Roman Architecture*, has rightly insisted on the importance of this phenomenon in all the subsequent history of vaulting, and its influence on the architecture of the Middle Ages. Another new feature is the existence near the great hall of a large apse with external buttresses, which also creates a precedent in architecture. There is a window in the centre; and one can see that the architect originally intended to have added another on each side, but changed his mind as the building progressed. Such alterations of plan are very common in Roman buildings, and are interesting, as showing the manner of procedure adopted. Yet another point of interest in this villa is the frequency of small light shafts, due to the great height of the building and the concentration of its various parts, which are a distinctly modern feature.

Besides the main block of the villa there are a number of detached buildings. One is a long, narrow store-house (?) at the further end of the garden, which, a century and a half ago, had a doorway at one end in ornamental brickwork: this formed the subject for a plate of Piranesi's —the only one he dedicated to the villa, which, considering its size, had been rather neglected by artists and architects

158

25. CENTRONI (p. 159).

26. VILLA OF THE QUINTILII (p. 185).

To face p. 159.

until the last quarter of the eighteenth century. **Another** is a large reservoir, supplied by a branch aqueduct, the arches of which can still be seen ; it came probably from the Anio Novus, as the foulness of the deposit seems to indicate.

S. of the whole group, on a knoll overlooking the Via Latina, there is a little detached building with a large vaulted hall in the centre, the purpose of which is uncertain. It belongs to about the same period as the rest of the villa, but it is perhaps a few years later.

The line of the old road continues to be traceable across the fields : but much of its pavement has been removed of recent years ; and this has occurred quite lately at a point about 2 miles further on, where it could perfectly well have been preserved as a vineyard path instead of being mercilessly torn up. It would have been one of the best stretches of ancient pavement in the neighbourhood of the city.

Just before this point the line of the old road has crossed the Marrana Mariana, which made use of the underground channel of the Aqua Claudia for a considerable distance, from the mineral spring called the Acqua Acetosa downwards, being diverted into it from its natural course towards the Anio. Above the spring, on a rocky spur—the end of a lava stream, as a matter of fact—are the remains of a large villa which is known by the name of Centroni (Fig. 25). This can be traced back as far as 1204, and may quite well be a survival of the name of one of the most famous builders of villas round Rome of Juvenal's day : " Centronius was a builder, and now he prepared towering villas on the curving shore of Gaeta, now on the summit of Tibur's citadel, and now on the mountains of Praeneste, with marbles sought from Greece and distant lands, outdoing the temples of Fortune and of Hercules." Nothing is left but the platform on which the house itself was built ; the exterior of the cryptoporticus has, however, an interesting series of blind arches springing from half columns—a form of decoration which was to play a great part in later architecture. In the mass of rock below is a remarkable series of passages, branching off at right angles from two main lines, which served as quarries for pozzolana earth (so important in Roman concrete), well arranged so as to exhaust every part of the hill which it was safe to excavate. They are certainly of Roman date, for a regular entrance to them was left in the embanking wall of the villa ; and one of the passages is lined with concrete to prevent a collapse. The largest passages are some 40 feet high and 13 wide ; and those who wish to explore them had better be provided with a light. The modern road—whether even the first part of it (the Via Tuscolana) is of ancient origin is extremely doubtful —by this time has fallen into the line of the Via Latina, and bears the name of Via Anagnina, as a reminiscence of the days when it was still open as a posting route, which it ceased to be at some time in the eighteenth century—I find it still given as a possible route in a post-book of 1717. On the opposite side is the Casale di Morena, picturesquely placed on a knoll, once occupied by another very large villa, which its construction has largely obliterated. Whether the name, which is quite an old one (fourth century), is derived from the Roman cognomen Murena is not certain, though perhaps not improbable.

Quite a number of antiquities have been found here or hereabouts, among them busts of Sophocles (?) and Hippocrates, acquired by Charles Townley in 1770, which are now in the British Museum.

A mile of gradual ascent brings us across the Naples main line, and the Frascati branch, which passes under the road in a tunnel : an amusing description of which was given in a little pamphlet in 1856, when the railway—the first in the Papal States—began to run : " All you, who quietly fly through the silent cave opened by the hand of man, you know not what a barrier Nature opposed to his courage ! Thanks to those who were not frightened by the difficulties caused by the springs, which threatened to destroy the works, we too have our tunnel ! " [1]

Here is the Casale Ciampino (also called Villa Senni,

---

[1] It is marked on the map as *F^(ta)* (Fermata) *Galleria.*

from its present owner), which takes its older name from a learned prelate of the late seventeenth century, and has passed it on to the railway junction and the aerodrome a couple of miles to the W. : and here was the site of the tenth ancient milestone from Rome. This being a post-station and the point of intersection of the so-called Via Cavona, the mediaeval name of an important cross-road from the Via Appia—and even further S., though we do not know how much—to the Via Praenestina, with a prolongation to the Via Tiburtina—a small village sprang up here. Like Ad Quintanas on the Via Labicana, it took its name from the distance, and its inhabitants became known as the Decimienses—the people who lived at the tenth milestone. But inscriptions show that it was also called Vicus Angusculanus, and was dependent on Tusculum, whose Senate and people had a shrine of the Lares Augusti restored by one of their aediles. The whole vineyard above Villa Senni is full of buildings belonging to this village; and above are the remains of some large villas which were cut through in making the electric tramway to Frascati about twenty years ago. An interesting little catacomb was also found—rather a rarity so far out of Rome—the key of which is kept at the Abbey of Grottaferrata.

On the other side of the modern road from Villa Senni (the old road lies rather further E.) remains of a shrine or temple were found in the nineties, and a number of terra-cotta votive objects have come to light at various times, similar to those found near Ponte di Nona. But we have no proper record of any of the discoveries in the area of this country village, which might have been, as Lanciani remarks, extremely instructive to us.

Besides the Via Cavona, two other ancient roads turned off from the Via Latina at this point, both of them to the left. One kept parallel with the Via Latina for some way and then joined it a mile further on; but the other takes us into an important district and we must briefly speak of it now. It was indeed, unless we accept the modern Via Tuscolana as an ancient road (a point about which it is difficult to make up one's mind),[1] the best route from Rome to Frascati (itself in Roman days nothing more than a large Imperial villa), and the north-western slopes of the ridge of Tusculum, which were a resort even more favoured in ancient days than in the Renaissance. Here, as in the territory of Tivoli, it would be useless to attempt to mention these ruins individually—those who require further details may be referred to the Bibliography—and I shall only mention a few of the more important and interesting ruins.

The first is a large round tomb known as the Torre di Micara, and often called—for no satisfactory reason that I can make out—the tomb of Lucullus. As at present preserved, it is a circular wall of hewn volcanic stone, with false joints, about 90 feet in diameter inside and 28 high ; it was turned into a fortress in the Middle Ages and is now a farmyard. There are some remains of tomb chambers in brick ; but how it terminated above in antiquity is not easy to see, as it has been so much altered.

Here four roads meet, and there were two different routes to Frascati. Taking the longer, which keeps a good deal higher up among the olives, we pass the remains of a very large villa. Nothing but the platform is left ; but this occupies an area something like 550 feet square, and the S.W. part of it is entirely artificial. It contains arched chambers of the most complicated description, the planning of which has led both Kircher and Canina astray (it is necessary to work with a light, for these chambers—once one passes inside the cryptoporticus which runs round the outer edge of the platform—were only intended to increase the area of the platform, and were not used even for the accommodation of slaves). What further complicates the matter is that the platform was built in front of an earlier cryptoporticus, the windows of which can still be recognised, which is hidden inside

[1] As the portion down from Frascati to the Via Cavona at Fonte Vermicino must be ancient, we may, if the sinuousness of the rest makes us reject it as a Roman road from Fonte Vermicino, suppose that the old line went on in a northerly direction to the Via Labicana at Torre Nuova.

its innermost recesses. It was divided into two, longitudinally, by a row of brick columns covered with stucco and with Roman Doric capitals, only a few of which are still standing ; and it has been rendered still more difficult of access by the construction of a later supporting wall along its whole length, close to the columns. The outside of the later platform is decorated with half columns, with semicircular arches between them, and a flat architrave above—another case of an interesting architectural feature.

Two branch roads return from here to the Via Latina, taking advantage of the comparatively level ground—for the ridge of Tusculum begins soon afterwards. One of them goes on to the district of Castrimoenium (Marino). We now pass under the Villa Muti and the Villa Montalto on its outlying slopes—both occupying the sites of ancient villas—and then pass close to the Villa Torlonia with its wonderful fountains and ilex groves. Here, too, scanty remains of Roman construction may be seen—nothing else is left—and whether the foundations in the garden terrace on a level with the present villa are of Roman date or not is doubtful. It is, however, possible that lead pipes were found here by Annibale Caro, the poet, in 1565, bearing the name of Lucullus ; and in that case here was the famous villa of this most luxurious of Romans. Frascati itself has grown considerably of late years : but the mediaeval nucleus of the town, confined within its old walls (on which the arms of Henry Stuart, Cardinal York, the last of his house, who lived here for many years as bishop, and died here, may still be seen), occupies almost exactly the site of a great Roman villa, of which some remains of no great importance (including some remains of the lower terrace, in the centre of which is a small rectangular chamber with an apse at the back against the hill-side, called the nymphaeum of Lucullus) have been seen at various points. It appears to have belonged to Passienus Crispus, whose second wife, Agrippina, the mother of Nero, compassed his death for the sake of his property. After her death it passed into Nero's hands, and it certainly belonged to the Emperors of the Flavian House, and presumably remained Imperial property right through, though we have no positive evidence one way or the other. It does not appear among the donations of parts of the Imperial domain made by Constantine to various churches in Rome and its neighbourhood ; and its subsequent history is quite unknown (for the legend of its donation to S. Benedict has no foundation in fact) until it appears again in the ninth century as a village called Frascata (from *frasche*, bushes—derived either from the material of the huts under which the inhabitants sheltered or from the bushes which covered its ruins) which gradually grew in importance, and had three or four churches of its own even before the destruction of Tusculum.

Only a little way above the modern town lies the splendid Villa Aldobrandini, with its fountains and its magnificent hemicycle, which Lanciani well compares with an ancient nymphaeum. The Villa Mondragone rests upon the remains of an ancient villa which certainly belonged to the two Quintilii, and fell into the Imperial domain when Commodus put them to death. Below it is the so-called Barco Borghese, i.e. the Parco, or enclosure, in which wild animals were kept. It, too, was the site of a great villa, and has a platform entirely artificial, resting entirely on vaulted chambers, now (as they always were) pitch dark, and displaying an almost diabolical ingenuity on the part of their constructor. For, though all the angles are right angles, they form a veritable maze, and the making of the plan—the work of the late Mr. F. G. Newton—was a very long and difficult business ; for there was only one way, as a rule, of getting to each group of chambers, and that a long and devious one ; and so a single wrong turning would mean retracing one's steps. Doubtless this plan has something to do with the distribution and weight of the buildings on the upper terrace, but, as this is now merely a garden, one has unluckily no notion of what they were like. And such speculations seem idle as one looks down from the terrace of Mondragone

164

and admires one of the finest views in the whole world on a sunny day—supposing, indeed, that one is lucky enough to get in. For the Frascati Villas are less easily accessible than they were, the public, if what is told is true, having proved themselves not too worthy of the confidence their owners had placed in them ; and either a carriage or a guide has, strictly speaking, to be hired, even by those who wish to go through the Villa Aldobrandini up to Tusculum, so that the longer route by Camaldoli is the only one that is entirely free from restraint.

Below Frascati, too, there were numerous villas ; but what is preserved in most cases amounts to a long, rectangular platform, supported by lofty walls, the upper surface of which has been used for a vineyard or oliveyard ; and while there are often some subterranean chambers preserved in the platform, we see little or nothing of the superstructure. The only adjunct of the villa which generally survives is its water reservoirs—and that owing to the massiveness of their construction. These vary much in size—some of them are quite small single chambers, while others may have six arcades each way and measure as much as 100 feet square : and they are sometimes above-ground, sometimes subterranean. The open circular tank also occurs sometimes.

This district to the N. of Frascati was reached by numerous ancient roads descending the slopes, some of which end at the Via Cavona, while others descend still further into the lower Campagna. One of the largest villas is attributed, on the faith of an inscription on a water-pipe, to the Emperor Tiberius, and another to Galba ; and the evidence in both cases seems to be sufficient— especially as in the former case another pipe bearing Vespasian's name came to light, which showed that it remained Imperial property. Half a mile to the E. of the Barco di Borghese, above the road to Monte Porzio, we have another Imperial villa, of which nothing is left but two huge platforms known as the Cappellette (the little chapels), from the niches in the supporting walls. This is

165

shown by lead pipes to have belonged to Matidia, the niece (or the grandniece) of Trajan.

We have already seen that the villa on the site of Mondragone became Imperial property about A.D. 183 ; and, as all the villas that we have named lie fairly close together, and in the same district, it may not be too much to suppose that, by the time of Commodus, the Imperial domain extended for a radius of about a mile round Frascati on the N. and E. A mile further down the hill, just below the Naples railway, between two of the ancient roads leading down from Frascati, is a small extinct crater, now full of vineyards, and bearing the name of Pantano Secco (the dry marsh). It was once a lake, and was drained at some unknown date—perhaps in the Middle Ages—and it is this that, from the time of Nibby onwards, has been held, and in my opinion rightly, to be the famous Lake Regillus, as being the only site proposed that can safely be said to be in the territory of Tusculum—except Prata Porci, which never was a lake at all.

Returning to the Via Latina, which we left at Villa Senni, we find on the left of the modern road the picturesque castle of Borghetto, built by the Counts of Tusculum about the end of the eleventh century, astride the old road, which was avoided thenceforth as far as possible by those who did not wish to have toll levied on them. The deep valley to the right (which looks like an extinct crater) is called the Valle Marciana ; the name is an old one (ninth century), and it can be by no mere chance that a freedwoman of Marciana, the sister of Trajan, made a dedication of some object unknown at the Vicus Angusculanus, as an inscription found there records. The natural inference, therefore, is that it takes its name from some property which she had in the district. At the southern extremity of it is the Sorgente Preziosa, a tepid spring which has rightly been recognised as that of the Aqua Tepula. It is not, and never was, very copious, and it is rather a mystery why it was thought worth while to convey it to Rome.

At the modern tramway junction (about the twelfth

ancient mile) the Via Latina is running almost due E., and continues to do so henceforth for about 3 miles, until it comes under Tusculum. To the S. of us is the famous abbey of Grottaferrata, the seat of the Basilian monastery founded by S. Nilus. It may perhaps take its name (Crypta Ferrata) from a square chamber under the campanile of the church, which was probably the cella of a Roman tomb. The monastery itself contains various objects of interest, and notably a well-kept museum of local antiquities, inscriptions, and works of art.

It stands upon the remains of an ancient Roman villa —one of the many candidates (they are about as numerous as those for identification with the Lake Regillus) to be considered the famous Tusculan villa of Cicero. But this is a tradition that cannot be traced earlier than the middle of the fifteenth century : and most modern writers think that it is to be sought half a mile further to the S.E. —on the southern extremity of a hill called the Colle delle Ginestre, now covered with vineyards and modern houses, but once, as its name would imply, with broom—where the remains are more scanty, but the evidence seems to them more favourable. But after having carefully examined it, I am bound to state my opinion that the only serious argument is this—that Cicero paid a water rate for the Aqua Crabra, the springs of which are at about 2,000 feet above sea-level, below Rocca Priora— so that the villa cannot have been on the heights of Tusculum, which rules out a good many candidates. We really know no more about its site than this (unless we could be sure that the Villa of Lucullus was on the site of the Villa Torlonia, and then we only know that the two were " near "—not how near) and the various passages in ancient authors, traditional names, and discoveries of works of art and other objects which are brought in as evidence do not help us to determine the site more closely. The tramway company has, however, followed local usage in calling the place Poggio Tulliano.

In the valley to the S.—which, under the abbey,

167

widens out into a great ravine—are the springs of the Aqua Julia, now the source of the Marrana Mariana.

At La Pedica, which, being at the thirteenth mile, must correspond with the post-station of Roboraria, the modern road from Frascati intersects the Via Latina at right angles. It probably follows an ancient line, and a mile S., at the Ponte Squarciarelli, divides into three branches. One runs southward to Marino, another due S. to the E. shores of the Alban Lake, and on to Nemi and Velletri, while the third ascends to Rocca di Papa.

A little further on an ancient road, the pavement of which was cleared about 1850, ascends the southern slopes of Tusculum, and, like the road approaching from the N., reaches the city at the amphitheatre, passing the tomb of one M. Coelius Vinicianus, who was a contemporary of Cicero's. The amphitheatre was placed at the western extremity of the primitive city in a depression in the narrow neck which almost divides the ridge into two parts, and was thus an important element in the defence : for here was the only easy entrance, which could have been held by a small force.

At a later date this neck naturally became an important traffic point, and three different ancient roads have been traced as coming up here from the N. The amphitheatre was, indeed, only built about the middle of the second century after Christ. It has only been very partially cleared, and is much filled in and overgrown ; it is only of moderate size (the total diameter being about 260 feet by 175 feet). To the W. is a large flat rectangular meadow surrounded by pines, above the Villa Rufinella—the site of a large villa, which most writers wish to call that of Cicero ; while on the E. is a great platform supported by arched substructions, which in considerable measure have fallen away down the slope. This was thought to be the villa of Cicero in the sixteenth century, but lately has often been called the villa of Tiberius. But on the platform there is nothing but a large core of concrete, which seems quite clearly to be the podium of a temple facing S.W., and, though somewhat small in proportion to the size of the platform on which it stands, is very well placed as regards position, commanding as it does a magnificent view over the lower ground over the slopes of the crater lake of Albano, and right away down to the sea. The site is thus eminently suitable for one of the chief temples of the city. As the temple of Castor and Pollux must be sought at the highest summit, we may, if we will, assign this temple to Jupiter. Macrobius says that " there are some who record that this month (May) came into our calendar from that of Tusculum, in which Maius is still called a god, who is Jupiter, so called, that is, from his greatness and majesty." And Livy tells us that it was struck by lightning in 210 B.C., and almost the whole of the roof was removed. To the left of the ruins the main road ascends the ridge in a south-easterly and then in an easterly direction, while a branch goes off parallel to it at a rather lower level, leading to some private houses on the slopes to the N.

A few hundred yards further up an open level space seems to mark the site of the forum, the remains of which were discovered by excavations in the first half of last century, together with a number of inscriptions and works of art, several of which, until quite recently, were built into a small house on the site ; most of the latter have now been removed for safe keeping. The forum was soon, however, covered up again, and whether the plan that we have of it is trustworthy is a little uncertain.

On the E. side of the area lay the theatre, the stage of which still has the chamber under it, reached by rectangular shafts, from which the curtain was drawn up. But the best-preserved portion is the cavea, where the rows of seats, resting against the hill-side, may still be seen. To the right are three or four steps on a curve —probably a fountain fed by the large square reservoir just behind the theatre. On the left of the forum a road descends to an interesting fountain ; the basin, a rectangular trough of volcanic stone, bears on the front an inscription of two aediles of the time of Cicero. The chamber at the back is interesting as having a pointed

roof and not a rounded arch—which has induced some
to attribute to it a very high antiquity, though I myself
am not inclined to do so, and the embankment wall in
which it is enclosed does not seem to be very early either.
Only a little way further on the ground rises steeply to
the summit, where undoubtedly stood the citadel—now,
however, entirely covered with ruins of the mediaeval
buildings and fortifications destroyed in 1191, when Tusculum ceased to exist, its place being taken by Frascati.

The position is of great natural strength, as the ground
falls steeply away on all sides ; and it has been still further
strengthened by cuttings in the rock, though of fortifications of the Roman or pre-Roman period there is no
trace.   At the very top of the hill is a cross, planted there
in October 1899[1] by the students of the English College
during their *villeggiatura* at Monte Porzio, where their
country house was until they acquired Palazzola a few
years back.   Among the blocks of stone used to support
it was an inscription of about 70 B.C., probably set up by
the attendants of the temple of Castor and Pollux.   That
the inscription was brought up here afterwards (unless
as building material in the Middle Ages) is unlikely ; and
we may, therefore, suppose that the temple stood up here.

The history of Tusculum may be briefly sketched
as follows.   According to tradition it was founded by
Telegonus, the son of Ulysses and Circe.   The first mention of it is on the occasion when its chief, Octavius Mami-
lius, espoused the cause of his father-in-law, Tarquinius
Superbus, on his expulsion from Rome, and led the thirty
cities of the Latin League against Rome at the battle
of the Lake Regillus.   The history of the subsequent
period is not very clear ; one authority states that it
was taken by the Romans in 484 B.C.   Coins of the late
Republic allude to its relief by Rome when besieged by
the Latins in 374 B.C., and it was one of the oldest of
Roman municipalities, and seems to have remained friendly
to Rome, with two exceptions.   In 211 B.C. Hannibal

[1] It took the place of several earlier ones (*The Venerabile* (Rome,
1926), iii. 27).

appeared before its gates, but was not admitted and did not attempt to force an entrance. It may have been in vogue as a *villeggiatura* as early as this : at the end of the Republic, at any rate, as Cicero says, it was full of men of consular rank : it was so favourite a summer resort that it had become almost a suburb of Rome : but during the Imperial period the town itself is hardly mentioned.

Its mediaeval history is obscure, and in the ninth century we have the rise of the famous Counts of Tusculum, from whom the Colonna family traces its descent. In 1167 the people of Tusculum, with the help of a small band of Germans, defeated the Romans at Monte Porzio ; but three years later it had to surrender to the Pope : while in 1191 it was handed over to the Romans, who left not one stone upon another.

A road diverging to the left of the theatre avoided the ascent to the arx, keeping under it and continuing along the top of the ridge beyond it. From this road, traces of the pavement of which still exist, we may command a view of the Via Latina ; it runs in the deep valley below (the Valle della Molara) between the ridge in which we are, which is the rim of the original larger crater of the Alban volcano, and the smaller crater which was raised by a later eruption in the centre of it. There are a certain number of villas on the ridge and its southern slopes ; while lower down on the N. lie the villages of Monte Porzio (derived from the mediaeval name *Mons Porculus*, and having nothing to do with Porcius Cato) and Monte Compatri. The road passed to the S. of the highest point of the ridge, the Monte Salomone (2,536 feet), on which there are the remains of a large mediaeval castle, covered by mounds of earth. To the W. of it is a path (probably on an ancient line) descending steeply to the N. through a narrow valley to the monastery of S. Silvestro above Monte Compatri, while another branch road ran down more gradually along the slopes on the S. to the Via Latina. Keeping up and straight on, Rocca Priora is reached in another mile and a half. This high-lying village is probably identical with the ancient Corbio. Its order in the various lists of the ancient cities of Latium may or may not be topographical, and it would be hazardous to try and determine its position from them. But it is quite clear from the account of Horatius's campaign against the Aequi of the mountains to the S.E. that it was not far from Algidus; while of Ortona, which is mentioned in connexion with it, we know nothing at all. The Arx Carventana, which was an important post in the continual warfare with the Aequi for the pass of Algidus—which meant the command of the route to the S.E.—is equally undiscoverable, and it is not bound to correspond with any site at present inhabited. An equal disappointment will probably be the lot of anyone who attempts to find the temples of Diana and Fortune *in Algido*—the former often mentioned by Horace, the latter once by Livy. I have ascended every summit along the rim of the crater and have found no traces of anything that can with any certainty be identified with them.

At the actual pass, which is just beyond the twenty-eighth ancient milestone, and is a narrow gap in the crater rim, very easily defensible, there is nothing but the remains of the post-station of the Osteria dell' Aglio or della Cava; while on the Maschio d'Ariano, the prominent summit a couple of miles to the S., there is nothing but a very large mediaeval castle : and those who have thought that the Temple of Diana was here have simply mistaken for it the apse of the church of the castle—which, of course, may have obliterated the temple. The view from the summit is, of course, magnificent; but so it is from any of the summits as we go S.W. along the ridge, over the Monte Peschio (the highest point of all, 3,080 feet above sea-level) and on to the deep depression through which the post-road to Velletri crossed the Macchia della Faiola, by a steep ascent on which brigandage was so frequent that a hill close by acquired the name of Monte degli Appesi, or Hangman Hill.

Returning to the pass, we find the Via Latina descending fairly rapidly, with a branch going off to the Via

Labicana almost at once. The line of the road can be clearly traced, but the country is less interesting, and there are few remains of buildings. As we have seen, there are several branch roads connecting these two main roads; while two branch roads led to the S. through the gap between the Alban Hills and the Volscian mountains.

The modern village of Artena lies on a spur projecting to the N. from them; and high above it are the massive walls of unhewn limestone blocks of an old town, the ancient name of which is uncertain. Our road keeps far below it, and eventually is joined by the Via Labicana at Ad Bivium.

O

VII

THE VIA APPIA

DESPITE THE FAME of the Via Appia, a monograph
dealing with it fully has never been written. The
reasons for this are various. If we take the road
as a whole there are very few writers who have ever
studied, still less followed, its entire course. Mr. Robert
Gardner and I are among them : but the publication
of our results has been delayed chiefly by a difficulty
which affects more especially the first part of the road.
This is the non-existence till now of indices to vol. vi.
of the *Corpus Inscriptionum Latinarum*, in which will
be found the inscriptions, mainly sepulchral, of the first
9 miles of the road ; and as the tombs of the Via Appia
were in origin more numerous and are certainly better
known and preserved than those of any other road—thanks
largely to the excavations conducted and described by
Canina under the order of Pius IX, as we shall see in the
sequel—the lack has been a serious one.

When we pass beyond the Alban Hills and reach the
Pomptine Marshes, considerations of a different order
have deterred us. It is this section of the Archaeological
Survey of Italy, extending as far as Terracina and the old
Neapolitan frontier, which still forms the boundary between the *compartimenti* of Latium and Campania, between
the province of Rome (which is co-extensive with the
former) and the province of Caserta (which is the north-
westernmost province of the latter), that has been selected
by the Italian authorities for the commencement of their
labours : and these are already well advanced.

From what I have said it will be clear that the moment

174

has not yet arrived when the history of the Via Appia and its monuments as a whole can profitably be written, though we shall before long have before us all the available material, so that the task will not need to be greatly delayed.

In the meantine, there is a somewhat bewildering maze of general works and special monographs : and I would suggest as a useful indication for those who desire to pursue the subject in detail an article of my own in the *Mélanges de l'Ecole Française,* xxiii. (1903) 375 *sqq.*, in which they will find much of the bibliography.

It is a short *catalogue raisonné* of a collection of 226 drawings of the various monuments of the Via Appia from Rome to Benevento, drawn by Carlo Labruzzi in 1777, in which year he accompanied Sir Richard Colt Hoare, of Stourhead, in a tour along the road. Sir Richard, in his *Recollections Abroad* (reprinted in his *Classical Tour*), has described the journey in some detail. The drawings themselves, bound in five splendid folio volumes, were in Sir Richard's own library. They were sold with the rest of the Stourhead treasures in 1883, came up again at Christie's in 1901, were knocked down for a ridiculously low figure, and soon passed into my possession.

Another set, which contains only 188 drawings, which are Labruzzi's preliminary drafts for Sir Richard's set, is in the Biblioteca Sarti in Rome, and there are a few others in private collections which are not to be found in either series.

Only 48 of them have been engraved, 24 in full size by Labruzzi himself, and 24 more by Parboni and Poggioli, on a reduced scale.

The only modern general work on the subject is Ripostelli and Marucchi's *Via Appia*, and that does not go beyond the sixth mile.

The Via Appia was constructed in 312 B.C. as a military road by the famous censor Appius Claudius Caecus. Livy speaks of the march of the mutineers of 342 B.C. from Campania as far as the eighth mile of the road

175

quae nunc Appia est.[1] It runs in an absolutely straight line from just beyond the Almo as far as Terracina (with only one slight divergence just beyond Aricia), and this is probably due to an autocratic order by the blind old censor.

It seems very doubtful whether the primitive track which led from Rome to the southern shores of the Alban Lake would have taken a line of this kind : such is not a characteristic of early roads, and we have probably found already in the Via Castrimoeniensis the original track to Alba Longa and the southern portion of the Alban Hills. Aerial photography may, of course, resolve our doubts, and, indeed, until this test has been applied it would seem advisable to reserve judgment.

The successive prolongations of the road to Venusia, Tarentum, and finally to its termination at Brindisium, need not detain us here, and we may turn our attention to the study of the course of the road itself.

Remains of the Porta Capena of the Servian wall were found by Parker in 1867, and its site is now marked by a brick ruin in the middle of one of the lawns of the Passeggiata Archeologica.[2] The principal artery of this park, a road about 50 feet wide, follows a tortuous course, and has completely obliterated the line of the older road which was previously to be seen running between narrow walls. Excavations down to the ancient level would, it is true, have been difficult, as the water would have been reached very soon.

The distance from the Porta Capena to the Porta Appia of the walls of Aurelian (corrupted into Porta d'Accia in the Middle Ages), the modern Porta S. Sebastiano, is just over a mile.

There are a number of interesting monuments, both Pagan and Christian, which, however, are generally dealt with in connexion with the city of Rome itself, and need not, therefore, be described here.

[1] VII. 39.
[2] A branch of the Aqua Marcia passed over it, and both Juvenal and Martial allude to the dripping of the water from the arch.

The site of the first milestone would thus fall, not outside the Porta S. Sebastiano (where a modern inscription has been set up), but just inside, as Lanciani had already determined.[1]

A milestone set up by Vespasian, with an additional inscription of Nerva, was found in the sixteenth century, and was placed on the balustrade of the Capitol, where it still stands. It is perhaps the best known of Roman milestones, and its shape is typical of the period.

The gate itself is one of the most imposing of the whole enceinte. It is flanked by two semicircular external towers of brick, which (as they stand) do not form part of the original structure. This has, indeed, been completely transformed by restorations after the period of Aurelian.

The lower part of these towers has been masked and strengthened, as in the Porta Flaminia, by rectangular bastions of blocks of marble resting on a base of blocks of travertine. These bastions were probably added by Honorius, and the same I believe to have been the case at the Porta Flaminia. The marble blocks doubtless came from tombs : a number of them have projecting bosses.

Immediately outside the gate, on the high ground on the left, was a celebrated temple of Mars, the ascent to which was known as the Clivus Martis. An inscription, now in the Vatican, records that its steepness was reduced at the public expense. Every year the knights rode in procession from here to the Capitol. The temple gave its name of *Ad Martis* to the whole neighbourhood, even down to Christian times ; and the poet Terence had a garden hereabouts.

The house on the right, immediately before reaching the railway, is built upon an ancient tomb of the first or the second century after Christ. Some of the ornamental brickwork of the exterior is still visible; and the interior, a chamber with a barrel vault decorated with reliefs in stucco, is fairly well preserved. The niches for the urns may still be seen.

[1] *Storia degli Scavi*, iii. 11.

On the other side of the railway a lane goes off westward to the Via Ostiensis (the so-called Vicolo della
Travicella, i.e. Traversella), which is probably of ancient
origin. Immediately beyond it we cross a brook,[1] the
ancient Almo, by a bridge which has been restored in
the Middle Ages. Tomassetti [2] states that traces of the
ancient bridge, and of the artificial bed of the stream made
of peperino slabs, can be seen when the water is low enough.
The river god was worshipped by the Romans, and at
the confluence of the stream with the Tiber the statue of
Cybele, and the objects connected with her worship,
were solemnly washed on March 27th. The stream itself
must in ancient times have had its origin near Capannelle,
on the Via Latina: the arrangement by which it still
receives the greater part of its waters from the Marrana
dell' Acqua Mariana is mediaeval.

As soon as we have crossed the Almo, the series of
tombs on each side of the Via Appia begins to be prominent.
We first see a huge mass of concrete on the left, which is
generally attributed to Geta ; and a similar mass on the
right, with an internal chamber, which is usually called
the tomb of Priscilla, the wife of Abascantus, freedman
of Domitian. The grounds for these attributions are in
both cases insufficient.

At the second mile, according to Pliny the Elder, was
situated the *Campus Rediculi*, where a pet crow of Tiberius
was buried, and there is every likelihood that it was
connected with the *fanum Rediculi*, the sanctuary of the
divinity who, it was believed, caused Hannibal to turn
back from his advance on Rome.

On the left is the church of *Domine quo vadis ?* which
takes its name from the well-known legend that S. Peter,
flying from Rome, met Our Lord, and asked him the
question. Our Lord replied, *Vado iterum crucifigi*, and
S. Peter returned to the city to meet his death. A paving-
stone of the road, with the imprint of Our Lord's footsteps
(as is believed) is still preserved in the church. The

---

[1] The modern name Acquataccio is a corruption of Acqua d'Accia.
[2] II. 40.

legend can be traced back as far as the third century, and was accepted as genuine by St. Ambrose.

Just beyond it are the divergence of the Via Ardeatina (on the right) and the Valle della Caffarella (on the left), and here is a circular chapel erected by Cardinal Reginald Pole. Here the straight line of the Via Appia actually begins.

Beyond it the road begins to rise, and on the left again is the huge concrete core of a tomb ; while on the same side, at the top of the hill, is a large columbarium, now the wine-cellar of an osteria. Its niches are empty : it is generally called that of the freedman of Augustus, but without reason; while that of the slaves and freed-men of Livia, found in the eighteenth century, was destroyed, and its inscriptions conveyed to the Capitoline Museum.

On the right, occupying the whole space between the Via Appia and the present course of the Via Ardeatina, as far as the Via delle Sette Chiese, is the property which has been assigned to the Trappist monks of Tre Fontane, who are the guardians of the catacombs of S. Calisto.

Here may be seen the remains of several tombs, one of which is interesting, as giving the transition between the rites of cremation and inhumation at the beginning of the third century after Christ—both being found in use in the same tomb.

Numerous inscriptions which have been found in the course of agricultural operations are built into the walls of the farm.

The catacombs themselves can hardly find description here. An ancient road may still be seen in the garden above them, running E.S.E., i.e. in a direction which, if prolonged, falls into the line of the Via Appia Pignatelli, which makes the antiquity of the latter probable if not certain. The Via Appia Pignatelli, which diverges to the left of the Via Appia a little further on, takes its name from Innocent XII, who belonged to this family, and who constructed it as far as the Via Appia Nuova, which it joins between the fourth and the fifth mile. It is very likely that it follows the line of an ancient road which served as a mediaeval variation of the Via Appia, very likely after the establishment of the castle at Capo di Bove.

On the left, beyond the divergence, are the Jewish catacombs of the Vigna Randanini ; while others lie on the Via Appia Pignatelli. Tomassetti points out that these cemeteries form a group, and are doubtless connected with the fact of the existence of a Jewish colony near the Porta Capena.

Before we follow the Via Appia itself further, it may be well to study the Triopion, an estate of Annia Regilla, the wife of Herodes Atticus, to which the Via Appia Pignatelli leads. Herodes was a Greek philosopher, the teacher of Marcus Aurelius and of Lucius Verus. The death of his wife, in A.D. 161, left him a widower, and he was accused by her brother of being concerned in her death. Suspicion continued to weigh on him, and he tried to justify himself in the eyes of the world by extravagant expressions of grief. Inscriptions now in Paris (there are facsimiles of them in the Villa Borghese) and at Naples mention a temple consecrated to Ceres and Faustina and a field sacred to Minerva and to Nemesis, well guarded and enclosed by a wall.

Little remains of these buildings, and of all the magnificence with which they were decorated. For Herodes Atticus was the richest man of his time (owing his wealth, so the story goes, in great measure to the accidental discovery by his father of a very large hoard of treasure in the foundations of a house he owned in Athens), and spent enormous sums in embellishing various cities of Greece ; and the Stadium of Athens, where his tomb was placed, was his gift to the city. A few interesting relics of his estate are still to be seen. First there is the church of S. Urbano, no doubt the temple of Ceres and Faustina, in which was the statue of Annia Regilla herself—a brick building with a portico of four columns. Inside are some interesting frescoes of the year 1011, illustrating the lives of S. Urban and three other saints, which are of importance in the history of the art of the period. Near

180

S. Urbano are scanty remains of other buildings : high up on the right is a prominent water reservoir, and on a lower knoll a grove of ilexes, which, of course, has nothing to do with the nymph Egeria, the counsellor of Numa Pompilius, whose grove was outside the Servian wall.

Below in the valley is a nymphaeum, called the grotto of the nymph Egeria under the same misconception—an oblong chamber with niches and a fountain at the end, with a recumbent female statue from a sarcophagus over it to typify the nymph. It was all once faced with marble, but now is unadorned except with maidenhair. It has frequently formed the subject of sketches and studies by artists and architects of all nations.

Above on the hill is the entrance to the catacombs of Praetextatus ; and further down the valley towards Rome, standing in a farmyard, is a picturesque brick tomb, finely decorated on the outside with columns and cornices in cut brick, of great elegance in design : while the use of yellow bricks in combination with the dark red gives a very beautiful colour-effect. It is thought by Lanciani and Lugli to have been the tomb of Annia Regilla, and though the interior will be seen, by those who penetrate into what is now a fowl-house, to be faced with brickwork of far less careful construction, the identification will probably stand. It is generally known as the temple of the Deus Rediculus, but there is of course no warrant for the name.

Returning to the Via Appia, we find the church of S. Sebastiano on the right, with its memories of SS. Peter and Paul. Without entering deeply into the controversies which have been aroused by the recent discoveries there—and which, as they mainly concern Christian archaeology, do not belong to our present subject—we may notice that it was found that the church was built on the edge of a low cliff some 25 feet high, at the foot of which were three finely preserved tombs, originally columbaria, but later changed into burial vaults and used by Christians in the first half of the third century A.D. These tombs must have given the origin to the name *catacomb* from κατὰ κύμβας (in the hollows), while at the top of the depression was a line of still earlier columbaria along a branch road of the Via Appia. About the middle of the third century the tombs were destroyed and covered over, and a large open court built over the whole, joining on, it would seem, to a villa which already existed near the earlier tombs, parts of which, however, were at the same time destroyed. The walls of it bear inscriptions showing that in this century and the next the place was visited by pilgrims, because it was in some way connected with the Apostles—perhaps their bodies were removed here from their resting-places by the Via Ostiensis and the Via Cornelia for temporary security during the persecution of A.D. 258.[1]

On the left, at the bottom of the hill, is a farmhouse, built on the foundations of the circular temple-tomb of Romulus, the son of Maxentius, who died in his childhood. It stands in the centre of a large square courtyard, in which must have assembled the processions before they entered the circus which lies behind. This circus is extremely well preserved, and was doubtless erected for the funeral games in his honour. An inscription erected to him after his deification served to identify it—previously, for some strange reason, the whole group was associated with Caracalla—and was placed at the curved end of the circus after the excavations of 1828, in which it was completely cleared and planned. We may note especially the *spina*—the long wall down the middle, which divided the arena into two halves, and was decorated with fountains, etc.—and also with egg-like objects, which marked the number of laps run. On it stood an obelisk, which originally belonged to some monument of the time of Domitian, and was brought here by Maxentius ; it was excavated in 1649, and taken by Innocent XII to adorn Piazza Navona, which, being built on the ruins of the stadium, is of precisely the same shape as the circus.

[1] A summary of the discussion will be found in Professor Stuart Jones's article on " The Apostles in Rome " in the *Quarterly Review* for October 1925.

The vaulting which supported the seats has fallen, but we may see the empty jars which were built into it in order to decrease its weight. The outer walls and the towers (*oppida*) on each side of the *carceres*, or starting gates, are well preserved. On the N. side of the circus, which runs due E. and W., is the Imperial box, in communication with a large villa, with two ruined apses with half domes. The greater part of it was erected by Maxentius, including a gallery or portico over 200 yards long connecting it with the circus, under which traces of earlier buildings may be seen.

We now ascend again steeply, and on the left find the circular tomb of Caecilia Metella. Whether her husband was the triumvir Crassus or not has been treated as doubtful : but from a careful study of the decorations it seems clear that the tomb should be attributed to the beginning of the Augustan period, whereas the triumvir fell at Carrhae in 53 B.C. It is therefore more probably his son (or even grandson) who is in question.

The tomb itself, a great drum of concrete faced with blocks of travertine, stood on a square base, of which only the core remains. It was some 60 feet in diameter outside. Two corridors, one above the other, led into the brick-lined chamber in the interior of the core, which now has no roof. This is generally believed to have been supported by a conical vault, but we really do not know much about it, though a conical termination to the whole, projecting above the drum, is the most probable. In any case, it was removed when the monument became the keep of the castle, which first belonged to the Counts of Tusculum, and passed to the Caetani in the time of Boniface VIII, when it was restored. The baronial palace was built close against the keep, and opposite it was the Gothic church : the castle itself occupied a rectangular space defended by towers, enclosing the road for a length of over 200 yards. This, no doubt, led gradually to its abandonment in favour of the Via Appia Pignatelli.

The castle was called Capo di Bove from the ox skulls on the frieze of the tomb, and a lofty tower a mile or so to the S. was called jestingly Zampa di Bove (the hoof of the ox).

The Via Appia has now reached the summit of a long ridge, formed by a lava stream from the Alban volcano, and runs along it for over 3 miles, commanding the most magnificent views over the whole Campagna, the flatter district between it and the Sabine mountains, the Alban Hills, and that desolate country between itself and the range of high sand dunes that shuts out the view of the sea. In this straight stretch it is flanked by an almost continuous line of tombs, all of them in a more or less ruined condition. They were excavated in the papacy of Pius IX under the direction of Canina, and the fragments discovered have in some cases been set up on or near the tombs, while in others they have been dispersed. The excavators were not able to go as far inwards from the road as might have been advisable, in order to lay bare the monuments of minor importance which probably lay behind the more prominent tombs in the front row— if we are to judge by the analogy of other roads, and also by such excavations as have been made, e.g. on the right just beyond the fourth mile, in the Lugari property. Here there is a large brick tomb built on an ancient cross-road, which once led to a large villa. The plan of this has been recovered and published ; when excavated, it was remarkably complete in all its details, the rooms being grouped round three sides of a peristyle with a garden on the fourth. Many of them could be identified with more or less certainty, and the baths and one of the store-rooms, with a series of huge jars as at Ostia, were especially well preserved. The original house was a small structure of the Republican period, with a little courtyard, and a cistern under it. To this the larger building was added in the time of Antoninus Pius and altered later, a Christian oratory and baptistery being added.

The large tomb is probably that of S. Urban the bishop, a contemporary of S. Caecilia, who suffered martyrdom under Marcus Aurelius ; and the house is then that of Marmenia, who herself was beheaded with her daughter and some twenty-two others, all of whom were very likely buried on the spot, as exactly this number of bodies was found. Other houses were also found on the same estate : and indeed it is likely that the ground on both sides of the main road for some considerable distance was occupied by buildings, as it offers such splendid sites.

At the fifth mile on the left there are far more considerable ruins—those of the great villa of the Quintilii, which cover a large extent of ground, of over a quarter of a mile square. I have studied them in detail and published plans of them, so that I need only refer briefly to the villa here.[1] The earliest buildings, which are the first we come to, belong to the time of Hadrian, including the large and prominent buttressed reservoir, to which a mediaeval tower has been added, which is now the farmhouse of S. Maria Nuova (Fig. 26). To the second period belonged a long, narrow garden in the shape of a stadium, with the curved end towards the Via Appia. This garden ran north-eastward towards the brow of the hill, where the principal buildings of the villa were situated, looking down on the Via Appia Nuova. There was a private branch aqueduct, starting probably from the channel of the Aqua Marcia : and the names on the water pipes showed that the villa had belonged to two wealthy brothers, Quintilius Condianus and Quintilius Maximus, whose death was compassed by Commodus for motives of jealousy and perhaps for the sake of their property, in which he certainly afterwards lived.

It seems to me probable that some of the extensive alterations in the villa are due to him—and, in particular, the change in the garden. The curved end of it was given up, and pierced by an entran:e with three openings leading into a small courtyard, upon which fronted a large monumental fountain, with a semicircular arch above it : but the rest of it was much enlarged, and became rectangular in shape. Further changes were made in the villa proper at various periods, and notably the two great rectangular halls, which still tower above the

[1] See *Ausonia*, iv. 25.

rest, were inserted at a comparatively late period. One of them is interesting inasmuch as it was undoubtedly a hot bath—for the terra-cotta flue-pipes can still be seen in its walls—and yet it had a number of very large windows on all four sides, which must in some way have been closed. Window-glass was not unknown to the ancients, but large panes were never made ; and if these were windows at all, and cloths were not employed—as sometimes in the Renaissance—to close the openings, we must suppose that the frames were massive. At S. Sabina, for instance, the sixth-century round-headed windows of the nave had heavy gypsum frames, with small panes of selenite let into them.

In contrast to the comparative concentration of Sette Bassi there is such a lack of unity in the appearance of the various parts of the villa, as it is at present, that it is not surprising that its true nature was not suspected until the excavation of 1828 ; and it was previously called Roma Vecchia. We have seen that most of the objects found there at the end of the eighteenth century are in the Vatican, though one of the best—a boy with a goose, from an original by the sculptor Boëthius, is in the Louvre —while those found in the later excavations are in the inaccessible Museo Torlonia. The plan was unluckily not taken on either occasion—which is unfortunate, as as the recent appearance of the motor-plough, now busy here as elsewhere in fighting what Mussolini calls the " battaglia del grano," simultaneously brought to light and destroyed the remains of a long row of pilasters, which belonged to a portico, as it would seem, though now it is difficult to assign them to their proper place.

Two mounds on the opposite side of the road are groundlessly called the tombs of the Horatii and Curatii : they probably conceal large mausolea of the Imperial period. A little further on, in a field on the same side, is a curious monument, made out of blocks of marble from tombs (some of them still bearing inscriptions), which seems to have been an oil press with basins for refining the oil— currently known as the *farmacia,* or chemist's shop.

27. VIA APPIA AND ALBAN HILLS (p. 187).

28. CIRCUS, BOVILLAE (p. 190).

To face p. 187.

Half a mile or more on the left is the large round tomb known as Casal Rotondo, with a house (the base of a lofty mediaeval tower, now gone) on the top of it.

To whom it belonged is unknown—the inscription of Cotta, which some associate with it, cannot be said to belong to it with any certainty. Here the new railway to Naples passes under the Via Appia; and an ancient branch road ran off due S., being joined near the Casale Torricola (it has given its name to a railway station which may be a convenience to walkers when the train service improves) by another, which diverged from the Via Appia near the tomb of Caecilia Metella, and kept at half a mile or so from it all the way: it led on to the district of Fiorano. Half a mile further is the Torre di Selce, a mediaeval tower of grey peperino, with a band of white marble to render it visible from a distance (as elsewhere in the Campagna). It stands on a large round tomb, the concrete foundations of which are in the form of a wheel: the intervals between the spokes were no doubt filled with earth, the mass of which was thus better supported than would otherwise have been the case.

A little further on the road descends sharply in a curve, and there is another prominent tower on the right. The route to the Alban Hills (Fig. 27) was evidently well guarded by its masters. On the same side, by the road, are some ruins of a sanctuary of Silvanus, which is not far from a temple of Hercules reconstructed by Domitian, 8 miles from Rome and 6 from the Arx Albana (his Alban villa on the site of Alba Longa). There, too, was the estate of the satirist Persius, where he died. Other tombs are to be seen here and there, though they become rarer. On the right, about the ninth mile, we may note a large round mausoleum, which may be that of Gallienus: for we know it to have been at this distance from the city.

Here or hereabouts, too, Gavin Hamilton found the Discobolus preparing for the throw (a copy of a work of the sculptor Naucydes) in 1792: it is now in the Vatican.

Here is the farm of Fiorano, within which are various remains of interest. The district seems to have been

187

P

thickly inhabited, and we notice here, for the first time, considerable traces of the regulation of the course of the streams which traverse it, by artificial tunnels cut through the volcanic rock.

A couple of miles to the S.W. are the remarkable ruins of La Giostra—the jousting-place. A long narrow hill, the shape of a stadium (whence its name), has an embankment wall of hewn stone fairly well preserved on three sides of it ; and upon the top of the hill are remains of a Roman villa, mostly consisting (as usual !) of reservoirs (one of which is open, and is circular, some 70 feet in diameter), the strength of which has caused them to resist the action of time.

The stone walls have generally been attributed to the ancient city of Tellenae, ever since Nibby first visited them about a century ago. We know little of its site, but it was another of the old cities of Latium. But the weak point of the theory is that there is no trace of a cutting or of any other defence on the S.E. (unless it has been completely filled up by the villa, which seems doubtful), so as to isolate the position on the most vulnerable side : and this seems to me a fatal objection ; for the wall (which is much ruined) would have had to have been far more massive and lofty than it appears to have ever been, in order to be of any use. We may add that the stone walls are backed into concrete, and that the blocks are approximately 2 Roman feet high—though they vary a good deal.

As to the supposed remains of two other early villages (Apiolae and Mugillae) which have been identified a little further to the E., towards Le Frattocchie, I am bound to say that I feel even more sceptical. There are remains in blocks of hewn stone, which may belong to the late Republic or early Empire ; but interesting though they are, they belong too much to a study of the Campagna in detail to find a place in this rapid survey. Let us hope that it may be possible for the Italian authorities to test these hypotheses by excavation, in the course of the Archaeological Survey of Italy which is now in progress.

188

We may now return to the Via Appia, which continues in its straight course, with a few interesting tombs on each side of it. Shortly after the site of the eleventh ancient milestone, and close to the modern one, it is joined by the modern highroad, which follows it right up to Albano. The hamlet where they meet is called Le Frattocchie, and here was an important road centre in ancient days.

We have first of all the so-called Via Cavona, of which we have already spoken more than once. It started from the Via Praenestina, and linked up the main roads which it intersected. But beyond the Via Appia it is not so clear, and we cannot trace a cross-road further W. than Falcognana. Then to the E. of the Via Appia there is a regular network of ancient roads, which communicated eventually in one way or another with Castrimoenium, which is represented more or less by the modern Marino. Its territory, too, is full of the remains of ancient villas, which we cannot here attempt to describe in detail.

A little further on the road to Antium, still followed by the modern highroad, diverges to the right : and in the fork between it and the Via Appia we find the site of the ancient village of Bovillae. This village must early have acquired some importance as the successor of Alba Longa ; though much of what is related about it is purely legendary, for it is situated on gently sloping ground, utterly unsuitable for defence. This was doubtless chosen by the Romans to prevent any possibility of its rising against them—and, if so, is the first example of a principle which they frequently applied, even in Britain. When the Via Appia was constructed, Bovillae was the first post-station out of Rome : and it was so far that the road was paved in 292 B.C.

But what we have left of it dates from the time when it was given a new importance by the connexion with it of the Gens Iulia, the family of Julius Caesar and Augustus and the early Emperors, which was supposed to have originated from Iulus, son of Aeneas, the founder of Alba Longa. The family ancestor-cult was situated here ; and at Bovillae Augustus's body lay for a night

189

on its way to Rome, and was escorted from here to the city by the knights. The family worship became a State worship, and was carried on by the Augustales : Tiberius reconstructed the shrine, in which a statue of the deified Augustus was placed, and instituted games in the circus ; a few of the arches of the straight end of this may still be seen among the vineyards (Fig. 28), and the hollow which it occupied is quite clearly marked. The municipal inscriptions refer to the inhabitants as Albani Longani Bovillenses, showing the connexion clearly. And Clodius's villa, which stood above the high-road a little further on, in the gardens of the house now occupied as a summer residence by the North American College, had, as we are expressly told, been constructed on the site at the expense of the shrines and sacred groves of Alba Longa, which had been preserved when the city was destroyed. Indeed, the Vestal Virgins of Alba dwelt at Bovillae after that. Close here, too, Milo dragged Clodius from an inn in which he had taken refuge, and slew him.

But except the circus there is little left. The attempt to trace the city walls has been made unsuccessfully— I doubt if there ever were any ; the shrine cannot be identified with any certainty (though an altar erected to Jupiter Pater by the family in the days of Sulla or earlier, " according to the laws of Alba," was found a century ago) ; and we are reduced to a few ruins and quantities of debris among the vineyards and the ground-plan (hardly more) of a small theatre.

Above Bovillae a cross-road runs to the Anzio road on one side and up to Marino on the other, passing up through the ravine now occupied by a beautiful wood (the Parco Colonna), in which some have wished to find the site of the Aqua Ferentina, the meeting-place of the Latin League, though, I think, wrongly.

The road ascends more and more rapidly between walls, and a branch (perhaps of ancient origin) ascends steeply to the modern village of Castel Gandolfo, which occupies a splendid position on the W. edge of the extinct crater in the depths of which the Lake of Albano lies.

The " long white town " recalls the ancient name so irresistibly that one would be inclined to place Alba Longa here, even were other evidences lacking : but that they are not. The discovery near here of important cemeteries of the Iron Age would not suffice by itself, for others have been found on the N. of the lake : but stronger arguments may be found in the close connexion of Bovillae (which lies just below) with Alba Longa, and the fact that Domitian's great villa [1] is called invidiously *Arx Albana* by Juvenal and Tacitus. This once splendid structure lies in the lovely grounds of the Villa Barberini immediately to the S. of the little town, commanding a wonderful view over the sea and the Campagna on the one side and the lake on the other, in which, on clear, still days, the wooded cone of the Alban Mount is reflected. The residential part has not yet been excavated. From the garden terrace (on which are the remains of a little private theatre, with remarkably well-preserved stucco decorations, and also a number of nymphaea, while below lies a stadium or hippodrome) a tunnel led through the summit of the ridge to a road which zigzagged down to the lake shore. Some earlier structures situated down here were incorporated in the Imperial domain, and notably two cool grottos, architecturally decorated— veritable " abodes of the nymphs "—well known to artists and architects from Piranesi's plates. He also studied the famous emissarium of the Alban Lake, hewn through the rock, so it was said, in 397 B.C. at the bidding of the Delphic oracles, which declared that Veii could only be taken when the waters of the lake reached the sea. It is more probable that it was in reality intended to carry the water rapidly through the porous strata, so that it could not soak through the sides of the crater and render the districts below marshy and waterlogged. The channel is over a mile in length, about 6 feet high and 4 broad, and has a sluice chamber at its egress from

[1] For this and the whole district, see Lugli's articles.

the lake. And here, if anywhere, we may notice Piranesi's genius for exaggeration : for the chamber would seem immense, whereas in reality it is small. Sometimes, too, his mind seems to run riot, as when he imagines complicated foundations to buildings such as the mausoleum of Hadrian and some of the bridges in Rome, over which, as they lay below-ground, he could exercise his fantasy freely : though even in such plates as those, Professor Hind finds much to admire. But, except in scale, he is trustworthy in details, and faithfully represented what he saw ; and for that his evidence has often been too lightly set aside.

At certain points round the lake shore were embankment and landing stages for small pleasure boats—but they ran by no means all round, as has hitherto been generally believed : and on the S. side there was but one isolated house, with a long, arcaded façade, now hidden among the woods, and accessible only by water or by a steep path. On the upper edge of the lake a good many more Romans naturally dwelt—for the Imperial domain does not seem to have extended over the whole of it by any means. It does seem quite likely, however, that the Roman villa which once existed on the site of Palazzola (Fig. 29), on the E. of the lake below the summit of Monte Cavo, belonged to the Emperor Augustus, and may have passed on with other Imperial properties. It is, however, more important to insist that we cannot possibly (despite the testimony of Dionysius) attempt to place Alba Longa here : for the position is quite indefensible on the upper side of the escarpments behind Palazzola, which have attracted the attention of many writers. If we examine the space above them, between the lake and the mountain, which is traversed by a number of paths, probably ancient in origin, we shall find that it is utterly unsuited for the site of an ancient city and does not correspond in the least to Livy's description : " It was called Longa Alba because its site stretched along a ridge." The remains of the Roman villa at Palazzola are scanty, but it must extend under the garden terrace of the old monastery ;

29. PALAZZOLA (p. 192).

30. ARICCIA (p. 194).

To face p. 192.

this has an interesting history, and is now the summer residence of the English College in Rome, who were fortunate enough to secure it only a few years ago.[1]

From Castel Gandolfo two lovely roads, fringed with old ilexes, the Galleria di Sopra and the Galleria di Sotto (the latter followed by the electric tram), lead to Albano. If we keep to the upper one, along the crater rim, we soon come to the Capuchin monastery of Albano. The old wood behind it occupies a lofty hill, and one would imagine that some temple had once stood there; but not a vestige of antiquity is to be seen. Just below it is an amphitheatre, the upper side of which is mostly cut out of the solid rock, while the lower is built of arches of concrete and supported on a terrace, the supporting wall of which is decorated with niches. It has been computed that it might have held about 16,000 people at most: and the method of its construction showed that it can have had nothing to do with Domitian, but must have been erected by the second Parthian Legion; and indeed two of the brick-stamps bear the name of this corps. It lies, too, just above the camp that was erected for it by Septimius Severus, who, having dissolved the Praetorian Guard, brought in this legion to take its place. A number of tombstones of Parthian soldiers were found in the woods between Albano and Ariccia some sixty years ago. The massive walls of the camp, built of blocks of hewn stone, still enclose a roughly rectangular space of about 450 by 250 yards, which is occupied by the upper part of the town of Albano, but do not extend as far as the Via Appia. The camp is very long in proportion to its width, and the closest parallel is found in the camp of Borcovicus (Housesteads) on " Hadrian's " wall. One of the side gates is preserved, and also one of the corner towers: while as well as the barracks, etc., belonging to the camp (of which only scanty remains exist) there are some earlier buildings within the enceinte, notably a round building, now the church of S. Maria della Rotonda, which dates from the time of Domitian and was probably an isolated nym-

[1] See the College magazine (*The Venerabile*), i. 189 ; ii. 3, 132, 222.

phaeum, and a huge reservoir measuring about 150 by 100 feet, divided into five aisles by four rows of nine pillars each ; it is very finely preserved, and was till recently used for the supply of the town.

Below the road and the camp are other ruins, of which the most important are the thermae, which also belong to the Severan period, and may indeed be a trifle earlier than the amphitheatre : while the Villa Doria, to the N.W., contains the remains of a large villa, which is generally supposed to be that of Pompey. Cicero twice mentions it in such a way as to show that it lay beyond that of Clodius, while it was still in the Alban territory : and this is the only possible site. There are here remains of a Republican villa enlarged in the time of Domitian and Hadrian until it became a palatial structure, now largely concealed by trees. On the other hand, the lofty tomb on the other side of the highroad, called the Tomb of Pompey, is of a later period, and in any case could have nothing to do with him, for Plutarch tells us that his family tomb was in his property : and in it he buried his young wife Julia.

The foundation of the basilica of St. John the Baptist by Constantine, and the donation to it of the deserted barracks, was the beginning of the city of Albano (*civitas Albanensis*), which soon became an episcopal see of considerable importance.

The Via Appia runs straight through the town, and at the end of it the old road descends steeply to the right by the curious tomb wrongly attributed to Arruns, son of Porsenna, or to the Horatii and Curiatii, while the modern road passes over a deep ravine (in which are the lovely woods of the Parco Chigi, with their variety of trees) by a fine viaduct erected by Pius IX, and enters the upper part of the village of Ariccia, between the Palazzo Chigi and the circular church erected by Bernini. This is a building in his more restrained style : but even more successful is the little church of Castel Gandolfo, though more fantastic in detail.

The modern village of Ariccia (Fig. 30) must occupy the

194

citadel of the ancient town, most of the buildings of which are in the valley below. They comprise the remains of a temple, some traces of the post-station—we shall all remember that Horace spent his first night out of Rome here *hospitio modico* (in a moderate inn)—and a few other indeterminate ruins.

Here the road was intersected by a cross-road, which came up from the coast, one branch beginning at Ardea and another at Antium, and led on up through the modern village, and along the space between the Lake of Albano and the Lake of Nemi, until it reached the slopes of the Alban Mount. Here it begins to ascend in a long sweeping curve (in the latter part of which the pavement is well preserved, and has only been cleared of recent years) until it reaches a bend above Rocca di Papa, where it turns sharply to the right and begins to zigzag up the mountain. It then joins the regular path (which is of modern origin) from Rocca di Papa at a small chapel and ascends to the summit. Here once stood the federal sanctuary of Jupiter Latiaris : but the excavations of the seventeenth century show that there was little left then up there, and certainly it is quite impossible to maintain the charge brought against Cardinal York of having destroyed the well-preserved remains of the temple, with its columns of marble, in order to erect the now disused Passionist Monastery, which is the only modern building on the summit.

It is, indeed, doubtful of what nature the temple was and where exactly it stood : for more recent excavations have never been carried to a decisive point. But that will not disturb us in our contemplation of the magnificent panorama of Latium which unfolds itself before us. We are on the highest point of the rim of the inner crater, which is ringed round by wooded hills, enclosing a depression popularly known as the Camp of Hannibal. Outside this ring of hills is a narrow depression between it and the outer ring of the original crater, which had a diameter of 9 or 10 miles.

The road by which we have ascended Monte Cavo is

the only route by which it was accessible to wheeled traffic in ancient times ; and as there was naturally a regular network of roads leading to the mountain from the various cities of Latium, they all had to approach the mountain from the S. The cities of the N. and E. would have made use of the road later followed by the post road to Velletri and Naples through the woods of the Faiola, but not Rome itself. Had this been the intention the Via Triumphalis would have been placed on the northern slopes of the mountain, so as to form a continuation of the Via Castrimoeniensis. It is, therefore, most likely that the Via Appia was followed from Rome—a fact not without importance, for many a general who failed to attain the honour of a triumph on the Capitol was allowed to celebrate one at the temple of Jupiter Latiaris. And the rock-cut tomb near Palazzola, being decorated with the priest's cap and staff, as well as the fasces, has been reasonably taken to be that of Cn. Cornelius Scipio Hispalus, who furnishes, so far as we know, the only instance of a man who, being both pontifex and consul, died during his tenure of the latter office, in 176 B.C. As his illness was caused by a fall on his return from the Alban Mount, where he had been to celebrate the Feriae Latinae, it is probable that he was buried here because at Palazzola was situated the house at which the consuls stayed when they took part in such ceremonies ; though it is rather out of the line of the Via Triumphalis, it would certainly have been a pleasant lodging.

From the deep depression in which the post-station of Aricia lay, itself an extinct crater, the Via Appia ascended upon an embankment (Fig. 31) which is the finest structure of the kind to be seen in the neighbourhood of the city. It is about 200 yards long, and there is little doubt that it is the beggar-haunted *pons Aricinus* of which Juvenal speaks : the steep ascent providing a favourable opportunity for members of that fraternity. On the upper side the hill-side ascends steeply to the modern road : but the two routes rejoin at Genzano, a village of mediaeval origin, famous for its wine, which lies on the S.W. edge

31. EMBANKMENT OF VIA APPIA BELOW ARICCIA (p. 196).

32. LAKE OF NEMI (p. 197).

To face p. 196.

of the Lake of Nemi (Fig. 32). The lovely little crater, with the " mirror of Diana " glistening below, is best seen from the garden of the Villa Sforza-Cesarini, the pines of which are seen in the foreground of some of John Richard Cozens' finest water-colours. Below the garden the path following the Roman branch road descends steeply to the lake. Its shores are precipitous on the E., and in the scanty bits of more or less level ground violets and daffodils are grown for the Rome flower market. It is heavily cultivated on the W. and N., where the remains of the great platform on which the temple of Diana stood can be seen : it is probable that there was no large monumental building, but only a group of small chapels ; or else some large architectural fragments would surely by now have come to light. The origin of the cult is certainly an old one, for even in Imperial times the priest, usually a gladiator or fugitive slave, won his priesthood by killing the previous holder in fight, having previously plucked a mistletoe bough (the *Golden Bough* of Sir James Frazer's well-known work) from the sacred grove. Off the temple were anchored two great floating " barges " (like the College barges at Oxford), equipped with marble pavements and lead water-pipes, and with beam-heads of bronze decorated with the heads of lions and wolves, holding mooring rings for small boats. They are some of the finest bronzes of the kind that we have, and are in the Museo delle Terme in Rome. They are generally attributed to Tiberius, though the name on the water-pipes is that of his successor, Caligula.

Above the temple lies the picturesque village of Nemi ; it is dominated by a mediaeval castle with a large round tower : and behind it is the mediaeval post-road (following, probably, an ancient line) which was in use until the time of Pius VI, and crossed the outer rim of the crater by a steep ascent through the Macchia della Faiola and by a still steeper descent to Velletri. A house on the road still bears the name of Casale dei Corsi, from the Corsican police who were responsible for the safety of the road ; and a hill some way off bears the grim name

197

of Monte degli Impiccati—another Hangman Hill—in allusion no doubt to the execution of brigands.

If we cross this road we enter the Valle Vivaro, and after a few miles may reach the Via Latina at the pass of Algidus, passing by the Lago della Doganella—another unsuccessful candidate for identification with Lake Regillus.

Returning to the Via Appia at Genzano we find that the modern road coincides with it for about a mile ; and then the old road is left to its own devices until it reaches the Pomptine plain a mile below Cisterna. At the point of separation the eighteenth milestone, erected by Nerva, was found a few years ago, and has been re-erected near to its old site : and from here we obtain a remarkable view of the flat plain and the straight line of the ancient Via Appia (there once more followed by the modern road) leading through it towards Terracina, which is just hidden from us by a projecting hill. On the right is the great limestone rock of Monte Circeo, looking like an island— as it must have been in ancient days—and the Ponza group of islands are further out to sea.

From this milestone the old Via Appia descended rapidly in a straight line, and its pavement is quite well preserved for over a mile, until it reaches the undulating post-road of Papal days, which it soon crosses, after passing over two torrents by massive stone single-arched bridges, still well preserved.

Some ruins on the left belong to the post-station of Sublanuvium, and this part of the road is also dominated by the mediaeval castle of S. Gennaro.

After this the remains of the ancient Via Appia, clear enough a century ago, have been obliterated by cultivation for a while, and its line is not easy to find at first, but it can be traced with a certain amount of patience, and then is better preserved. It descends fairly fast through undulating country.

The most interesting point is that called Solluna (perhaps the site of a post-station called Ad Sponsas, but this depends upon the identification of Tres Tabernae, the

Apostolic Three Taverns, which is, unluckily, quite uncertain), where it was intersected by an ancient road
from Velletri towards the sea, called the Via Mactorina.

Here a number of interesting pagan inscriptions have
been found from time to time, several of them used up
later in a Christian cemetery. Further on are the remains
of a small aqueduct, and shortly after it crosses the
modern road and runs parallel with it to Cisterna, where
we may leave it, as to follow its course through the Pomptine Marshes would take us too far afield.

The present road to Velletri diverges to the left from
the ancient Via Appia at the eighteenth milestone and
keeps high along the hill-side. It has no remarkable
features except the fine views which it commands, and
was only made a few years ago, when the electric tram
was constructed. The undulating road constructed by
Pius VI, to take the place of that over the Faiola, turns
off to the right, keeping round the lofty Monte Cagnoletti,
which (one would have thought) owed its name to several
statues of dogs which have been found among the remains
of one (or more) of the villas on its summit, and its southern
slopes, by Gavin Hamilton, were it not that the name is a
good deal older.

After a mile the road diverges to the right to Civita
Lavinia, the ancient Lanuvium,[1] built on a hill which
projects forward into the Campagna. The acropolis of
this primitive Latin city occupied a vine-clad hill, on the
southern slopes of which are the remains, of the Imperial
period, of great arcades. This has generally been attributed
to the famous temple of Juno Sospita, from whose treasury,
as from that of Diana, Octavian borrowed the money
that he needed for the equipment of his fleet against
Antony. This temple, however, has not yet been found :
and the only sanctuary which has come to light on the
acropolis is one with three *cellae*, resembling in plan the
temple of Apollo at Veii ; it is certainly not sufficiently
ornate to be identified with a sanctuary of that character,

[1] For a detailed study see Colburn in *American Journal of
Archaeology*, xviii. (1914) 18, 185, 363.

Q

and is probably the Capitolium, dedicated to Jupiter, Juno, and Minerva. It goes back to the fourth century B.C. : but some of the architectural terra-cottas (many of which are in the British Museum) go back to the fifth century B.C. The landed property of the temple of Juno seems to have extended as far as the coast at Fogliano, where a tile has been found with the words *Sacro Lanuvio* impressed upon it.

Below the acropolis was the Roman town, on the site of which the picturesque mediaeval village, with its two gates and towers, was built. Remains of a temple of Hercules and the back of the stage wall of the theatre may still be traced, some of the seats of the latter having been found many years ago. From the lower end of the town an ancient road ran straight down the slopes and across the plain to the coast, and its pavement may still be traced through that desolate region and through the woods of Nettuno to Antium or Astura.

A mile to the N. are the remains of a large villa, which tradition has connected with the Antonine Emperors, who are known to have possessed a country house here : and it is further confirmed by the discovery of portrait busts of them, which are now in the Capitoline Museum.

Returning to S. Gennaro, we are some 5 or 6 miles from Velletri, the ancient Volscian Velitrae. The post-road which goes to the upper end of the town, rejoining the new route followed by the tram a little before it, may follow an ancient line : but there was certainly also a short cut, with several steep ascents and descents, to the lower end of it. Velletri stands on a large hill between two deep valleys, and the present town, though it has some 20,000 inhabitants, does not occupy the steep lower slopes of the hill. Of Roman buildings there are hardly any traces, except for a large building unearthed a few years ago near the railway station : but a series of painted terra-cottas from an early temple have recently been found in the town. A large villa to the W. of the town is by some authors believed to be that of the Gens Octavia, the family of Augustus, though the remains so far brought to light belong to a later date. But the lofty fourteenth-century campanile of the cathedral and a number of houses of the mediaeval period are of interest : though the once magnificent baroque Palazzo Ginnetti is now so sadly neglected as to look out of place in its surroundings. It has the merit, at least, of commanding an extraordinarily fine view over the fertile vineyard-clad lowlands to the limestone heights of the Volscian range in front, while behind the town rise the steep edges of the outer rim of the Alban crater, largely covered with woods and almost without a human habitation. Only a few paths lead up to the top of the ridge, and even fewer make the short, abrupt descent on the other side into the high-lying Valle Vivaro. And here, having made the complete circuit of the Alban Hills, we may leave them and begin our study of the low-lying region between them and the sea-coast, by setting forth once more from Rome by the Via Ardeatina.

III

*THE ROADS LEADING TO
THE SEA-COAST*

*VIII. THE VIA ARDEATINA,
THE ROAD TO SATRICUM,
AND THE VIA LAURENTINA*

*IX. THE VIA OSTIENSIS (WITH THE
VIA CAMPANA AND THE VIA
PORTUENSIS)*

III

PRELIMINARY NOTE

THE DISTRICT BETWEEN THE LOWER SLOPES of the Alban Hills and the sea-coast is very different from those which we have so far studied. It is at the present day very sparsely populated, largely owing to the scourge of malaria : and this was the case even in ancient times. Those who have read the *Aeneid* will probably picture it as enjoying a prosperity which never afterwards fell to its lot—mainly, I imagine, for this reason. The portion of it now traversed by the new railway to Naples is remarkable for its desolate loneliness, being served by no modern highroad. The neighbourhood of the Via Ardeatina is one of the few districts in the Campagna where fox-hunting can still be enjoyed ; while when we approach the coast and the large Royal park of Castel Porziano we find that these extensive forests were used for preserving game in Roman times, just as they are at present. The tombstone of a certain Tiberius Claudius Speculator, a freedman of the Emperor, records that he had been the administrator of the Imperial property at Formiae, Fondi, and Gaeta, and also of the Laurentine park, where the elephants were kept : and in 1906 the excavations conducted by the Queen of Italy at the Vicus Augustanus Laurentium led to the discovery of another inscription, which records how the president of the guild of gamekeepers (*saltuarii*) had offered to the members a set of portraits of the Emperors, to be set up in an appropriate hall in the village.

Of the cities so famous in the *Aeneid*, Ardea had come down to a mere shadow of its former self : while Lavinium,

205

in its higher and healthier situation, still enjoyed a certain measure of prosperity.

The coast, on the other hand, was healthy, and the nearer we come to the mouth of the Tiber, and consequently to Ostia and to Rome, the more plentiful are the remains of villas along the shore. At Ostia, the port of Rome, we come into a centre of busy life and trade : but even the hilly district along the Tiber valley on the left bank was not very thickly populated in Roman days, and on the hills of the right bank there are hardly any traces of ancient habitation.

VIII

THE VIA ARDEATINA, THE ROAD TO SATRI-CUM, AND THE VIA LAURENTINA

THE VIA ARDEATINA AT PRESENT diverges to the right from the Via Appia at the church of *Domine quo vadis ?*, and I think we must suppose that it always did so. The name is therefore correct, even though it is quite impossible to get anywhere near Ardea by it, at present. It then ascended the hill and passed between the catacombs of S. Calixtus and those of Domitilla, which last are on the Via delle Sette Chiese, an old branch road connecting the Via Ostiensis and the Via Appia, and reaching the latter at San Sebastiano. This church was, strictly speaking, one of the seven basilicas which had to be visited during the Holy Year of Jubilee, though S. Maria del Popolo was substituted for it by Sixtus V owing to its distance. Our road, on the other hand, leads on to the church of the Annunziatella, which made the ninth pilgrimage church. It presents no particular features of interest until well beyond this church, which lies a little off on the right : for nothing is now to be seen of the ancient villas in the *tenuta* (farm) of Tor Marancia, which produced so many works of art in the excavations of 1817–23 that a large folio volume was devoted to illustrating them. The most important are a number of paintings depicting the mythical heroines of amorous adventures of antiquity, which are in the Vatican Library, while several of the mosaics now decorate the floor of the Braccio Nuovo.

At the sixth kilometre from Rome the road forks, and both branches are ancient : the left-hand one, which is followed by the modern road to Castel di Leva and thence to Falcognana and Frattocchie, is really the first portion of the road to Satricum : while on the right hand is the Via Ardeatina proper. We may first speak briefly of the former, as it ran along the lower ground below the Alban Hills, not far from the new railway to Naples, which keeps more or less parallel to it. It therefore crosses a large number of streams descending from the lower slopes of the crater, but in most cases before they have had time to become formidable obstacles : so that it followed a fairly easy line, and no engineering works of importance were required.

Remains of antiquity are comparatively few, and in this regard there is a contrast to the district adjacent to the Via Appia. There is really nothing worthy of particular notice, except for a road going off near the eighth kilometre to Zolforata, until we reach Castel di Leva. Here is a mediaeval castle on a hill, with the small church of the Madonna del Divino Amore, celebrated for the festival which takes place here on the first Sunday in May, when numerous carriages decorated with flowers drive out from Rome and Albano, and there is much merrymaking. The road is practicable for carriages as far as Falcognana (there are two farmhouses of the name, one on each side of the road).

Beyond this the straight road becomes a track, but there are continual traces of antiquity—pavement and cuttings through the hills. It is intersected by various roads leading from the Alban Hills to the coast, and finally, after passing through Campomorto (which is quite in the low ground, and was till lately most unhealthy), reaches Satricum. The site of this ancient Latin city, several times won and lost by the Romans—for it was on the boundary of the Volscian territory—is to be fixed on the low hill, surrounded by tufa cliffs, with scanty remains of defensive walls in the same material, which is now occupied by the farmhouse of Conca and was a regular citadel in this flat district, once desolate and unhealthy, but now fast coming under cultivation.

A mile to the W. an archaic temple, with fine terra-
208

cottas of the seventh or sixth century B.C. (now in the Museo di Villa Giulia), was found in 1896, and is supposed to be that of Mater Matuta, from a fragmentary inscription.

Tombs, remains of buildings, etc., were also found, and the desolate woods were once occupied by a city which was able to boast of a sanctuary decorated with the finest products of Greek art. We are only 5 or 6 miles from the sea-coast at Nettuno, from which the place is most easily accessible, and about the same distance from Cisterna, on the edge of the large Sermoneta estate. The other roads leading down towards the coast do not carry us nearly so far afield, and may be briefly dismissed.

We left the Via Ardeatina at the sixth kilometre. From there it continues to run due S., passing E. of the large farmhouse of Cecchignola, with its lofty water-tower. Its course is marked by pavement, tombs, and cuttings through the hills : for it cuts across numerous small tributaries of the Tiber.

The modern road to Ardea (called Via Laurentina) falls into it about 14 kilometres from Rome : and after traversing some very desolate undulating country it passes E. of the farmhouse of Zolforata or Solfatara. Close to this are sulphur springs, and here is to be sought the Albunea of the seventh book of the *Aeneid*, to whose grove King Latinus went to consult Faunus, and not at Tivoli, where the water of the Anio is not sulphurous. Here was an important road centre in old days, and the branch hence to Lavinium, which is still in use, is probably of ancient origin. But there are two other roads from Rome which lead more directly to Lavinium, further still to the W.

A controversy which has long vexed the souls of men is in regard to the correct nomenclature of this whole group of roads ; but much of the difficulty disappears if we are willing, as I think we must be, to accept M. Carcopino's demonstration in a recent work (*Virgile et les Origines d'Ostie*, Paris, 1919), that there never was any such place as Laurentum (which does not appear by name in the *Aeneid*), and that Lavinium, the home of Latinus, is the city of the Laurentes. This city, which in Imperial days bore the name of Lauro-Lavinium, as inscriptions show, occupied the site of the modern Pratica di Mare, which will be described below. It satisfies Vergil's description of the military operations which occurred in its neighbourhood, while it is the only site between Ardea and Ostia which would satisfy the requirements of an ancient city.

We thus get rid of the distinction between the Via Lavinas or Lavinatis (a modern name for the road leading to Lavinium) and the Via Laurentina, the only road of which we hear in ancient authors : and we only have two comparatively small difficulties to solve—the existence of two roads leading to the same place. One of them issued from the small gate in the Aurelian wall which Antonio da San Gallo destroyed to make his bastion, crossed the Almo by a separate bridge a few hundred yards W. of the Via Appia, and led into the modern road to Ardea, near the Torre d'Archetto, leaving it again at Pizzo Prete and going on by Trigoria and Castel Romano ; while the other diverged from the Via Ostiensis at Vicus Alexandri, and ran on by Decimo and Capocotta. The first of these is called by Lanciani[1] (who takes it to Tor Paterno) the Via Laurentina, the second the Via Lavinatis —the reason being that an inscription mentions a certain Diadumenus as contractor for the Via Ardeatina and the Via Laurentina, so that they must have been close together. But let us take Pliny's description of his villa [2] : " There is more than one way to get to it : for both the Via Ostiensis and the Via Laurentina lead there : but you must turn off from the former at the eleventh mile and from the latter at the fourteenth " ; and we shall find that it suits the second road and not the first. The ·best way out of our difficulty is to suppose that, as in so many cases, one road was called the Laurentina vetus and the other the Laurentina nova ; and, though we may not be able to determine with certainty the relative date of the two, we can probably say that the first road is the earlier,

---

[1] *Mon. Lincei*, xiii. 133 ; xvi. 241.   [2] *Epist.* ii. 17, 2.

and the second, with its milestones of Tiberius and Maxentius, the later.   There is no necessity to suppose (though it may have been the case) that the *vetus*, however, ceased to be called Laurentina : and the fact that the two roads are never more than a couple of miles apart until they join just outside Lavinium, and are connected by three crossroads at least, renders it unnecessary to suppose that the contractor who looked after the repairs of the Via Ardeatina could not have attended to both of them.

Having reached the coast-line, it will be best to describe it as a whole from the Tiber to Monte Circeo.   Leaving Ostia aside for the moment, we may follow the line of the Via Severiana, which ran along the coast, behind the almost uninterrupted line of Roman villas which faced upon the sea for several miles S.E. of the Tiber mouth. The coast-line has advanced considerably, and the ruins of these once splendid residences lie concealed under the sand, and are hidden from the sea by lofty dunes of comparatively recent formation.   The whole coast-line beyond Castel Fusano belongs to the King of Italy, and as game is preserved in the forests, the solitude, in contrast to the gay life which once prevailed here, is almost oppressive. Pliny's own Laurentine villa has not yet been excavated with care, though trial pits have been made between the great oaks which cover its ruins, and further excavation would be necessary before it would be possible to see how far the remains correspond with the elaborate description which he gives of it in one of his letters.

But the remains of the village (the Vicus Augustanus Laurentium) which lay next but one to it have been in considerable measure cleared, and the mosaic pavement which has been laid in one of the cloisters of the Museo delle Terme in Rome was found here in the ruins of some baths : while in another villa there was found the fine replica of the famous Discobolus (or discus-thrower) of the Greek sculptor Myron, which was also presented to the same museum by the Queen.

Further along the larger trees disappear, and the sand dunes become more apparent, while the scrub becomes thicker. Even in Roman times the district cannot have been very different from what it is now, for the Imperial elephants were kept in it. We soon reach Tor Paterno, a farmhouse built into the remains of a large villa, perhaps also Imperial property. Here most archaeologists have placed the ancient Laurentum : but personally I find M. Carcopino's demonstration that it never existed to be quite convincing, and the site never seemed satis-factory, to my mind, for an ancient city.

The earth brought down by the Tiber is not deposited any further along the coast than this, and the ancient coast-line is thus practically identical with the modern : but it still continues to be low and desolate, and there are very few traces of ancient buildings until we reach Antium. Not long after leaving the Royal property we see on the left, over 2 miles away and about 300 feet above the sea, the village of Pratica di Mare. It occupies a very strong site, high enough up to be healthy : it is almost entirely isolated by ravines (Fig. 33), and is thus eminently suited for the ancient city of Lavinium, the home of Latinus, whose daughter Lavinia Aeneas married. Various inscriptions of the Imperial period mentioning the Lauro-Lavinates have been found here : and a certain number of archaic objects point to its habi-tation in earlier days, as the tradition tells us.

From Pratica we can look S.E. towards Ardea, which lies less than 6 miles away—the capital of Turnus, King of the Rutuli, the adversary of Aeneas. It stands on a naturally strong position on an almost isolated rock (Fig. 34), and its artificial fortifications consisted of a massive stone wall on the N.E. (Fig. 35) where alone it is connected with a long ridge running up towards the road to Satricum, which is reinforced by outworks—two massive mounds and ditches—at a considerable distance away from the city, protecting the approach to it. The reed huts of the miserable modern village may give us an idea of those of antiquity. Tombs and dwellings were also cut in the rocky sides of the neighbouring ravines.

The desolation of this immense expanse of country

33. LAVINIUM (THE MODERN PRATICA) (p. 212).

34. ARDEA (p. 212).

To face p. 212.

35. WALLS OF ARDEA (p. 212).

36. COAST AT ANZIO (p. 213)

To face p. 213.

reaches perhaps its climax in the neighbourhood of Ardea, especially to the S. of it ; but on a fine day the fresh sea air and the beauty of the woods render the scene very attractive ; and in many cases they are beginning to give place to pasture or cultivation.

The shore grows somewhat higher as we approach Antium, the modern Anzio, which we reach at the end of a line of sandy cliffs. The old Volscian town, which lay a little inland, on a site defended by deep ditches, was once the foe of Rome : and in one of her first naval battles Rome took the beaks (*rostra*) from the prows of the conquered ships of Antium and used them to decorate the front of the orators' tribune on the edge of the Comitium.

In Roman days the whole shore of the bay was covered with seaside residences (Fig. 36), one of which belonged to Nero : and in it was found that much-discussed statue, the so-called " Fanciulla d'Anzio," which probably represents a boy-priest of Apollo.

Here, too, was a famous temple of Venus, mentioned by Horace. The picturesque fishing village of Nettuno, with its castle, lies in the bay, at the other side of which is the lonely tower of Astura, in which Conradin of Swabia was treacherously murdered in 12.8. It is built on an enormous Roman villa, now half submerged, with a tiny harbour of its own—not, probably, that of Cicero, who owned a favourite villa here, to which he withdrew after the death of his daughter, Tullia. Even in Roman days it was none too healthy, and both Augustus and Tiberius are said to have contracted here the illnesses of which they eventually died : while Ardea must have been even more subject to the scourge ; *et nunc magnum manet Ardea nomen ; sed fortuna fuit,* as Vergil says.

From Astura a single sweep of low sandy coast, with lagoons inland of it, runs to the foot of Monte Circeo, which, as one approaches it, dominates the whole landscape. Inland is the vast expanse of the Sermoneta property, mostly forest and pasture, which takes us right up to the Pomptine Marshes and the Via Appia.

IX

THE VIA OSTIENSIS, ETC.

THE ROAD TO OSTIA leaves the Aurelian walls of
Rome by the gate now known as Porta S. Paolo,
close to the Pyramid of Cestius and the cemetery
where Keats and Shelley lie. It follows the valley of
the Tiber for the first half of its course, then crosses a
chain of hills, and then descends to the low ground where
Ostia stands. The modern road, until recent improvements, coincided with it closely, and considerable traces
of it were to be seen : while the last half was more like
an English lane than many of the other roads out of
Rome, being shaded with trees. A few of the small
bridges still retain traces of antiquity ; but there were
not many ancient buildings of any particular importance
along its course, though the deep cuttings recently made,
first for the road itself, and then for the electric railway,
have brought a few remains to light. We may note
especially the aqueduct which brought water from springs
in the hills to Ostia : its low arches were still fairly well
preserved in the sixteenth century, but have now completely
disappeared.

The salt marshes which surrounded Ostia itself until
recent days have now been drained and cultivated, and,
like the whole of the coast strip, this flat expanse has been
made habitable by the discovery of the true cause of
malaria. The decisive experiments were, indeed, made
about a quarter of a century ago at Castel Fusano, in
the immediate neighbourhood.

The most prominent building in our view of Ostia is
the fine Renaissance castle (Fig. 37) built in 1483–6
by Baccio Pontelli for Cardinal Giuliano della Rovere,

37. CASTLE, OSTIA (p. 214).

38. PALAESTRA OF BATHS, OSTIA (p. 216).

To face p. 214.

nephew of Sixtus IV, and afterwards himself Pope under the title of Julius II. It was placed so as to command a bend of the Tiber, which, however, in the great flood of 1557 completely changed its course, and now runs nearly half a mile distant from it. Only just beyond it lies the entrance to the excavations, which have made great progress during the last few years and are still being continued.

Ostia was the port of Rome : and what we see before us are the ruins of a great commercial city. Though tradition alleges that it was founded by Ancus Martius, which would make it the oldest of Rome's colonies, there is no real evidence for the existence of any permanent habitation on the site of Ostia before the fourth century B.C. How much earlier the salt marshes at the mouth of the Tiber existed is quite another question, but in any case Ostia is not mentioned as a port until late in the third century B.C., in the history of the second Punic Wars.

The first settlement was a small rectangular fort ; but by the first century B.C. it had expanded very considerably, as is shown by the line of its walls, which has recently been traced. The road from Rome ran right through the town and served as the main street : and, before the flood of 1557, the river ran more or less parallel to it. The side-streets were therefore laid out at right angles to them both, especially in the northern part of the town. As we come nearer to the coast, we find that the main road turned to the left and approached it at right angles. The excavations are of very great interest and importance, and only a brief description of them can be given here.[1]

Of the original fort and the Republican city some remains have been incorporated into later buildings : and it is an interesting conjecture that Vergil's description of the castle founded by Aeneas at the mouth of the Tiber was inspired by what was still visible of the remains of the fort. There was apparently a reconstruction in the

[1] See Calza's *Ostia*, translated by R. Weeden-Cooke.

time of Augustus and Tiberius, to which, among other buildings, the original theatre is due. We must place rather later than this some baths with a fine mosaic pavement, which were afterwards entirely razed to the ground, a street being built over them; while the new thermae were constructed by Hadrian and his successors on an adjacent site. They are remarkable for a number of fine mosaic pavements, attributable to the Antonine period, in which, as is natural, marine deities and monsters predominate; and also for the abnormality of their plan, the palaestra (Fig. 38) taking up a considerably larger part of the building than is usual in such establishments. Some very interesting mosaics may also be seen in the colonnades behind the theatre; they surround a temple, which has been thought to be that of Ceres, the goddess of the crops; for here were the offices of many of the trading corporations concerned with the importation of grain, which was, of course, one of the most important functions of Ostia.

But the most imposing temple of all is that which has generally been called the temple of Vulcan, but which is now considered to be the Capitolium—the temple of Jupiter, Juno, and Minerva—which was not lacking in any Roman colony. It may be, like the theatre in its present form, a reconstruction of the time of Septimius Severus and Caracalla; for the foundations of the original Capitolium have been recognised elsewhere. It stands on the right of the main street, at the top of a lofty flight of steps (Fig. 39), and faces on to the Forum, in the centre of which stood the temple of Rome and Augustus, unluckily much destroyed by quarrying for building material in the Middle Ages. Ostia was indeed ransacked for material for the building of the cathedrals of Orvieto and Pisa; and some of its buildings have suffered considerably, while others have not been nearly so badly treated.

But the most extensive part of the town was devoted to storehouses and private dwellings. In the former the store-chambers themselves are generally grouped round

39. CAPITOLIUM AND DECUMANUS, OSTIA (p. 216)

40. RIVER NUMICUS (p. 217).

To face p. 216.

a courtyard, in two stories or even more ; but they display considerable variety in their plan. The houses are remarkable for their surprising modernity. They are not in the least like the type of house with which Pompeii has familiarised us ; there are hardly any which have an atrium : and light is generally derived from numerous windows opening either on to the street or on to a garden or courtyard. In the latter case the similarity to a Renaissance house in Rome is surprising. Their internal arrangements are equally different from what we have been accustomed to : they are divided into tenements which are quite independent of one another, and are separately approached from below, the plan being often quite identical for three or four floors. External balconies are almost universal, and the warm red brickwork with which the walls are faced, and which is now, especially in the evening light, so pleasing to the eye, was probably not faced with plaster, but left exposed to view, the tiled arches being picked out in a darker red.

Outside the city the roads were flanked with tombs—many of them *columbaria*, with niches for urns like those of a dovecot—whence comes the name. Some of the most interesting have been found on the Via Severiana, which led to the S.E. It soon crossed a stream which may very likely be the Numicus (Fig. 40), in which Aeneas was drowned (though this is more generally identified with the Incastro, which flows past Ardea), which forms the boundary of the lovely pine forests of Castel Fusano (Fig. 41). Here its pavement has been discovered in the woods. Its further course along the coast has already been described.

At Ostia there were always two difficulties to contend against—the dangerous southerly winds which blew into the mouth of the river, and the silting up brought about by the enormous amount of solid matter brought down by the Tiber—and the combination of the two proved fatal to the new harbour which Claudius built on the right bank of the river, $2\frac{1}{2}$ miles to the N. of the mouth. He connected it with the open sea by a large opening with

217

a lighthouse on a breakwater in the centre, and with the river by a canal.

Trajan built a large hexagonal basin between the harbour of Claudius and the sea, with which he connected his own part by a new canal, which is still called Fossa Traiana and serves for navigation by small craft. The new harbour, known as Portus, was, however, administratively dependent on Ostia until the time of Constantine, who placed it directly under the city of Rome, and gave it, apparently, greater importance than Ostia.

The basin of Trajan has recently been cleared, and is used as a reservoir for the irrigation of the land to the N. of it : but the extensive warehouses which surrounded it, and the docks which lie near it, are still half hidden under vegetation, and it is only to be hoped that they may one day be excavated with care and left visible.

For here we have one of the finest examples of an ancient harbour in existence, which, despite the spoliation which it has undergone, is still probably in a relatively good state of preservation. The harbour was defended by a wall, the creation of which is attributed to Constantine, though the gateway, called the Arco di Nostra Donna, may possibly have been erected by Trajan in the first instance (Fig. 42).

To the E. is an isolated building in brick—it is circular, and the interior is decorated with niches ; the dome is interesting as having radiating ribs projecting from the face of the vault ; while another feature is an external balcony, carried on arches resting on brackets, like those of Ostia. It is called the temple of Portunus, but without real warrant : and probably belongs to the middle of the third century A.D. (Fig. 43).

Claudius's harbour, on the other hand, lies in the middle of the plain, and its outline can barely be traced, as its breakwaters are covered with the accumulation of earth. The coast-line has advanced at least a mile and a half on the N. side of the river-mouth also, though the distance gradually diminishes as we go up the coast. The Roman shore-line can be traced clearly here also : but

41. CASTEL FUSANO (p. 217).

42. ARCO DI NOSTRA DONNA, PORTO (p. 218).

To face p. 218.

43. "TEMPLE OF PORTUNUS," PORTO (p. 218).

44. FLOODS NEAR PONTE GALERA (p. 219).

To face p. 219.

this district was far less in favour with them than the neighbourhood of Lavinium, and there are very few villas indeed for a long distance, though there are undoubted indications of the existence of the coast road.

The lovely pinewoods of Maccarese (the ancient Fregenae, situated on the Arrone, the stream which issues from the Lake of Bracciano) and a few solitary towers are almost all that breaks the monotony of the flat sandy shore until we reach the neighbourhood of Palo, the ancient Alsium, where the Via Aurelia comes down to the coast.

A road was constructed from Rome on the right bank of the Tiber, for the service of this harbour of Claudius, starting from the Pons Aemilius. Not far outside the Porta Portuensis of the wall of Aurelian (a double gate destroyed in 1643), it diverged to the right into hilly country from a far older road, the Via Campana, so called because it led past the sanctuary of the Arval Brethren (an old priesthood revived under the Empire, whose records, inscribed on slabs of marble, are preserved to us in part) to the Campus Salinarum Romanarum, the salt marshes on the right bank of the Tiber, which were probably in existence before those on the left bank. This last inference is based on the fact that the roads which approach Rome from the N. and N.E. (and especially the " saltway," the Via Salaria) are making for the crossing over the river, which may have existed just below the island before Rome became a city at all : and this they would not have done had the salt marshes of Ostia on the left bank been those principally in use.

There are practically no remains of antiquity and very few features of interest to be seen on either road. The two rejoin at Ponte Galera, where the mouth of the Tiber was situated in remote days, before it had begun to extend the coast-line by the earth it brings down : and a return to this early state of things sometimes occurs (as in the flood of 1915) when the river bursts its dykes and overflows the whole of the low country. It then becomes clear that the low hills, at the foot of which the railway to Pisa and Genoa runs, were once the coast-line (Fig. 44).

S

IV

THE ROADS LEADING
INTO ETRURIA

X. THE VIA AURELIA

XI. THE VIA CLODIA AND THE
VIA CASSIA

IV

PRELIMINARY NOTE

IT IS QUITE POSSIBLE that the first Roman road to Veii, which later became the Via Clodia, originally started from the Pons Sublicius and ran along the right bank of the Tiber for some way, until it left the river valley at the same point where it did in later days. For we have unmistakable traces of a road diverging from the Via Clodia on the right at the sixth mile and going direct to Veii; while there are grounds for supposing the existence of the Via Clodia as early as the end of the fourth century B.C., but it is difficult to suppose the existence of a bridge on the site of the Pons Mulvius at so early a date. On the other hand, it would also be possible to suppose that the original road to Veii was that which was later called (for reasons that we do not know) the Via Triumphalis; and this would certainly give us a better line out of Rome. The discovery near the railway station of S. Onofrio, behind Monte Mario, of a Bronze Age settlement (pre-Etruscan, of course, though it was afterwards occupied by that people and the site was in use even in Roman days) is, I think, a sufficient ground to modify the opinion which I have previously expressed, that an early date for the Via Triumphalis is improbable : though what was the political or historical relation of this settlement to Rome or to Veii we do not know.

The distances along both the Via Clodia and the Via Cassia were reckoned, like those along the Via Flaminia, from the Porta Ratumena of the Servian wall; while the Via Cassia, though it afterwards became the more important road of the two, did not, strictly speaking, begin its independent existence until the eleventh mile from Rome.

It must have existed in some form about 217 B.C., but was probably not constructed in its permanent form as a highway until about 187 B.C., and Florentia (Florence), at which the road ended, was very likely founded at the same time.

The other road which led from Rome into Etruscan territory, the Via Aurelia, crossed the river at once and led through the fortifications of the Janiculum over undulating country to the coast, which it only reached at about 20 miles from Rome. Its construction is attributable to about 175 B.C.

With the exception of Veii, which lost its importance when it became subject to Rome, we may notice the almost entire lack of centres of population in all this district : otherwise the little crater lake, E. of the Lake of Bracciano, now known as the Lago di Martignano, would not have been assigned to the territory of Alsium, down on the coast 20 miles away.

The hills above the right bank of the Tiber are of marine formation—oyster shells, for example, may be met with in quantities on Monte Mario ; and the vegetation is characteristic of the sea-coast. But we soon get into a region where these strata are overlaid by volcanic rock, the main crater being that occupied by the Lake of Bracciano. This district is furrowed with ravines, and is difficult to traverse with ease or rapidity. It was, therefore, sparsely inhabited even in Roman days : so the conclusion that much of it was thickly wooded is an eminently probable one ; for the cross-roads, though not very frequent, are still out of proportion to the scanty traces of habitation with which we meet. The desolation of mediaeval and modern days is even greater ; but the high ground in the immediate neighbourhood of Rome, with its fine views of the sea and the hills, has recently begun to come into favour : and the transformation which we have seen at work in the Campagna will probably extend over this region as well in course of time.

X

THE VIA AURELIA

THE VIA AURELIA VETUS climbed the hill from the crossing of the Tiber to the culmination of the fortified *tête de pont* on the heights of the Janiculum, where Aurelian later on placed his Porta Aurelia, close to where the American Academy in Rome now stands. Leaving the entrance to the lovely Villa Doria Pamphili on the left, it passes along its boundary wall, in which the opus reticulatum and brick of Trajan's aqueduct may still be seen. It runs on as a narrow, shady road between walls and trees for nearly 3 miles, being about the only highroad out of Rome which has preserved the quiet and secluded appearance which all of them had some thirty or forty years ago. Several narrower lanes branch off it to the right and left. One of these goes off due N. to the Via Triumphalis and is followed by the aqueduct. It passes close to the pinewood known as the Pigneto Sacchetti, a prominent feature on the skyline to the left of Monte Mario : the tops of the trees are so close together that they present the appearance of a line of arches. Below is the Valle dell' Inferno, largely formed by digging for brick-earth in Roman days, and still the site of many brick-fields, which continually encroach on its cork woods, the nearest to the city. In it lie the scanty ruins of a villa designed by Pietro da Cortona for the Sacchetti family in the seventeenth century, which appears to have collapsed owing to the insecurity of its foundations. Three miles out, the Via Aurelia Vetus is joined by the Via Aurelia Nova. This probably ascended to the Janiculum just S.E. of the Porta S. Spirito, crossed it at once, and then redescended to the neighbourhood of the Porta

Cavalleggieri. Thence it climbed the hill behind the Vatican, and so reached the main road.

The Via Cornelia, on the other hand, upon which the tomb of S. Peter lay, came from the Pons Aelius (Ponte S. Angelo) along the N. side of the Circus of Caligula, so that S. Peter's is built upon its axis. It then ran on through the Vatican gardens out of the Porta Pertusa of the Leonine wall, and perhaps rejoined the Aurelia Nova a little further on. They soon separated, however, and the Via Cornelia turns to run westward, to the S. of the modern road, passing by frequent cuttings through undulating country for a few miles, and then completely disappears, so that its course is quite uncertain. On the modern road we may note the modern chapel of S. Rufina at the eighth mile from Rome (though the site of the old episcopal see, that of Silva Candida, was half a mile away, at Porcareccina) and the large farm of Boccea further to the N., where the road turns W. to the lonely farm of Tragliata, in the middle of a district furrowed deeply by streams running southward through large ravines, difficult of access, and sparsely populated even in ancient times. The only satisfactory way to explore it (and it will well repay those who care to do so) is on foot, starting from the Viterbo railway, which keeps close to the Via Clodia, and coming down to the coast railway for an evening train.

The Via Aurelia crosses the streams rather lower down, when their number has considerably diminished : but even it has a good many ups and downs, attenuated to some extent by cuttings through the hills. None of its paving is actually *in situ*, though plenty of paving-stones are to be seen.

Before the eighth modern mile we cross the stream known as the Galera, one of the largest of them, at a place called Malagrotta. There is a picturesque legend of a cave inhabited by a dragon or a serpent : but the prosaic truth is that the name is a corruption of Mola rupta (broken mill), which can be found as far back as the tenth century, and was no doubt destroyed by a flood.

Here a track, of ancient origin, goes off to Maccarese, which *may* be the enigmatic Via Vitellia ; though the description of it given by Suetonius " from the Janiculum to the sea " does not fit any road that I have been able to find ; and it is just possible that it is really the same as the Via Portuensis, which is not mentioned under that name until the fourth century (Suet., *Vitell.* i).

The ancient Via Aurelia ascended to the N.W., and is not rejoined by the modern road until the top of the hill. At the twelfth ancient milestone lay the post-station of Lorium, near the site of an Imperial villa, which was the favourite resort of Antoninus Pius and Marcus Aurelius. Excavations made in 1824 led to the discovery of some remains of the villa, with inscriptions and works of art. A bishop seems to have had his see here in 487 : but the village was abandoned after the damage which it suffered in the Gothic wars.

In the seventeenth and eighteenth centuries the place had become so unhealthy that Eschinardi notes that a carriage was always kept ready there by Prince Doria, to whom the farm belonged, to carry the sick into hospital.

There are a few other ancient buildings, but the district was thinly inhabited, and there is nothing of special interest until we reach the two-arched bridge over the Arrone, which still shows traces of antiquity. From here a road may have led northward to the Via Cornelia.

Some way further on to the W. is the large and picturesque group of farmhouses known as Torrimpietra : a certain number of antique sculptures and a large number of paving-stones are to be seen here, but it is doubtful where they were found.

A couple of miles further on we cross another stream, the Fosso di Palidoro, which has changed its course, for the large farmhouse on the W. of it, which gives its name both to the stream and to a station on the main line (which we have now reached), is built upon an ancient two-arched bridge of large blocks of limestone which has been high and dry for centuries. The name Palidoro is derived from *Paritorum,* which refers to a large tomb

227

faced with marble which must once have stood here and can be traced as far back as 1018.

From Palidoro a path leads northward to the ruins of the large mediaeval castle called Castel Campanile, on a most remarkable site—a long, narrow peninsula of rock between two deep, wooded valleys. It has been identified with Artena in the territory of Caere, but I have never been able to see any trace of anything earlier than the mediaeval period, except a pagan sepulchral inscription on a block of marble, with a draped figure in a shell niche in very high relief, the provenance of which I do not know.

There is also an altar from the mediaeval church, which was dedicated, as the inscription records, in the year 1000.

About 2 miles from Palidoro is another ancient bridge, and beyond it a small mediaeval castle on a mound, which perhaps marks the site of the post-station of Ad Turres. Here a road diverged to the N.W., and led straight to Caere, the modern Cerveteri (with a branch to Ceri—see below), while another led due N., rising gradually.

In a prominent position on high ground, commanding a fine view of the coast, is a large white farmhouse known as the Casalone ; and near it are the remains of a large Roman villa, showing that the site was appreciated in those days. To the N. of this the modern path, which has so far followed the ancient line, divides into various branches. Here we are close to the little village of Ceri, which under the name of Caere Nova was founded about the beginning of the thirteenth century.

The Via Aurelia ran on straight for another mile, and then turned to run N.W., parallel to the coast, keeping at a certain distance from it, and passing a line of mounds called the Monteroni, which are partly natural and partly artificial *tumuli* of Etruscan tombs. The modern road follows what are probably old branch roads along two sides of a triangle, in order to run into the little village of Palo and out again. Here there are a few villas along the shore (one of them is very large, with five porticos, a large courtyard, and several gardens : it was excavated in 1866, but is now covered with sand), for here was the site of Alsium, one of the oldest cities of Etruria. As such it was not of any importance, except as one of the harbours of Caere, Pyrgi (now S. Severa) being the other [1] : though in Roman times, owing to the lack of other towns in all this district, its territory was very extensive, while Pompey and Caesar both had villas there, and it was also in great favour in the second century : we hear of the Younger Pliny's friend finding here a " nest for his old age "; Fronto, the tutor of Marcus Aurelius and (Ep. vi. 10) Lucius Verus, enjoyed here the pleasures of the seaside, and actually wrote a short work about his holidays in Alsium ; and the former also owned a villa here.

The villas continue to the W. of Palo also, where the modern bathing place of Ladispoli has recently grown up, to replace the village of Palo, which has been allowed to fall into ruin, only the fine castle of the Odescalchi family remaining. Close to it are foundations, now projecting into the sea, which belong to a villa rather than a harbour, as they have no opening seaward.

From Alsium there must have been a direct road to Caere, and this is represented by the modern highroad from Palo to Tre Ponti, where it rejoins the old Via Aurelia, and by a track going due N. from this point to the town of Cerveteri. This, with its picturesque mediaeval castle, occupies the site of the citadel of the ancient town of Caere. We are told by ancient writers that its old Pelasgian name was Agylla. It was one of the twelve cities of Etruria, and the Tarquins took refuge here after their expulsion. We know of its greatness and power chiefly from the magnificence of its tombs : for of its buildings little or nothing remains.

After the invasion of the Gauls in 390 B.C. the Vestal Virgins were conveyed here for safety ; and some ancient authorities derive the word " ceremony " from this fact. In 353 Caere took up arms against Rome, but was defeated,

[1] It is interesting to notice that both these names are derived from Greek words—ἅλς (salt) and πύργοι (towers).

and was therefore admitted to a limited form of Roman citizenship, without any internal autonomy. Its prosperity, which had decayed considerably, was restored under Augustus or Tiberius, and in its theatre a number of inscriptions and statues of Emperors were found which may have decorated the wall of the stage. They now occupy a room in the Lateran Museum. Nothing is now to be seen of this building, and in the whole area of the city we can only trace a few remains of road pavement in the modern paths through the vineyards which cover the site. The city walls in rectangular blocks of tufa can be traced along the top of the cliffs on the inner edge of the (artificial) fosse, by which the defences are strengthened in places, for a length of about 4 miles, and there appear to have been eight gates in the circuit. To the N.W. is the hill known as the Banditaccia, where the principal necropolis is situatèd—though there are also a number of outlying tombs. The tomb chambers are either hewn in the rock or covered by large round mounds, and they are interesting, some for their architectural and decorative details (which are reproduced in the natural rock), others from the fine objects (vases, etc.) discovered in them ; and though full details of these found in the recent Government excavations are not yet available, a great deal that is of interest can be seen on the spot. The most important tomb of all, the so-called Regulini-Galassi tomb, lies to the S.W. of Cerveteri ; the objects found in it (a chariot, a bed, silver goblets with reliefs, splendid gold ornaments, etc.) belong to about 650 B.C., and form one of the chief treasures of the Etruscan Museum of the Vatican.

From Cerveteri a road runs northward to the Via Clodia, which it reaches a little before Bracciano, and it may fittingly be taken as the boundary of our study of this region, which, as a fact, lies well outside the limits of the Roman Campagna proper, and belongs rather to Southern Etruria.

XI

THE VIA CLODIA AND THE VIA CASSIA

THE VIA CLODIA, after the construction of the Via Flaminia at any rate, left this road immediately after the Pons Mulvius, and ascended the hill straight in front of the bridge. It soon descended again into the valley of the stream known as the Acqua Traversa, and then ran along it for a while. On the hill facing the traveller from Rome at the fifth mile was the villa of Lucius Verus, in which two busts of Marcus Aurelius and four of Lucius Verus have been found. Some remains of a substruction wall, once far more extensive, may still be seen below the huge modern villa which has just been built on the top of the hill, in the garden of which a portion of the ancient villa itself, consisting of several rooms with mosaic pavements, is still preserved. Beneath them is a network of passages for the storage of water, running right through the hill.

Not far off (though we do not know exactly where) was the grove of Robigus, which was at the fifth mile of the Via Clodia—a deity who, if not propitiated, Ovid tells us (*Fast.* iv. 907), would cause rust in the corn and ruin the crop.

The pavement of the Via Clodia was found in making the munition works in the valley ; behind them it ascended a small gulley and reached the modern highroad (which goes round the villa of Verus to the right) a few hundred yards before the so-called tomb of Nero. Here the Clodia itself turned N.W. ; but a road has been found continuing on in the same direction, which has been supposed, not without good reason, to have been the original road to Veii, which it reaches in another 5 miles or so. We may note on it the ruins of a massive tomb in concrete, with

231

a cruciform chamber in the interior, lined with large blocks of stone (Fig. 45), but otherwise there is nothing of great importance to be noted until (after passing by a well-preserved Roman fountain—a small brick-lined chamber, known, I cannot say why, as the Fontana di Rè Carlo) it arrives at the foot of the citadel of Veii, where its pavement is still preserved in the low ground.

Considerable remains of a building belonging t a large farm house have recently been found on the right of the road and covered up again.

The so-called tomb of Nero, which has often been sketched by artists of all nations, is really a huge marble sarcophagus which, as the inscription plainly shows, is that of one Publius Vibius Marianus. The present name does not appear before 1516, and the connexion with Nero is purely arbitrary, for his real tomb was somewhere on the Pincian Hill. Mediaeval legend, however, was always busy with him as a monster of iniquity, whose unquiet spirit wandered here and there in search of rest and might well have haunted this lonely tomb.

The Via Clodia has now reached the summit of a narrow ridge between two valleys, and follows it for several miles. A few remains of ancient buildings may be noticed, but, despite the splendid view, there is nothing of any great importance, except some interesting mediaeval farmhouses —one of which, La Giustiniana, is built right on the line of the ancient road, which keeps on the right of the modern, and passes through some cuttings in the hills. Here the Via Triumphalis (followed by the now subterranean Aqua Traiana and by the modern railway to Viterbo) comes in to join the Via Clodia. There are no remains of interest along its course, except for the Bronze Age settlement already mentioned near the lunatic asylum of S. Onofrio. Unfortunately the excavations did not make its nature altogether clear : and the site is now covered by a group of modern houses, though an Etruscan tomb cut in the rock may still be seen.

Half a mile further on another branch road turns off to the citadel of Veii : and just after it we see the lofty

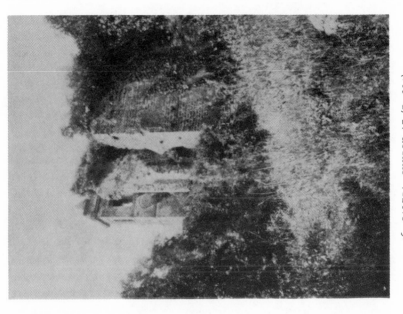

46. GALERA, CHURCH AT (p. 234).

To face p. 234.

45. TOMB ON VIA VEIENTANA (p. 232).

mediaeval watch-tower of Spizzichino, perhaps of the eleventh century, one of the oldest and best-preserved towers in the Campagna.

A mile or more brings us to the Osteria della Storta ("the inn of the crook in the road"), the first ancient post-station out of Rome, which went on through mediaeval and modern days. It takes its name from the bifurcation of the Via Clodia and the Via Cassia, rather less than a mile further on. An inscription of A.D. 379–383 records the construction of stables for the horses of the State posting service, that they might no longer be worn out by an excessively long stage. A chapel on the way to the station records the appearance of Christ to S. Ignatius Loyola, the founder of the Jesuits, on his journey to Rome—an account of which has recently been written by a learned member of that Society, Father Fonck.

From La Storta a path runs southward, which seems to follow an ancient line for a while and probably reached the Via Cornelia eventually : but the country is difficult, being furrowed by deep valleys. Still, it is a significant fact that it lies in the same straight line as a direct path to Veii, which at present shows no traces of antiquity : and, as we know that the territory of Veii was very extensive before her conquest by Rome, it may be that this was one of the routes by which she reached the southern part of it ; and it may even have led on to the coast. Half a mile further the Via Clodia goes off N.W., and then almost W. The ancient road traversed a series of deep cuttings which the modern road avoids ; and the aqueduct soon leaves it and makes off due N. It is mostly subterranean or at ground-level, though some fine arches were preserved near Cesano station until the restoration by Paul V : but now only a little ancient brickwork is visible at their base.

The road passes through a lonely stretch of country for a few miles until the Osteria Nuova (probably the post-station Ad Careias, close to Careiae) is reached, where it is intersected by a road going N. to Cesano village, and so on to the Via Cassia, and S. to the large

233

T

farmhouse of S. Maria di Galera, and perhaps further on still. The modern highroad running N.W. to Anguillara probably does not follow an ancient line. A mile to the W. of this is one of the most picturesque spots in the whole Campagna—the village of Galera. It is situated on a rock almost surrounded by the deep valley of the Galera stream —for here the streams from the southern slopes of the extinct crater (now occupied by the Lake of Bracciano), which to the N. have run in shallow beds, suddenly find softer strata beneath them, and plunge abruptly over waterfalls into huge ravines, which they are ever widening and deepening. The lines of communication—the Via Clodia, and a little later a branch of it (which may have run to Caere, though after a few miles it divides into several branches, which I have never been able to follow out as yet)—thus kept along the ridges between the ravines as far as possible, only crossing them where it was unavoidable, as the country is extremely difficult.

It probably occupies the site of the ancient Careiae— about which we know very little—and it has an interesting mediaeval history. There are no traces of great antiquity to be seen, and indeed the village was only deserted in 1809, when the malaria drove the inhabitants away. The picturesque desolation of its streets, half grown up with vegetation, and of its crumbling buildings, makes it one of the most attractive places to visit for those who love the remoter parts of the neighbourhood of Rome (Fig. 46).

The Via Clodia may be reached direct in half a mile from Galera by keeping along the bank of the stream. For the next 3 miles it rises gradually, crossing some other streams, which are here only insignificant obstacles. At the modern post (and railway) station of Crocicchie the Via Clodia is again intersected by an ancient road, almost at right angles. Going south-westward, it passes, after rather less than a couple of miles, the remains of a very large villa, with an outer platform some 360 by 310 feet, supported by a wall with low arches in front of it, upon which rises the villa terrace proper. There is a large reser-

234

voir for the supply of the villa, with nine chambers, each measuring 60 by 17 feet inside : and there are other traces of habitation in this now desolate district. If we follow the road a mile or more further we shall find ourselves joining the branch road from Osteria Nuova to Caere ; beyond it is the Casale della Tragliatella, and near it the Fontanile delle Pertucce or Pertugie, i.e. the caves or holes. It lies in a valley, which has been drained by an artificial tunnel : the cliffs on its N. side are full of caves— at first quarries and then habitations, for the most part, though several of them are tombs—all of the Roman period, including some *columbaria,* which presumably belonged to the first century A.D. The largest tomb is the so-called Grotta della Regina, with an arched entrance flanked by columns, cut in the rock, and a niche for a sarcophagus within. Several cuttings for ancient roads descend into the valley from various directions. The Grotta della Regina was quite unknown to me when I set out from Crocicchie ; and I had intended to make for Caere westward, only altering my plans when I was told of its existence at Tragliatella. The unexpected is, indeed, one of the joys of exploration in the Campagna ; and one must always be ready to vary one's itinerary.

Going N.W. from Crocicchie, on the other hand, we soon find pavement well preserved ; and another path, also ancient, soon diverges to our right, and runs eastward—probably as far as the Via Cassia at Pisçiacavallo. Here the main track turns due N., and passes close by the remarkable ruins of S. Stefano, which attracted the attention of Pirro Ligorio. He planned and drew them in the sixteenth century ; and his representation is on the whole very accurate. The main building is about 50 feet square, and stands to nearly the same height. From the analogy of a similar building at Hadrian's Villa, the so-called barracks of the Vigiles, it is fairly clear that it was really a storehouse in three stories.

The path goes on to Anguillara ; and, though there are no traces of antiquity upon it, it is almost a necessary line of communication : for there are numerous other ruins in the neighbourhood. Outside Anguillara, indeed, there is a meeting-point of seven or eight roads, radiating from it in all possible directions—all of them probably of ancient origin. The little village stands on a small pèninsula overlooking the lovely crater lake of Bracciano, the ancient Lacus Sabatinus—a great relief to the eye after the somewhat desolate district that we have traversed. The name is not, as one might suppose, derived from the eel-fishers, but goes back to classical times, in the form *Angularius*, so that it comes from the situation of the place in the corner of the lake, near the place where the Arrone [1] leaves it : though the eel has found its way into the arms of the family of that name, and hence into those of the Orsini, who became lords of Anguillara in 1493. There was probably no village here but only a villa, of which scanty but sufficient traces may be seen among the modern houses.

The Aqua Traiana ran along the E. and N. banks of the lake, its springs being situated at various points on the N.W. side of the crater : the Acqua Paola follows its course, but also receives a certain amount of water from the lake itself. No ancient road can have run along this E. bank—there is barely room for the aqueduct : but a path runs westward from Anguillara along the lake shore, past the airship sheds of Vigna di Valle, to join the Via Clodia S. of Bracciano, which has more claim to be considered ancient.

Bracciano itself, with its strikingly interesting mediaeval castle, does not occupy an ancient site, though it lay on the line of the Via Clodia a little beyond Ad Novas, where the road from Caere came up to join it ; but a couple of miles beyond it, the road, which had descended into the lake basin, re-ascended through the woods to Forum Clodii, the site of which is marked by the little

[1] The name is very likely connected with the Etruscan praenomen Arruns or Aruns, and the *tribus Arnensis*, which is associated with the *tribus Sabatina*, probably derived its name from this river, and not from the Arnus (now the Arno) further to the N. Strabo makes a strange mistake in speaking of it as navigable, and in saying that it falls into the Tiber.

chapel of S. Liberato. Here are preserved a number of inscriptions, in which the people of this little posting village are mentioned under the name of Foroclodienses; and it seems to have been the headquarters of a praefecture, by which the neighbouring villages were administered. A villa erected here in the time of Augustus by one Mettia Edone not unnaturally acquired the name of Pausilypon; one may even wonder whether the owner brought the name with her from her native town of Naples, for her own name seems to show that she was a Greek.

Further on, in a little valley, are the modern Bagni di Vicarello, with springs which were used in Roman times—though whether the Aquae Apollinares are to be placed here or at Stigliano, some miles to the W. of Manziana, is a difficult question. There are remains of a huge villa overlooking the lake under the modern Casale di Vicarello.

Further E., along the lake shore, is the little town of Trevignano, which was defended by ancient walls, now hidden or destroyed. The rock above the town, which was probably the citadel, is now crowned by a mediaeval castle. The name probably comes from an estate called Trebonianum: but what was the name of the town that once stood here—whether it was Sabate, or whether this name has arisen from a mistaken reading of the *Itineraries* —is another question. From it a modern road leads to Sette Vene, a post-station on the Via Cassia, to which we must now return.

We left this road at the junction a little beyond La Storta. A few hundred yards further on, we see a deep cutting on the right, and here the modern road to the village of Isola Farnese turns off, by which the site of Veii can best be reached. A path soon diverges to the left and falls into the line of the Formello road, which is also of ancient origin. Isola Farnese, a small modern village (which I will not call miserable, because almost everyone who has written about Veii has already done so), lies on a hill just outside the perimeter of the city, which, even so, is extremely large, exceeding in size both Volaterrae and Tarquinii, while it is only slightly smaller than that of Rome as enclosed by the Servian wall. Its importance in Etruscan times was very great, and it is not surprising that Rome found its rivalry intolerable. The position, too, is one of great natural strength, as it is almost entirely surrounded by two deep ravines, traversed by streams which met at its S.E. extremity, below the citadel : and only on the W. is it connected with the surrounding hills by a neck, now traversed by the road to Formello, which has, I suspect, been artificially deepened. Under this neck passes a long tunnel in which for over 400 yards a stream was carried by the Etruscan engineers. The steep cliffs which surround the rest of the city have been further defended by walls of large volcanic blocks of stone. But on this vast tableland—for it is not sub-divided by any considerable depression—there is hardly a vestige to be seen of what was once a great city, which even in Imperial times knew a certain revival of prosperity. Excavations have in recent years brought to light much that is interesting, and above all, near the mill, where the stream is usually crossed by a plank (unless it happens to be in flood, when one must go a long way round), the now famous temple with three *cellae*, in which was found the splendid life-size statue of Apollo (to whom it was probably dedicated) in painted terra-cotta, which is now one of the chief ornaments of the Museo di Villa Giulia. It formed part of a group representing the theft by Hermes of a sacred stag : and is of the highest importance as showing us how the first temple of Jupiter Capitolinus must have been decorated. Here, too, was a large open water-tank of the Etruscan period.

Ascending hence by an ancient road to the area of the city, we cross it until we reach the Ponte Sodo, on the N. side. Originally it was quite a small channel for the stream, about large enough for a man to walk through (and this was the usual size of such tunnels), but time has con-siderably enlarged it, and made it much more picturesque. Above it was one of the city gates ; and outside this, to the N., was one of the cemeteries of the city, the only tomb of which that is worth seeing is the Grotto Campana, with its interesting archaic paintings of the first half of the sixth century. We may return to the city a little further E., past a *columbarium* cut in the rock, often called the *spezieria* (or grocer's shop), and notice on the way up some small archaic houses found in 1917. From here one must traverse almost the whole length of the site to arrive at the narrow neck which communicates with the citadel, popularly called the Piazza d'Armi. On the S. of this the road from Rome ascended : and just to the W. of it thousands of votive objects in terra-cotta were found in 1889—heads and feet predominating, belonging to some temple in the neighbourhood. Excavations in more recent years have brought to light remains of the gate by which the citadel was defended (it was closed in Roman times, when the citadel seems to have been deserted), of private houses, and of a large depression lined with stonework, which may have been an open water-tank.

The contrast between the active life of ancient times and the desolation of modern days can nowhere be more strongly felt than here : and Dennis, in his *Cities and Cemeteries of Etruria*, helps us to realise such an impression on this and many another site that he describes in that most delightful work.

The road to Formello, as we have seen, passes just to the W. of Veii, and runs due N., leaving on the left an extensive cemetery in which some 1,200 tombs of various periods have been brought to lig . A large number of them were the tombs of the " Villanovan " people, who occupied the site of Veii, and many others in Etruria, before the Etruscans came. Beyond this, as far as For mello, the interest of the district on each side of the road lies mainly in the fact that it was, more than any other in the neighbourhood of Rome, most carefully drained, no doubt for agricultural purposes. Many of the streams are, wholly or partially, artificial channels hewn in the rock, and this fact is accurately indicated in the representation of these streams in the detailed maps of the Campagna. In many cases the roofs of these tunnels, which were originally not of very much larger dimensions

239

than would enable a man to pass along them, have fallen in; while in others they are still preserved for quite a distance. The name Ponte Sodo (solid bridge) is thus not confined to Veii itself.

The Via Cassia runs almost parallel to the Via di Formello for 3 or 4 miles N. of Veii, but ascends a good deal more rapidly; on the ascent, the modern road hardly ever coincides with it, but keeps slightly to the right or the left. Before the ascent begins at the Osteria di Pisciacavallo a road from the Via Clodia at Crocicchie falls into our road. At the top of the hill is the old Osteria della Merluzza (the "smelt," probably so called from an old relief representing a fish), and here, too, an ancient branch road came in from the W., passing below Cesano village: while another joined the Via Cassia from the same direction a mile further on, this last being followed by a modern road. There were quite a number of villas in the district. The main road in Roman times passed through the largest cutting I have seen in the Roman Campagna; it is 60 feet deep, 18 wide, and about a mile long, thus traversing the rim of the extinct crater of Bracciano, which takes its name from the Roman post-station of Vacanae or Baccanae. High up on the hill to the right, called Monte Lupoli, are deep shafts communicating with a drainage channel far down in the bowels of the hill, which discharges into the stream which since 1838 has drained what would otherwise be a swamp. On the hill one writer, who describes the channel and shafts with fair accuracy, wishes to put the site of Veii, taking them to belong to the *cuniculus* excavated by Camillus during the siege! For the site of Veii was in dispute until the forum of the Imperial period was found in the nineteenth century—just as was that of Gabii. Baccano was indeed noted for its unhealthiness; and the many travellers of all nations who have passed the night at the post-station at the bottom of the crater have expressed various opinions as to its comfort. On the western rim of the crater is the Monte S. Angelo, on the summit of which was an Etruscan settlement, and to the N. of it a path leads through a deep cutting—a " neck " which can be seen from a long distance off—to the Lago di Martignano, and thence on to join the various ancient roads in the neighbourhood of Anguillara. Other roads placed Monte S. Angelo in communication with other parts of the country.

To the right of the Via Cassia a probably ancient road, cutting off the windings of the modern road, runs up to Campagnano, which occupies a characteristically Etruscan site, though we know nothing of any traces of antiquity in the town itself. Tombs have been found in the neighbourhood. The whole country is contorted by volcanic action, and furrowed by deep ravines. The Via Cassia leaves the crater on the N. by another deep cutting through a hill which once again bears the grim name of Monte dell' Impiccato, or Hangman Hill. Other cuttings hereabouts may belong to ancient roads, though as the soil is soft one cannot always be certain.

The forest of Baccano was indeed so infested with brigands that the simple expedient of burning it all down was eventually adopted early in the sixteenth century.

After a sharp descent we reach a modern bridge called the Ponte del Pavone, crossing a small stream, which, however, rapidly fills after rain : in fact, the ford was so dangerous in bad weather that Pope Gregory XIII, on his return to Rome in September 1578, sent a messenger on ahead to report, before he would come on himself ; and we soon come to a small single-arched ancient bridge, just before the large post-house of Sette Vene. Here the modern road from Bracciano and Trevignano (on the line, no doubt, of an ancient branch of the Via Clodia) comes in : and, if we will, we may round off the area which we have chosen for study by following a modern road through Campagnano to the twentieth mile of the Via Flaminia. The easternmost portion of it shows pavement *in situ*, and though the western does not give us definite indications, we may assume the antiquity of the whole line with at least a certain amount of probability.

V

THE ROADS LEADING TO
THE NORTH

XII. THE VIA FLAMINIA AND
     THE VIA TIBERINA

V

PRELIMINARY NOTE

THERE WAS PROBABLY a primitive route along the right bank of the Tiber long before the construction of the Via Flaminia, as far as the crossing of the river into Umbria below Otricoli. This was followed by the Via Tiberina, and was not as difficult a route as some writers have supposed. We cannot say when the shorter but more hilly road running W. of Soracte was made : but in any case it owed its establishment as a permanent highway to Gaius Flaminius, who built the road which has ever since borne his name in 220 B.C. It ran from Rome to Rimini, and formed the easiest route from Rome to Cisalpine Gaul and the fertile Po valley, which had recently come under the sway of Rome. It was therefore simply a short cut (gaining about 5 miles on the Via Tiberina), and it was, we may say, only by accident that it passed through any part of Etruria at all on its way to the crossing of the Tiber below Otricoli. By the time it was built, the Etruscan city of Falerii had already (in 241) been destroyed, and it passed a few miles to the E. of it, crossing the Treia valley by an extremely fine piece of engineering ; while the Roman city founded in its place was served, not by the Via Flaminia, but by a branch of the Via Cassia which ran through Nepi and on to Orte and Amelia.

The Via Flaminia must have been of considerable military importance to Rome, especially during the second Punic War ; and when Augustus undertook the restoration of the roads of Italy, it was for this reason that he took charge of this road himself, and rebuilt all the bridges (as he himself recorded) except the Pons Mulvius and one other : and it was evidently well kept up in subsequent times.

As a result it became a much-frequented road : and the most striking proof of this is perhaps furnished by four silver cups found at the baths of Vicarello, on the N. shores of the Lake of Bracciano. These are each inscribed with the itinerary from Gades (Cadiz) in Southern Spain to Rome, with the name and distance of each post-station : which proves that the land route was, in the time of Trajan or not much later, preferred to the sea route across the Gulf of Lions. The military importance of the road comes out in the history of Vespasian's advance on Rome, and later on in Constantine's victorious march : while it played an even larger part in the Gothic and Lombard wars of the fifth and sixth centuries. The road followed the old Tiber valley route for the first 9 miles, and then ran over hilly country for the next 27, returning to the river at the thirty-sixth mile.

It soon came into difficult country, and had to pursue a very sinuous course : while the collapse of the bridge and embankment by which it crossed the Treia valley led to the complete abandonment of that whole stretch of the road to the N. of Soracte. It does not touch any town, either Roman or Etruscan, in this portion of its course : Capena, the only one of any importance—and this probably diminished in Roman times—lay 3 or 4 miles off to the right, and the other villages of the district were still further off, by the Tiber, and more easily accessible by the Via Tiberina or even by ferry from the road on the left bank of the river.

XII

THE VIA FLAMINIA AND THE VIA TIBERINA

THE VIA FLAMINIA left the Servian city by a gate on the northern slopes of the Capitol; and the tomb of Bibulus, to the left of the monument to Victor Emanuel II, still stands to indicate the direction of the road. After this it turned almost due N., and ran for about 3 miles quite straight to the bridge by which it crossed the Tiber—the ancient Pons Mulvius, now the Ponte Molle. It was perhaps for this reason that burial on the Via Flaminia was a privilege granted, as it was to Bibulus, as a special honour to his merits at the bidding of the Senate and the people. Sulla and, later on, Paris, the famous actor, were among those who received it. A good deal of ancient work may be seen in the bridge, though it probably belongs to a restoration of 109 B.C. In the old days the ascent to it was a good deal steeper on each side; and this explains why Martial speaks of it more than once as a haunt of beggars.

From the bridge the road turned sharp to the right along the low ground by the river, and did not leave the Tiber valley until the post-station of Saxa Rubra or Ad Rubras, which stood at the further end of the red tufa cliffs, below which the road runs for 4 miles or so. In this first part of its course there is very little of interest to be noted. The picturesque caves in the cliffs of Grottarossa, which, whatever their origin, were used for habitation until a fairly recent period, are being thrown into the shade by a large quarry, which long ago destroyed the front of the tomb of the Nasonii, first discovered in 1674, in widening the road for the jubilee of the following year. Some of its paintings are in the British Museum, but a few can be faintly discerned on the spot. A few other tombs still stand in the fields to the right of the highroad, and show that the road must have run further out, where it would have been more liable to interruption from high floods than the modern road.

We pass the valley of the Cremera, which is formed by the union of the two brooks, the deep valleys of which serve to isolate the site of Veii. The acropolis may be reached from here in about two hours on foot. The stream is associated in our minds with the story of the Fabii, who may indeed have fortified themselves on the knoll, now crowned by a mediaeval tower, which almost seems to block the mouth of the valley. The bridge over the stream is Roman, though to some extent altered. Further on is a very large and prominent tomb on a cliff above the road, and about a mile further on, and a little less than 8 miles from Rome, we see in front of us the massive supporting walls of the villa of Livia, the wife of Augustus, as was shown by the discovery in it in 1867 of the splendid statue of the youthful Emperor, now in the Braccio Nuovo of the Vatican. On the hill-top there is still to be seen an underground room belonging to the villa, with paintings on the walls representing a garden. It commands a fine view down the valley towards Rome.

A bronze tablet was found in the Tiber in 1909, which, from the inscription on it, may have been originally affixed to a ferry-boat across the Tiber ; for a part of the villa was situated at Fidenae.

At the foot of the hill are the remains of a brick arch, perhaps of the Constantinian period, which gives its modern name to the hamlet.[1] The Via Flaminia ascends to the left, while a road called the Via Tiberina turns off to the right, and keeps along the Tiber valley. In the territory between the two roads, but rather nearer to the latter, are some enormous quarries, covering a very great extent of ground, and appropriately known as Grotta Oscura (the Dark Cave). From there was hewn the stone that served for the construction of the Servian walls after the fire of

[1] It is known as Prima Porta ("the First Gate"). See Fig. 47.

47. PRIMA PORTA (p. 248).

48. QUARRIES NEAR GROTTA OSCURA (p. 249).

To face p. 248.

the Gauls—a hard, yellowish tufa, whereas the cindery tufa which is found in the walls of the Palatine comes from Prima Porta or Fidenae, and takes its name from the latter. There are various other smaller quarries in the neighbourhood of Grotta Oscura (Fig. 48). The Via Flaminia, until a hundred years ago, and in great measure until the construction of the electric tram line, had a good many more remains of pavement to show than most other roads out of Rome.

There is little of further interest until we reach the modern farmhouse of Malborghetto (taking its name from a mediaeval castle constructed round it), which is built into a four-way arch of concrete faced with brick. This belongs to the time of Constantine, and marks, as Toebelmann, a German scholar who fell at Mons, pointed out in a work written before his death and published posthumously,[1] the site of that Emperor's headquarters on the night before the battle of Saxa Rubra. By going carefully into the accounts which we have of the battle, he showed that the only possible position which Maxentius could have taken up was a little N. of Prima Porta, on the hills and in the plain, with the river in his rear. In doing so he made precisely the same error of neglecting to secure his retreat which caused the defeat of the Romans at the Allia seven hundred years before : and when Constantine attacked the right wing on the plain with his cavalry (which he sent by four different routes, so that their arrival took the enemy completely by surprise) Maxentius's troops (except the Praetorian Guard on the left, who were cut down to a man) gave way in panic, and were driven down the Via Flaminia as far as the Ponte Molle, where many of them, including their leader, were drowned in the river.

Shortly after Malborghetto a road of ancient origin diverges to the right to Scrofano, which lies under the prominent Monte Musino, crowned by the scanty ruins of a mediaeval castle, in which some have tried to see remains of the *Arae Mutiae*, which once belonged to

[1] *Der Bogen von Malborghetto.*

Veii. From Scrofano roads lead across to the Via Cassia. At Malborghetto we are some 13 miles from Rome, and from here the road rises, following a winding course, and keeping to the watershed between valleys which grow deeper and deeper as we go on.

There is nothing of note until we reach the nineteenth mile, above the picturesque village of Castelnuovo di Porto, which belongs to the diocese of that name.

On the highroad is the old posting-inn (now a private house) of which Browning speaks in *The Ring and the Book*. The large kitchen chimney may still be noticed from outside. From here a road leads down to the Via Tiberina in the valley. A mile further on is the Madonna della Guardia, taking its name from a large mediaeval castle which guarded the road, just above the tram station of Morlupo. It is just 20 Roman miles from the Servian walls of Rome, and probably occupies the site of the post-station of Ad Vicesimum. An ancient road diverged to the right here, and another within half a mile ; and both of them led over difficult country to the ancient Etruscan city of Capena, about 3 miles away. It occupied a fine site on the north rim of an extinct volcanic crater. Tombs have been found, dating from the beginning of the Iron Age down to Roman times ; and inscriptions show that it was one of a group of three federated communities, to which belonged most of the territory in the V between the two main roads, going as far N. as the southern slopes of Monte Soracte. The other two were probably Flavinium, the modern Fiano, and Lucoferonia,[1] where was situated the famous sacred grove of the goddess Feronia, worshipped more by the Sabines, it seems, than by the Etruscans. Those who were possessed with her spirit walked with naked feet over heaps of burning coal and ashes without receiving injury. The site of the latter is a little to the N. of Nazzano, now marked by the old church of S. Antonio, on a hill above the Tiber. There is nothing standing now at Capena but one solitary ruin : and,

[1] The map, following De Rossi, places Lucoferonia where, I think, Capena should be.

as at Veii, I cannot but commend Dennis's delightful description of the site rather than attempt it myself. "The view from the height of Capena," he says, "is wildly beautiful. The deep hollow on the south with its green carpet, the steep hills overhanging it dark with wood [1]—the groves of Capena, be it remembered, were sung by Vergil— the bare swelling ground to the north with Soracte towering above, the snow-capped Apennines in the eastern horizon : the deep silence, the seclusion : the absence of human habitations (not even a shepherd's hut) within the sphere of vision, save the distant town of Sant' Oreste, scarcely distinguishable from the grey rock on which it stands ; compose a scene of more singular desolation than belongs to the site of any other Etruscan city in this district of the land."

After the second road to Capena has left it, the Via Flaminia turns W. to follow a narrow neck between two valleys, one running S. and the other N.; but this it only does for half a mile, turning N. again where the road to Campagnano goes off to the left. The country continues to be more and more furrowed by valleys, and, beyond its natural beauties, presents no special features of interest. But those who would gain an idea of it should not fail to go on as far as S. Oreste and ascend Soracte, which, from its isolated position, commands a view of Southern Etruria and of the fertile hills of Sabina, with the outliers of the Apennines behind them across the Tiber valley, which no other point affords. They will thus be able to survey the northern part of the territory we have been studying, just as from Monte Gennaro and from Monte Cavo they will be able to see the rest of it : and such general views may form a fitting conclusion to the somewhat detailed examination of the Roman Campagna which I have put before my readers in the foregoing pages.

[1] This has now disappeared and the hill-sides are bare ; but for the rest every detail still applies.

INDEX

[N.B. The new introduction has not been indexed]

INDEX

1. *Names of places outside the area of the Roman Campagna are not indexed.*
2. *Where a name is several times mentioned the page where it is most fully discussed is indicated by the use of heavier type.*

Acqua Acetosa (via Latina), 159
Acqua Felice, 147, 155
Acqua Traversa, 231
Ad Bivium, 152, 173
Ad Careias, 233
Ad Duos Lauros, 131, 146
Ad Martis, 177
Ad Novas, 236
Ad Pictas, 152
Ad Quintanas, 150, 181
Ad Rubras, 247
Ad Statuas, 151
Ad Turres, 227

Ad Vicesimum, 250
Aesulana, Arx, 122
Aglio, Cava d', 172
Agylla, 229
Alba Longa, 29, 31, 126, **190** *sqq.*
Alban Hills, 22 *sqq.*, 48, 50, 51, **125** *sqq.*, 134
Alban Lake, 168, **191** *sqq.*
Alban Mount, 23, 195
Albano, 127, **193** *sqq.*
Albulae, Aquae, 99 *sqq.*
Albunea, Grove of, 209
Aldobrandini, villa (Frascati), **164**
Algidus, 23, 126, 151, 153, **172**
Allia, 70 *sqq.*
Alsium, 229
Ambarvalia, festival of the, 29
Anagnina, Via, 160
Angelo, S., **117, 118**
Anguillara, 235
Angusculanus, Vicus, 161
Anio, 34, 58, 61, 65, 84, 93, 96, 101, 113 *sqq.*, 145
Anio Novus, Aqueduct, 119, 128, 149, 155, 159
Anio Vetus, 119, 149
Annunziatella, 207
Antemnae, 29, 30, 59, 61, 63 *sq.*, 67
Antium, 189, **213**
Appia, Via, 19, 31, 33 *sq.*, 40, 42, 126, 129, **174** *sqq.*, 213
Appia Pignatelli, Via, 149, 154, **179** *sqq.*
Aqua Alexandrina, 132, 136, 147
Aqua Appia, 144
Aqua Claudia, 119, 128, 149, 155 *sqq.*

Aqua Crabra, 167
Aqua Julia, 156, 168
Aqua Marcia, 119, 143, 155
Aqua Tepula (Sorgente Preziosa), 166
Aqua Virgo, 143, 144
Aquae Albulae, 99 *sqq.*
Aquae Labanae, 73, 92
Arcione, Castello, 98
Arco di Nostra Donna, 218
Ardea, 28, 32, 212, 213
Ardeatina, Via, 179, **205** *sqq.*
Aricia, 28, 194
Arrone, 32, 219, 227, 236
Artena, 141, 173
Artena Caeritum, 228
Arval Brethren, Grove of the, 29, 30, 219
Astura, 213
Aurelia, Via, 35, 45, **225** *sqq.*

Baccano, 240
Bagni, 100
Barberini, Villa (Castel Gandolfo), 191
Barberini Tomb (Palestrina), 139
Battista, Casale, 116, 117
Bernardini Tomb (Palestrina), 139
Bibulus, Tomb of, 247
Borghese, Barco (Frascati), 164
Borghese, Villa (Frascati), 148
Borghetto, Castle of, 166
Bovillae, 28, 33, **189** *sq.*
Bracciano, 32, 42, 236
Brutus (Villa of Tibur), (so-called), 120 *sqq.*
Buffalotta, Fossa, 70, 85 *sq.*

Cabum, 28
Caenina, 29, **90**
Caere, 32, 35, 139, **228** *sqq.*
Caffarella, Valle della, 179
Cagnoletti, Monte, 199
Campagnano, 241
Campana, Via, 29 *sq.*, 219
Campus Rediculi, 178
Capannelle, Le (below Tivoli), **133, 137**
id. (via Latina), 156
Capena, 32, **250** *sq.*
Capena, Porta, 33, 176
Capobianco, 89, 90
Cappellette, Roman Villa of the, 165

Casale Rotondo, 187
Casalone, 228
Casilina, Via, 146
Cassia, Via, 35, **231** sqq.
Cassius, Villa of (Tivoli), 120 sq.
Castel Campanile, 228
Castel Fusano, 211
Castel Gandolfo, 127, 190
Castel Giubileo, 67, 69
Castel di Leva, 208
Castel S. Pietro, 139
Castel Porziano, 205
Castellaccio, 145
Castelnuovo di Porto, 250
Castiglione, Torre di, 134
Castrimoenium (Marino), 28, 31, 126, 127, 154, 163, 168
Castrimoeniensis, Via, 3, 126, 176
Cavamonte, 137
Cavo, Monte, 23, 195
Cavona, Via, 133, 149, 161, 165, 189
Cecchignola, 208
Centocelle, 147
Centroni, Villa of, 159
Cervara, 144
Cervelletta, 144
Cerveteri (see Caere)
Cesano, 233
Cesareo, S., 48, 151
Cesarina, La, 88
Cestius, Pyramid of, 214
Ciampino, Casale, 160
Cicero, Tusculan Villa of, 167, 168
Circeo, Monte, 198, 213
Clodia, Via, 29, 35, **231** sq.
Clodii, Forum, 236
Clodius, Villa of (Via Appia), 190, 194
Coazzo, 87, 88
Coelius Vinicianus, Tomb of, 168
Collatia, 31, 32, 63, 67, **145**
Collatina, Via, 31, 32, 131, 133, **143** sq.
Collina, Porta, 58, 60, 139
Colonna, 150
Conca (see Satricum)
Concae, 99
Corbio (Rocca Priora), 28, 172
Corcolle, 137
Corioli, 28
Cornelia, Via, 226 sqq.
Corniculani, Montes, 57, 116
Corsi, Casale dei, 197
Cremera, 30, 72, 248
Crustumerium, 30, 71, 72, **86**
Cures, **77**, 78

Decimo (Via Laurentina), 40, 41, 210
Ad Decimum (Decimienses), (Via Latina), 41, 161
Diavolo, Ponte del, 80, 81
Diavolo, Sedia del, **83**, 87
Domine quo Vadis ? 178
Domitian, Alban Villa of, 191

Equites Singulares (Cemetery of the), 146
Eretum, 73 sqq.
Eurysaces, Tomb of, 128

Ficulea, 30, 31, **88** sqq.
Fidenae, 28 sqq., 59, 63, 67 sqq., 71, 249 sq.
Fiorano, Farm of, 187
Flaminia, Via, 34 sqq., 42 sqq., 66, 83, **245** sqq.
Flavinium (Fiano), 250
Formello, 239 sq.
Fortinei, 28
Fortune, Temple of, at Praeneste, 113 **139** sqq.
Fossae Cluiliae, 28
Frascati, 127, 150, **160** sqq.
Frattocchie, le, 189
Fregenae, 219, 227

Gabii, 28, 29, 31, 44, 67, **134** sqq.
Gabina, Via, 31, 128
Galera, 30, 226, **234**
Gallicano, 135, 137
Genazzano, 142
Gennaro, Monte, 115
Gennaro, S., 198
Genzano, 196
Gericomio, 121, 122, 137
Giostra, la, 188
Giovanni, Tor S., 86
Giubileo, Castel, **67**, 69
Gordiani, Villa of the, 131
Grottaferrata, Abbey of, 167

Hadrian, Villa of, 103 sqq.
Helena, Mausoleum of (Torre Pignatarra), 146
Hercules, Temple of (Tibur), 112 sq.
Horace, Villa of (Tibur), 114 sq.

Ilario, Catacombs of S., 152
Isola Farnese, 237 sq.

Janiculum, 225
Juno Sospita, Temple of (Lanuvium), 199
Jupiter Latiaris, Temple of, 195

Labanae Aquae, 73, 92
Labicana, Via, 31, 41, 43, **126** sqq., 141
Labici, 28, 32, 63, 67, 128, 150
Labico, 151
Ladispoli, 229
Lanuvium, 28, **199** sq.
Latina, Porta, 153
Latina, Via, 30, 34, 41, 126, 127, 129, 146, **153** sqq.
Latium, 26 sq., 174
Laurentina, Via, 32, 40, 41, **209** sqq.
Laurentini, 28, 32, 212
Lavinium, 28, 29, 209, **212**
Livia, Villa of, 248
Lorium, 227
Lucano, Ponte, **101** sqq., 116, 137
Lucoferonia, 250
Lungliezza, 133, **145**

Maccarese (Fregenae), 219, 227
Macchia della Faiola, 172
Mactorina, Via, 198

Maecenas, Villa of (Tivoli), 111
Maggiore, Monte, 75, 76
Magliana, La, 49
Malabarba, Via (Mola Barbara), 143
Malagrotta, 226
Malborghetto, 249
Mandela, 25
Marcellina, 115, 116
Marciana, Villa of (Frascati), 166
Marcigliana, Casale, 71
Marco Simone, Casale and Laghetto di, 88, 97
Maria Nuova, S. (Via Appia), 185
Marino, 127, 168
Mario, Monte, 22
Marius, the Younger, 139
Marozza, Grotta, 48, 74, **92**
Marrana Mariana, 156, 168
Martis, Clivus, 177
Maschio d'Ariano, 172
Matidia, Villa of (Frascati), 166
Maxentius, Circus of, 182
Mentana (*see Nomentum*)
Metella, Caecilia, Tomb of, 183
Micara, Torre, 162
Molle, Ponte (Pons Milvius, Mulvius), 61, **245** *sq.*
Mondragone, Villa (Frascati), 149
Montalto, Villa (Frascati), 163
Montecelio (Monticelli), 97, **116, 117**
Monte Compatri, 150
Monte Musino, 249
Monte Porzio, 165
Monte Rotondo, 73, 91
Morena, Casale di, 160
Moricone, 115
Muti, Villa (Frascati), 163

Nemi, 197
Nettuno, 213
Nomentana, Porta, 82
Nomentana, Via, 48, 57, 59, 62, 63, 65, 77, **82** *sqq.*
Nomentum, 28, 32, **91**
Nona, Ponte di, 41, 42
Norba, 28, 31
Novus, Vicus, 76, 81

Osa, stream, 133, 145
Ostia, 44, 47, 49, **214** *sqq.*
Ostiensis, Via, 36, 42, 43, **214** *sqq.*

Palazzola, 192
Palidoro, 227
Palombara, 87, 91, **115** *sqq.*
Pancratii, Tomb of the, **154**
Pantano Secco, 148
Parco Colonna, 190
Passerano, 137
Pastore, S., 138
Patinaria, Via, 84, 85
Pedum, 28, 32, 137
Pertucce, Fontana delle, 235
Pescara, La, 138
Pigneto Sacchetti, 225
Piombinara, Castle of, 148
Poggio Tulliano, 167

Poli, 137
Pompey, Villa of, Albano, 194
Pompey, Villa of, Alsium, 229
Pomptine Marshes, 24, 32, 49, 129, 174
Ponte Amato, 138
Ponte S. Antonio, 137
Ponte Galera, 219
Ponte Lucano, **101** *sqq.*, 116, 137
Ponte Mammolo, 96
Ponte Molle, 61, **245** *sq.*
Ponte Nomentano, 84
Ponte di Nona, 41, 42, 132
Ponte Sardone, 138
Ponte Squarciarelli, 168
Ponte di Terra (near Hadrian's Villa), 110
id. (Via Praenestina), 136
Porta Appia, 176
Porta Aurelia, 225
Porta Capena, 153, 176
Porta Collina, 59, 60, 139
Porta Esquilina, 128
Porta S. Giovanni, 154
Porta Latina, 153
Porta Maggiore (Praenestina), 128, 146
Porta S. Paolo, 214
Porta Pertusa, 226
Porta S. Sebastiano, 176
Porta S. Spirito, 225
Porta Tiburtina, **94**, 143
Portuensis, Via, 227
Portus, 218
Praeneste (Palestrina), 28, 32, 44, 113, 138, 139
Praenestina, Via, 36, 41, 102, 127, **128** *sqq.*
Prata Porci, 149
Pratica di Mare, 46, 210, 212
Prima Porta, 249
Primitivus, Church of S., 136
Pupinian tribe, 30, 148
Pyramid of Cestius, 214
Pyrgi, 229

Querquetulae, 28, 137
Quintilii, Villa of the (Via Appia), 156 *sqq.*, **185**
Quintilii, Villa of the (Mondragone), 164
Quintilius Varus, Villa of (Tivoli), 114
Quintanas, Ad, 41, **150**

Regillus, Lake, 148, 149
Regulini-Galassi Tomb (Caere), 230
Robigus, Grove of, 231 (*see* 30)
Rocca di Papa, 195
Rocca Priora, 23, 172
Roma Vecchia, 156, 186
Romulus, son of Maxentius, Heroon of, 131, 151, 182
Rospigliosi, Villa, 151
Rufina, S., 226
Rufinella, Villa, 168
Rustica, La, 144

Sabate, 32
Sacco, River, 139

Sacer, Mons, 84
Salomone, Monte, 171
Salaria, Ponte, 65 *sq.*
Salaria, Porta, 59
Salaria, Via, 30, 36, 57, 59 *sqq.*, 92, 115, 116, 219
Salone, Casale, 49, 144
Satricum, 28, 31, 126, 208
Saza Rubra, 249
Scaptia, 28, 33, 137
Schiavi, Tor de', 131 *sqq.*
Scrofano, 249
Sebastiano, Church of S. (Via Appia), 181
Segni, 141
Senni, Villa, 160
Sette Bassi, **156** *sq.*, 186
Settecamini, 97, 98, 116
Sette Chiese, Via delle, 207
Sette Vene, 237, 241
Severiana, Via, 211, 217
Sgurgola, 25
Solfatara, 208, 209
Solluna, 198
Soracte, 250 *sq.*
Spada, Villa (*see* Fidenae)
Spizzichino, 233
Squarciarelli, Ponte degli, 108
S. Stefano, ruins, 235
S. Stefano, Colle di, 109
S. Stephen, basilica, 154
Storta, 233
Stuart, Henry, Cardinal of York, 163
Stuart, Charles, 129
Sub-Augusta, Church of (ad duos Lauros), 147, 150
Sublanuvium, 198

Tellenii, 28 (*see* 188)
Terracina, 175, 198
Tiberina, Via, 36, 248
Tibur (Tivoli), 28, 32, 44, 52, 58, 103, **110** *sqq.*, 118 *sqq.*
Tiburtina, Porta, **94** *sq.*, 143
Tiburtina, Via, 57, 87, **93** *sqq.*, 145
Tolerini, 28
Tor Angela, 132

Tor Marancia, 207
Tor Paterno, 212
Tor de' Schiavi, 131, 143, 156
Torlonia, Villa (Frascati), 163
Torre di Castiglione, 134
Torre Centocelle, 147
Torre Fiscale, 155
Torre di Micara, 162
Torre Nuova, 147, 148, 162
Torre Pignattarda, 146
Torre Tre Teste, 132
Torri, Grotte di, 78, 79
Torrimpietra, 227
Travicella, Vicolo della, 178
Trevignano, 237
Triopion, 180
Triumphalis, Via (Alban Mount), 196
Triumphalis, Via (Via Clodia), 225, 232
Tusculum, 28, 30, 44, 126, 128, 148 *sqq.*, **167** *sqq.*
Tutia, 28

Urban, Tomb of S. (Via Appia), 184
Urbano, Church of S. (Triopion), 180

Valerii, Tomb of the, 154
Valle d'Inferno, 225
Valmontone, 152
Veii, 18, 28, 30 *sqq.*, 45, 71 *sq.*, **231** *sqq.*
Velletri, 24 *sq.*, 28, 197, **200**
Verano, Campo, 98
Vermicino, Fonte, 162
Vicarello, 41, 237
Vicesimum, Ad, 250 (*cf.* 41)
Vicus Angusculanus, 161
Vicus Augustanus Laurentium, 211
Vigesimo, Valle, 41
Villanovans, 26, 239
Viminalis, Porta, 94
Vitellia, Via, 227
Vitriano, Colle, 116
Vittorino, S., 111
Vivaro, Valle, 198

Zagarolo, 135, 137, 148
Zolforata, 208, 209